NATIONAL SECURITY IN THE
INFORMATION AGE

Books of Related Interest

Why Wars Widen: Predation and Balancing
by Stacy Bergstrom Haldi

Asymmetries of Conflict: War Without Death
by John Leech

International Security in a Global Age: Securing the Twenty-First Century
by Clive Jones and Caroline Kennedy-Pipe

Deterrence in the 21st Century
edited by Max G. Manwaring

Terrorism and Grand Strategy
edited by Paul B. Rich and Thomas R. Mockaitis

Dimensions of Western Military Intervention
edited by Colin McInnes and Nicholas J. Wheeler

Intelligence Services in the Information Age
Michael Herman

NATIONAL SECURITY IN THE INFORMATION AGE

Editor

EMILY O. GOLDMAN

University of California, Davis

FRANK CASS
LONDON • PORTLAND, OR

First published in 2004 in Great Britain by
FRANK CASS PUBLISHERS
Crown House, 47 Chase Side,
Southgate, London N14 5BP, England

and in the United States of America by
FRANK CASS PUBLISHERS
c/o ISBS, 920 NE 58th Avenue, Suite 300
Portland, Oregon 97213-3786

Copyright © 2004 Frank Cass & Co. Ltd.

Website: www.frankcass.com

British Library Cataloguing in Publication Data

National security in the information age
  1. National security 2. Information technology 3. Information
  warfare 4. Computer security
  I. Goldman, Emily O., 1961–
  355′.03

ISBN 0-7146-5600-3 (cloth)
ISBN 0-7146-8486-4 (paper)

Library of Congress Cataloging-in-Publication Data

National security in the Information Age / editor, Emily O. Goldman.
    p. cm.
Includes bibliographical references and index.
    ISBN 0-7146-5600-3 (alk. paper) — ISBN 0-7146-8486-4 (pbk.: alk. paper)
  1. National security – United States. 2. National security. 3. Information
  warfare – United States. 4. Information warfare. 5. United States – Defenses.
  6. United States – Military policy. I. Goldman, Emily O., 1961–
  UA23. N2497 2004
  355′.033073–dc22

                                                            2003019749

This group of studies first appeared as a special issue of *Contemporary Security Policy*,
ISSN 1352-3260, Vol.24, No.1 (April 2003) published by Frank Cass and Co. Ltd.

Printed in Great Britain by
Antony Rowe Ltd., Chippenham, Wiltshire

Contents

CONCLUDING REFLECTIONS

Introduction: Security in the Information Technology Age

EMILY O. GOLDMAN

The campaign in Afghanistan from the autumn of 2001 through the winter of 2002 and the war in Iraq to unseat Saddam Hussein's regime have given the world a glimpse into the capabilities of a US military that has undergone significant transformation in the decade since the Persian Gulf War of 1990–91. The US military has increased its ability to leverage information technologies to improve battlefield performance. GPS-guided precision munitions enable the US to target fixed positions at night and in poor weather. Unmanned aerial vehicles (UAVs) greatly enhance reconnaissance capabilities. Space assets assist in position location, precision attack, communications and data transfer. Information warfare operations have also become an important part of the repertoire of combatants in the information age.[1]

While information technology has had a significant impact on US battlefield operations, the capabilities and security challenges fostered by the information age extend far beyond the domain of war fighting. The explosive growth of the internet economy, for example, has added a new dimension to commerce, but internet-based industries also present new vulnerabilities. The internet economy requires reliable information security and infrastructure dependability. Protecting the main components of the civilian and government information infrastructure is not easy without regulation of the telecommunications industry and cooperation across the public and private sectors.[2]

The control and use of information and knowledge is a central engine driving human activity and progress – individuals, organizations and nations interact more and more in cyberspace; consequently political, military and economic leaders are under increasing pressure to manage, deter and reduce the level of associated risks. Threats to cyberspace range from the systematic and persistent, to the decentralized and dispersed, to the accidental and non-malevolent. The full impact of the information technology revolution on global stability and national security cannot yet be known. But what is clear is that the information age has led to important changes in threats, vulnerabilities and warfare. These demand new security practices. In the face of these challenges, national security establishments need new thinking.

This special issue examines from multiple perspectives how one of the most important social transformations in history – the information technology revolution – has affected the provision of security. Advances in computerized information and telecommunications technologies have been accompanied by related innovations in management and organizational practices and structures. These changes together have set in motion forces that challenge many of the conceptual and ethical premises that have been the stock and trade of national security experts for the past half century. The information revolution has redefined what it means to be vulnerable by making the most advanced societies the most vulnerable to attack, simply because they are more information dependent. The information revolution has redefined who can pose a significant threat by diffusing and redistributing power to traditionally weaker state actors and non-state actors, empowering them to do harm. The information revolution has altered expectations about conflict among democratic societies, too. Recent experience has shown that voters are uneasy with anything other than extremely accurate killing.

These essays seek to stimulate new thinking and to help clarify the core security dynamics and practices of cyberspace. They are organized around four key themes. In the first section, Richard Harknett and Damon Coletta examine the impact of the information revolution on the underlying premises of deterrence and crisis management. These core security concepts were critical for managing conflict during the Cold War. Harknett and Coletta assess how the information revolution has affected their relevance for security in the future. In the second section, Chris Demchak, Matt Bishop and Emily Goldman examine the strategic and organizational underpinnings of information war. They ask to what extent warfare in the information age marks a departure from previous eras, requiring new strategic principles and organizational structures. In the third section, Miroslav Nincic and Pat Morgan examine how security practices in the information age, enabled by dramatic improvements in the capabilities for perception management, monitoring and surveillance, and clandestine warfare, threaten democratic values of public accountability, liberty and privacy. In the last section, Walter Baer takes up several of the biggest challenges of securing cyberspace: coordinating between the public and private sectors to provide security, and preventing market failure in the provision of security by the private sector.

MANAGING CONFLICT IN THE INFORMATION AGE

Deterrence was the strategic paradigm for the nuclear age and proved quite successful in managing conflict between the superpowers. Great power conflicts were not to be fought and won, but avoided. Information warfare (IW) now poses two major problems for the existing deterrence framework: commensurability and attribution. The Cold War deterrence paradigm relied on the principle of retaliation in kind. The losses inflicted through retaliation would match losses incurred during the attack. But what if an attack reduces no buildings to rubble, kills no one directly, but only destroys information? What is the appropriate response? What would dissuade a state from contemplating a cyber attack? The adversary's information infrastructure may not be sufficiently important to his security to constitute an adequate target for retaliation. Should we then threaten physical destruction of national assets in response? Should attacks on societal connectivity be treated as acts of conventional war?

The retaliation–in–kind model faces an arguably greater problem of attribution. Attacks may not emanate from a state, but rather from terrorists, organized crime, or able hackers who have an incentive to hide their identity and who lack assets that can be held hostage – a prerequisite for deterrence by retaliation to work. While states may be deterred from cyber warfare because they are vulnerable in return, a non-state actor may not be deterred by the threat of retaliation. Theoretically, actors may be able to move themselves from the 'deterrable' to the 'non-deterrable' side as an integral component of IW. For example, a company engaged in industrial espionage could contract out to a hacker, rather than use company resources. States may engage in masking their strategic attacks to appear to be hackers' work. They may even involve themselves in 'deep coalitions' with nongovernmental organizations (NGOs), skilled individuals, multinational corporations (MNCs) and even organized crime syndicates to effect an attack.[3] As Richard Harknett argues, the reduced probability of finding perpetrators means one cannot rely exclusively on deterrence but must develop strategies to cope in an environment where greater disruption and destruction are possible by fewer, harder to find and harder to deter actors. If the conditions for our traditional model of deterrence do not hold in an IW environment, what strategic concepts should replace it? Harknett and others in this special issue present some alternatives.

While deterrence is viewed as a strategy to manage conflict and prevent the outbreak of war, then crisis management is an equally important task, one that received significant scholarly and policy attention during the Cold War. Crisis management focuses on preventing an escalation spiral that could precipitate major war. Information technology may perform several important conflict prevention functions: enhancing transparency and building confidence in arms control verification regimes and peace operations; detecting military build-ups and disseminating intelligence in order to reduce strategic surprise; tracking the movements and activities of terrorist and organized crime groups through the creation of global databases; and spreading information to counteract hyper-nationalist rhetoric that foments ethnic conflict and genocide.[4]

Damon Coletta is sceptical that increased capabilities for the collection, analysis and distribution of information will ease the crisis management problem. The prevailing wisdom treats crisis management as a less intense form of military conflict, implying that the same gains that revolutionary technologies have achieved in combat should also hold true during crises. However, crisis management often has its own dynamic apart from war-fighting. Wars are fought to eliminate competition, while crisis managers seek to induce cooperation and avoid war. Coletta has greater faith in diplomatic skill than in technology to de-escalate crises. American IT dominance may increase the danger of crisis management failure, and how the horizontal proliferation of a less sophisticated set of information technologies to other countries and non-state actors might hinder crisis management as well. While US organization to fight wars is taking advantage of new information technologies, it is less clear that US organization for crisis management is similarly adapting.

ORGANIZATION AND CONDUCT OF WARFARE IN THE INFORMATION AGE

Warfare in the information age will be shaped not only by the technology, but also by the concepts and organizations developed to employ the technology.[5] The promise and challenge of war in the information age lies as much in developing the concepts and organizations needed to employ the technology effectively as in developing or acquiring the technology itself. Two points are worth exploring here. First, how *are* militaries organizing to wage warfare today and what concepts are they relying upon? How *should* militaries organize for warfare in the information age? Second, are we witnessing the decline of wars of destruction and the ascent of wars of disruption? Are militaries being captured by the paralytic paradigm, or does the Clausewitzian model of destructive warfare still hold sway?

In the information age, the Clausewitzian industrial-era model of destructive war based on lethality may eventually be supplanted by an information-era model of war centred on disruption, paralysis and non-lethality. IT clearly can be used in a destructive mode, e.g., in combined-arms operations to improve the efficiency of high explosive attacks as recent operations in Iraq demonstrate. But IT can also be deployed in a non-lethal mode, as a substitute for high explosive attacks via cyber-attacks that disrupt connectivity. Logically, paralytic warfare would aim to incapacitate the opponent's war-making system by causing a complete or partial loss of function, short of destruction. Although IT holds out the prospect of a new paradigm of warfare, Chris Demchak argues that specific developments within the United States are hindering this development. The US military is leveraging IT to enhance lethality and others are likely to follow this model. Her analysis raises a series of questions about the emergence of new paradigms of warfare. What conditions must be met for a new paradigm to gain ascendancy? When two competing paradigms co-exist, technical superiority alone is often not enough for a professional community to embrace a new organizing framework and revolutionize its mode of operations. How can core organizational constituencies be convinced of a need for a paradigm shift? Finally, what patterns of warfare can we expect when old and new paradigms co-exist?

Matt Bishop and Emily Goldman examine how information warfare, specifically cyber attacks on physical and cyber targets, can be integrated into military campaigns. They ask whether the underlying strategic logic of warfare has been altered, or merely the tools to execute war? They argue that despite dramatic changes in technology, the logic of warfare today remains the same as in the past – sequencing and coordinating attacks to achieve lower order technical or 'cyber' goals as part of a broader campaign to achieve higher order political, material and/or symbolic goals. Most military operations can be characterized as either 'sequential' or 'cumulative'. Traditional military contests (such as the First and Second World Wars) were sequential. Battles were linked logically into campaigns that culminated in the attainment of a linear goal (conquering territory such as the Western Front in the First World War, or creating mutually supporting military bases as in the Pacific island-hopping campaign to Tokyo). During the Cold War, many low intensity conflicts were characterized by cumulative strategies. The control of territory was of little importance. Rather the cumulative effects of some variable (inflicting casualties, interdicting supplies, etc.) decided the contest. IW fits into both types of strategies. Cyber attacks on military targets can be the opening volley in a sequential strategy designed to facilitate the imposition of a physical attack to follow. Cyber attacks on societal targets can be used in a cumulative strategy of repeated homeland attacks to erode the will of the domestic population.

The integration of cyber attacks into traditional military campaigns may follow an enduring logic of warfare, but this mode of attack raises new challenges for strategic thinkers. If conflict becomes more disruptive than destructive, where does peace end and war begin? What electronic activity would lead to war? In the information realm, the skills that enable one to build robust defences (e.g., encryption, passwords, layers of firewalls) can be used easily to eavesdrop on, contaminate, or disrupt information flows. Given the technological potential for intrusion, the temptation is strong to pre-emptively disrupt in order to 'prepare the battlefield' before conventional hostilities begin, or before a crisis begins, or to incapacitate an adversary's war-making system by causing a complete or partial loss of function. Computer software operators disrupting other computers are not likely to be seen as dangerous or as acts of war, yet disruption can be as great a security threat as destruction. The technological promise of information warfare blurs the peace–war boundary and defies our traditional understandings of offence and defence. Where is the battlefield in an IW context? Which operations constitute legitimate defensive measures and which ones are reasonably considered offensive?

Finally, warfare in the information age has spurred a debate about the extent to which IT has levelled the playing field for warfare, making individuals as lethal as states. Harknett persuasively argues that the very capable few can wreak enough havoc to be a significant concern. Bishop and Goldman do not dispute this point, but emphasize that only states and state-sponsored groups will be able to launch sustained attacks and thus they retain considerable advantages over individuals or small groups.

GOVERNANCE IN THE INFORMATION AGE

If strategy is about the relationship of means to ends, it must reflect the will of the people. Public support is central to how a democracy organizes itself for national security, how democratically elected leaders decide to go to war and, once at war, how to conduct it. A major implication of the information revolution could be an ability to wage war with significantly fewer casualties than before. Yet information warfare capabilities compromise democratic values of accountability and privacy in significant ways and these are explored by Miroslav Nincic and Pat Morgan.

Nincic identifies three ways that information warfare confounds the democratic process. By blurring the peace–war boundary, IW makes it more difficult for the public and their representatives to control the initiation of war. By distorting information in an effort to confound the adversary, IW may inadvertently deceive the public, again undermining public controls that are the heart of democratic governance. Finally, IW lends itself to excessive government intrusiveness into the private lives of its citizens. Morgan focuses specifically on this last point when he argues that a logical tension exists between privacy and security. Security requires access to information about criminals and foreign threats. Privacy means protection from access for the ordinary citizen. Enhanced information gathering, processing and transmission enlarge the threat to privacy plus the threats of manipulation and control. Specifically, he fears that national-security-driven penetration capabilities *vis-à-vis* foreign information and communication systems, plus enhanced surveillance (public and private) for domestic security or other reasons, are likely to breed more possibilities for abuse by the security monitors that may escape public oversight. Carnivore, for example, which was developed by the Department of Justice to monitor internet connections, implied uncontrolled access to communications. Medical record privacy models address this explicitly by auditing access to patient data. Better efforts to anticipate threats in the design of technical and organizational systems will be vital.

The threat to privacy is no longer simply one of state control for two reasons. First, the communications revolution has globalized the domestic security problem. Talented exploitation of new technology now emerges anywhere to lend itself to privacy elimination and enhanced control (by public and private entities) and can readily escape domestic barriers and regulation. Second, the proliferation of private reconnaissance capabilities multiplies uncontrolled monitoring. Domestically, accumulation of sensitive personal information in public and private hands continues under measures and methods inadequate to bar unwarranted access and misuse.

The security–privacy nexus will be one of the most important for political leaders to address. Already twenty municipalities in the United States have passed resolutions that declare the USA Patriot Act a threat to civil rights, in some cases calling upon city employees not to cooperate with federal investigations that are thought to violate civil liberties.[6] How should society adjust its concerns for privacy and security, if detection and pre-emptive action become cornerstones of defence against information warfare as well as other forms of attacks on the homeland? In democratic societies, these answers are likely to turn on public perceptions of threats to both security and privacy. Paradoxically, while public concern about how information warfare violates democratic norms is growing, the prospect that wars of disruption might displace wars of destruction may make it easier to generate public support for such operations. We are only beginning to examine how the IT revolution may be changing expectations within democratic societies about what is considered legitimate military practice. Increasingly 'accurate' warfare may be a double-edged sword: the public now expects fewer casualties and ever-greater precision in detecting, deterring and responding to attacks, but this may mean violating democratic norms of privacy and accountability.

PRIVATE SECTOR INCENTIVES FOR MANAGING SECURITY

The information revolution raises important philosophical questions for American society in particular, and democratic societies more generally. Openness, and the open society, are ideals that permeate American interests, values and goals. If there is a 'Washington consensus' today, it is that open markets, open trade, globalization and the free flow of information are beneficial to the United States and to the globe. The global positioning system (GPS) and FLAG (fibre-optic links around the globe) project epitomize US efforts to create a global information infrastructure that interconnects the world.

Yet openness involves risks. Advanced information systems like GPS can be used by adversaries to guide their own weapons against US and allied forces, while the increasing dependence of commercial concerns on GPS makes it difficult to arrange for even a temporary wartime shutdown of the system. The United States remains far more open than most other states, and far more vulnerable because of it. One key risk in fostering greater interconnectivity (e.g., to improve trade) is that the United States exposes itself to attacks on its own information infrastructure, which could lead to serious economic and social damage. The military has long been the first line of defence, but in the information age, reliance of the defence establishment on the private sector has grown exponentially. Walter Baer raises very important questions in this regard. Can military security be assured if private sector security is not? How can we prevent market failure in the private sector? To the extent that security in the information age is as much a market problem as a military problem, what is the balance of public and private responsibility for providing security? Clearly the incentives for security in the private sector must exceed the social risks facing the rest of society if we are to protect our critical information infrastructure.

The creation of infrastructure rules governing IT security is inevitable. IT infrastructure rules will stipulate minimum levels of security and some common rules for implementation, much like building and public health codes protect the public. Technology alone will not produce good public policy. Nevertheless, most projects focus on designing better technological options for IT security while ignoring the governance issues for the rules. Baer points out that private organizations such as the Center for Internet Security are developing 'best practices' models of security policies for commercial, academic and government entities that are connected to the internet. These define *de facto* rules for management and affect the development of security techniques to protect the infrastructure and the traffic that passes through it. But what is the appropriate mix of public and private authority to establish IT infrastructure codes? How can IT infrastructure codes be reconciled and enforced across national borders?

Given that much of the security function will rest with the private sector, we should expect market failures if there are benefits for society from additional levels of safeguards that could not be claimed fully by the firm. For example, defending against 'denial of service' attacks requires all server operators to protect their systems. Organizing such cooperation can be challenging. Anticipating an under-supply of safeguards, we must evaluate other policy instruments, in particular market mechanisms, such as insurance requirements, that are discussed in detail by Baer. These could prove more flexible and efficient than detailed government rules. Another proposal involves the use of 'unsecurity credits' which are analogous to environmental pollution credits that allocate to industrial manufacturers the legal right to pollute the environment, as a by-product of their operations, up to a certain limit.[7] If the company pollutes past that limit, fines ensue. If they exceed expectations and operate more cleanly than required, they can sell leftover credits to other companies, at whatever price they can get. This arrangement gives all concerned parties a rational means to decide on an optimal course. In a network computing environment, by analogy, unsecure practices pollute and instituting credits is one way to assist companies in making balanced security decisions. Unsecurity credits force companies to evaluate their assets, determine the total amount of 'unsecurity' they are willing to sustain, and allocate credits accordingly.

The public and private sectors must jointly provide for the security of the nation in order to mount an effective defence against IW attacks. This involves understanding the incentives and obstacles to the sharing of information and know-how between government and industry, clearly identifying the likelihood and sources of market failure, and developing the right policy instruments to correct it. The military services, law enforcement agencies, industry and regulatory bodies made considerable progress when preparing for the Y2K rollover, yet the virus attacks that tied up portions of the internet in early 2000 demonstrate that much remains to be done.[8]

A related public–private problem involves the exponentially increasing reliance of the defence establishment on the private sector. With an increasing dependence on use of COTS (commercial off-the-shelf) technology, are we introducing new vulnerabilities into the system and do we understand our current vulnerabilities? The time has come for a more considered inventory and analysis of which critical components for defence must be developed by government and which can acceptably be outsourced to industry.

CONCLUSION

The information age is upon us. Accepting it is not a choice but a necessity. We must learn how to meet our needs for security in a new technological environment. The information age does not invalidate all previous premises about security but requires new and creative solutions, and reasonable adaptations of existing policies that remain valid. Like globalization, the challenge is to leverage the positive dimensions of the transformation while minimizing its more deleterious side effects. The information revolution is a double-edged sword for security managers. Comparing US and coalition operations in Iraq in 2003 to those against that same country in 1990–91, we see that war can be more discriminate, less destructive and more disruptive yet the 'knowledge burden' is exponentially greater. While leveraging IT has been a hallmark of US military operations in recent years, dependence upon IT has made advanced societies increasingly vulnerable to attacks by empowered small groups whose ability to act anonymously has made preventive and deterrent measures difficult. Moreover, not only have small groups been empowered by the information age; so too have states, leading to a potential for abuse that infringes upon the civil liberties of citizens.

There are no obvious solutions to the challenges that IW presents. The very solution to the information age that Demchak proposes for effective military operations – the atrium model of a global database based on broad information sharing – is precisely the type of policy most feared by Nincic and Morgan because of its threat to privacy. This is but one example of the difficult trade-offs facing security managers. These essays represent a considered treatment of the issues and the tensions among them, which we hope will stimulate new thinking in the halls of government, industry and academia.

ACKNOWLEDGEMENTS

I thank Leo Blanken for research assistance that supported the writing of this essay.

NOTES

1. There is some controversy over the impact of information warfare operations. Operation Allied Force, the NATO military campaign in 1999 to force Serbian troops out of Kosovo, was hailed by some military experts as the first ever cyberwar. To support its bombing campaign against Serbia, the United States established a team of information warriors to electronically attack

critical networks and command and control systems. Official post-conflict assessments suggest the IW efforts were used ineffectively and not exploited fully. Bob Brewin, 'Kosovo Ushered in Cyberwar', *Federal Computer Week*, 27 Sept. 1999.

2. Gregory Rattray, *Strategic Warfare in Cyberspace* (Cambridge, MA: MIT Press, 2001) points out that the pressure to cut costs has led to systems that meet only normal operating demands and do not provide sufficient redundancy. The loss of a single Verizon switching facility in lower Manhattan during the strikes on the World Trade Center caused major telephone tie-ups in the region; some glitches persisted for months. At the same time, the end of AT&T's long-distance monopoly forced the government to deal with multiple operators in developing security measures.

3. Alvin and Heidi Toffler, 'Foreword: The New Intangibles', in John Arquilla and David Ronfeldt (eds), *In Athena's Camp: Preparing for Conflict in the Information Age* (Santa Monica, CA: RAND, 1997), p.xix.

4. Joseph S. Nye, Jr. and William A. Owens, 'America's Information Edge', *Foreign Affairs*, Vol. 75, No. 2 (March/April 1996), pp.20–36.

5. See Emily O. Goldman and Leslie C. Eliason, *Diffusion of Military Technology and Ideas* (Stanford, CA: Stanford University Press, 2003).

6. 'Two More Cities May Join Patriot Act Revolt', <http://abcnews.go.com/sections/us/DailyNews/usapatriot_oakland021217.html>.

7. This idea was presented by Mark Graff at the 'Security in the Information Age' Workshop, Lawrence Livermore National Laboratory, 19 April 2002. See <http://www.markgraff.com/mg_writings/Unsecurity.pdf>.

8. Rattray, *Strategic Warfare in Cyberspace*.

Integrated Security: A Strategic Response to Anonymity and the Problem of the Few

RICHARD J. HARKNETT

The nexus of theory and policy in the area of international security studies is a somewhat awkward space. Theory and theoreticians can be too abstract for practical policy application; Policy and policy-makers can be too narrowly focused temporally and substantively. Yet, it is at moments in which basic principles are unsettled that thinking theoretically can have its most positive impact and when application in a prescriptive sense is most justified.

In academic studies, the framework of realism offers a simple starting point for the study of world politics: above all else, the material capability to harm (traditionally viewed as state-possessed military power) matters. According to realists, the distribution of such capability can explain much of the flow and dynamics in world politics. When applied to the contemporary international system, it is not unsurprising for realists that the focus of attention is directed at the behaviour and policies of the United States. And yet, since September 2001, it seems more clear than ever that a curious dichotomy (at least) is emerging: just as the power and influence of one particular state is overwhelmingly pervasive across the international system, that particular state is forming policy from an assumption of great vulnerability. To understand US policy it is necessary to understand how and why a great concentration of power is coexisting alongside a great fear over security. I will suggest that a focus on the notion of a material capability to harm is quite enlightening not only for answering this question, but for guiding real policy responses to the security problems of the twenty-first century. Simply put, the material capability to harm is not a state dimension characteristic and thus the most powerful state can not rest comfortably with regard to its security.

INTRODUCTION

While great caution should be used when labelling some phenomenon as 'new', this paper is premised on the assumption that current trends are likely to create conditions in which traditional models for organizing national security will prove inadequate.

My basic argument is that twenty-first-century conflict must be understood as multidimensional in character. There are new security consequences related to the globalization[1] of information and military technologies that pose serious challenges for traditional national security models of defence and deterrence and, by extension, challenges the basic security organization of the international system – the state. The critical factor in multidimensional conflict is the combinations of existing and new forms of organization with existing and new forms of destructive capability. In assessing these combinations, I suggest that a multidimensional threat environment requires a multidimensional response. Specifically, I conclude that if there is something new with the globalization of information and technology capable of causing great harm, it is the prospect for widespread *unattributable* disruption and destruction. This paper suggests that the missing umbrella organizing concept about future threats is not asymmetry (the buzz word of the past few years), but attribution. It is important to recognize, however, that as we begin to organize security to grapple with anonymity, we must remain attentive to traditional dimensions of conflict as well.

With this in mind, this paper presents the outlines of a strategy of Integrated Security, an approach that seeks to respond to traditional and new dimensions of conflict simultaneously. The key to IS is recognizing that strategic success will depend greatly on the interconnectedness of a continuum of security models, rather than the mere creation of more options. This interconnectedness must provide immediate security, but also serve a broader objective of changing the security environment. The overall objective of IS is to move security competition toward more easily managed dimensions. In doing so, IS reinforces the state as primary security actor.

In the Cold War, deterrence was the manner through which immediate security was found, but it also reinforced a larger grand strategy – containment – that sought to overcome the Soviet threat (through time). The threat of wide-scale anonymous destruction is a long-term problem that must be overcome as well, since it threatens the basic organizational structure of the current state-based international system. Integrated Security supports a grand strategy to reinforce the state system in that it emphasizes the goal of pushing security competition into the state (rather than proxy or network) dimension. As the importance of the state as a security tool is emphasized, the state system can be protected. In this manner, both the immediate and the underlying aspects of twenty-first-century conflict can be addressed.

CONCEPTUAL CLARITY

This paper is premised on the notion that one of the challenges we currently face is to develop the conceptual model through which we can organize thinking, state structures and policy. Strategy is an attempt to match military-related means to specified political ends in the most efficient and effective manner[2] How we conceive of our security environment is of critical importance in determining the priority of political goals and the appropriate means for achieving those objectives. We must step back in order to move forward.

For example, the Cold War not only structured actual state behaviour, but as a concept structured the manner in which politicians and security analysts thought about those state relations. That is to say, the actual competition played out between the Soviet Union and the United States required other states to react in certain ways. States defined their position in world politics as aligned with one of the two superpowers or in a catch-all category of non-aligned. The interactions between states simultaneously rested and reinforced a conceptualization that viewed security through a bipolar lens. The threat was relatively clear for both sides (or assumed to be clear as Third World conflicts were understood in terms of how they fit into an East versus West competition). This rather straightforward threat assessment paralleled the emergence of a technological development with profound military implications – the harnessing of the atom.

The strategic cornerstone of the Cold War – nuclear deterrence – fostered and was supported by a relatively simple strategic environment. The nature of the deterrent threat presented the adversary a prospect of incontestable costs and had the effect of 'focusing the mind'.[3] The threat of assured destruction was a rather crude, but direct message. The conceptualization of the strategic system as bipolar meant that such a clear message of security consequences had to be sent essentially in one direction to one recipient. The evolution of this strategy of nuclear deterrence created a unique security system in which the actual continued existence of one's adversary became the basis of one's own security. The mutual context of assured destruction placed significant constraints on the competition between the superpowers.[4] The constraints may have been so powerful that leaders of the Soviet Union may have accepted the internal collapse of empire as less risky than military efforts to retain central control.

Whether the effects of nuclear deterrence were as profound as suggested above is less important than the recognition that nuclear deterrence was a remarkable departure as a model for organizing one's national security. Prior to the nuclear–bipolar age, the offence–defence model assumed security rested in the ability to physically take and secure territory (or sea lanes as in the case of the British and other naval powers). It had been the dominant model of security for most of military history. Finding the correct mix between offence and defence was the critical strategic calculus that drove tactics, operations, procurement and organizations. The notion that security during the period of 1945–1990 would be organized under a different model would have been viewed as utterly radical in 1944. Particularly from the point of view of the Soviet Union and the United States, who were achieving their political goals through the successful application of the offence–defence approach. The emergence of deterrence as a dominant security model was a response to a profound shift in capabilities, which required a re-thinking of the relationship between war and survival. The conceptualization of the security environment as bipolar facilitated the general acceptance of deterrence, since it was seen as the best means of achieving the containment of each sides' principal adversary. (Note that the bipolar conceptualization itself was a major departure from the pattern of diplomatic history in which multipolar thinking and dynamics tended to dominate).

In 1945 a significant shift in the capabilities available for violence and the structure of political relations led to a reorganization of security around a different security model. As we move forward into the twenty-first century, more slowly, but assuredly, the need for reorganization and rethinking is arising again. In this regard 11 September 2001 may have accelerated such thinking (and may have narrowed such thinking too much), but the events of that day were only a premature manifestation of underlying trends in technology and information diffusion and organizational adaptation that are irreversible (although scope and speed of diffusion and adaptation are susceptible to manipulation). These trends undermine deterrence as a dominant security model and they can not be adequately addressed with a return to a primary reliance on offence–defence models.

The paper is structured as follows: first, I will turn to the underlying trends I see as effectively changing the security environment of the next few decades. I will identify those trends and importantly show why those trends are likely to persist, thus making them a serious security challenge. I take some time to develop this argument in order to show that these trends will have staying power, however, those more familiar with the literature on the information technology revolution may wish to skim forward. Second, I will introduce the concept of multidimensional conflict, which flows from the trends discussed previously. I will show why deterrence and offence–defence models are important, but inadequate. Third, I will introduce the remaining continuum of security models necessary in a multidimensional threat environment – recovery, preventive offence and pre-emption. Finally, I will conclude with an outline of a strategy of IS from the particular perspective of the United States.[5]

TRENDS IN THE INFORMATION AGE: SECURITY IMPLICATIONS

It had become commonplace by the mid-1990s to speak of living in 'the information age'.[6] The designation of a particular time of human history as an identifiable 'age' is meant to highlight its distinctiveness from the past. It signals that a transformation has taken place in the way human activity is conducted and/or defined. One of the central human activities that is greatly affected when such transitions occur is warfare. In fact, the movement from one 'age' to another has been intertwined with developments in the ability to conduct warfare. In other words, transformations in the conduct of war have brought about societal change and societal change has reinforced corrections on the battlefield.[7] The dynamic force behind such transformations has, at many times, been advancements in technology.[8] Thus, it is not surprising that the growing ubiquity of personal computers and other information technologies is viewed not only as the basis for a new societal age but as the foundation for a new form of warfare as well.[9]

The distinction of the late twentieth century as 'the' information age (has there ever been 'an' age without information?) rests specifically on the recognition that the micro-processing silicon chip has created a new level of combined computational and communicative power in the form of the networked computer. While individual computers in isolation represent powerful tools, it has been the connecting of these devices that has proven to be a truly significant advance. Computer networks support everything from local, regional and national banking systems to telephone switching systems and transportation structures. Information age technology also includes fax machines, cellular phones and satellite communications. While these technologies have important consequences in isolation, it is their integration into networked platforms that is significant. The progression of the information age will be dictated primarily by the growing significance and ubiquitousness of the networked computer. This trend is captured most vividly by the explosion of interest and usage of the internet – the network of computer networks. Initially conceived of as part of an American defence plan to improve communications during a nuclear attack, the internet has transformed computer usage.[10] While the creation, accumulation, and manipulation of information has always been a central part of human activity (warfare in particular),[11] the computational and communicative power of the networked computer has produced some distinctive consequences. By identifying these consequences we can analyse the potential changes in human practices that may emerge. There seem to be at least five inescapable features that can be ascribed to the information age. They revolve around the ideas of accessibility, availability, speed, affordability and recursive simplicity.

Accessibility

The networking of personal computers has led in turn to the networking of individual networks. The universe of these networks, what is now commonly referred to as cyberspace, carries data and information in all of its forms.[12] This high (and ever growing) degree of connectivity has decreased tremendously the obstacles to information retrieval. Through the use of modems or wireless devices, individuals sitting at home or outside a cave can now connect into cyberspace to access depositories of information worldwide. To a certain degree, access to information in the past had been geographically dependent. The purpose of creating collective depositories of information, such as libraries and archives, was to enhance common access to public information. One's ability to access these depositories depended on being able to travel physically to the collection. While there has existed the option to receive some of this information by courier, such a process typically has required requests that are both narrow and specific. This is difficult to achieve unless one has come into contact with related resources, which likely only occurs through direct physical contact with the related material. A tremendous advance in information access is created when retrieval of information is not primarily dependent on being in geographic proximity to the information storage facility itself.[13]

Availability

Housing information in central depositories to increase access to it has a number of important consequences. A system of information retrieval that depends on geographic proximity for access requires an enormous amount of duplication. Since many people may wish access to particular information, it must be distributed to all of the local depositories found in the system. If the information is not physically on-site it is not available for retrieval.[14] In this system, availability depends on how many copies can be made and stored in relation to how many information retrievers are at work. The difference between access and availability is important. Living near a library might mean one has access to a book, but if someone has already checked out the only copy, the book will not be available for some specified time. Cyberspace offers a significant advance in availability by creating the opportunity for multiple simultaneous retrieval of information. The limitation on availability is not dependent on how many copies of a particular instrument exists, but on how many users can access the particular digitized database. This should prove a less vexing and less expensive problem. Increasing a computer network's ability to handle more users will prove to be more cost effective than having to duplicate the actual source of information by the same number of users.

Aside from multiple simultaneous information retrieval, availability in the information age can also be discussed in sheer quantitative terms. Being less geographically dependent for access, means having available much more information than in the past. The existence of cyberspace allows the retrieval of information that was physically unavailable because of geographic distance. In fact, one of the growing problems with the information age is how to manage too much information.

Speed

A third feature of the information age is the enormous increase in computational and communicative speed. What is distinctive about this age is that vast sums of accessible information can be disseminated and processed in seconds. The computational speed of computers has grown exponentially and so has network connectivity. When the ARPANET was first developed, modem speed was about one-tenth the speed of the slowest modems in the late 1980s.[15] Other modes of information transmission, such as fax machines, cellular phones, and satellite television, now enable vast numbers of information seekers to have up-to-the-minute or even real-time knowledge of events. The implications for the decision-making process of individuals and organizations are significant. The time it takes to collect initial information, analyse and process that information, make a decision and implement it has been tremendously compressed. The speed associated with information age technology means that more information can be handled in a faster manner. Previously, to speed up a decision-making cycle, information retrieval and analysis had to be shortened (since they were the most time-consuming). Information technology, while not eliminating this problem, makes it much less vexing. A large amount of information from multiple sources can now be retrieved without putting undue time pressures on the overall decision-making cycle.

Affordability

The fourth distinctive feature, and perhaps most important overall, is that the resource base required to exploit the advantages of this technology is relatively low and is decreasing rapidly. The average price for computing power has been decreasing. Graphic based point-and-click software has now become standard with computers and wireless devices. This requires the user to know little more than the functions that certain icons (pictures) represent. Use and programming of VCRs now requires people to push a few buttons and speak in a clear voice to a voice-activated machine. Fax machines, cellular phones, VCRs, and even computers are following the same pattern of the digital hand-held calculator, which was a luxury item in the early 1970s and now are owned by elementary school students in most developed countries. For the median average income family in developed countries, the cost of computers and their related devices is no longer prohibitive.[16] This is, of course, not to imply that there exist no barriers either financial or skill based, but to suggest that such barriers are becoming less and less significant for general access. Information technology is affordable in the broad sense of that term. It is requiring the investment of less time for training and money.

Recursive Simplicity

The final general feature of the information age is the inherent recursive nature of computer technology, which supports a clear trend of ever expanding growth in access, availability, and speed with a simultaneous reduction in cost and skill barriers (although probably not at the rate experienced in the past 20 years). Recursion can be identified as self-similarity in structure, where symmetry runs across scale; in essence, pattern inside pattern.[17] Put another way, a recursive structure is one in which the whole is structurally identical to its parts.[18] While recursive structures exist in nature (snowflakes and ferns show this quality), they were originally discovered as mathematically based constructions. By identifying the principle of self-similarity across scale, mathematicians Helge von Koch and Benoit Mandelbrot, showed that fractal patterns could lead to infinite length in a finite space.[19] These observations laid the foundation upon which early developers of computer software constructed large programs out of existing smaller ones. The recursiveness of software tremendously simplifies its development. Instead of thinking of each independent part of a design separately, base commands can be re-used in similar but broader commands again and again. Thus, one need only know a fraction of the levels (essentially its foundation) to understand and construct multi-level designs. The application of pattern within pattern as a structuring principle allows for exponential growth factors. The microchip has been constructed recursively. In a broad sense, the faster chip is simply more chips pressed into one central component. The ability (through greater miniaturization) to construct a chip simply by compressing more chips into the same space means that the basic design of the chip is not radically altered from its slower antecedent and that no new design is necessary every time one seeks greater computational speed. Because there is recursive simplicity to both computer software and hardware the trend toward greater speed, access, and availability can be predicted. In the mid-1990s, for example, the world wide web portion of the internet had nearly 22 million pages of content and the internet, itself, was doubling in size every three months.[20] As with Koch's snowflake, the growth in these features may be infinite even though the principal device we use – the computer – represents a finite space.

Implications

These five general characteristics of the information age certainly promise to affect human relations in significant ways. There is a growing literature, particularly associated with military consequences, that argues that the information age amounts to revolutionary change. It is not the objective of this paper to discuss directly the revolutions in military affairs (RMA) debate,[21] but to highlight the revolutionary effects that may be related to the information age. Two implications that do portend a dramatic shift in human activity can be extrapolated from the five general characteristics discussed above.[22]

Individual Empowerment

Taken as a whole, having quick access to enormous amounts of available information at a reasonable cost has the potential to empower individuals.[23] Current and emerging information technology provides the single person the ability to collect, organize, analyse, and disseminate the same amount of information that only 40 years ago required a team of technicians and researchers.[24] The computational power that is now found in the small *personal* computer sitting on the desktop (or lap) of one individual could be found only in computers requiring large institutional support (university and government mainframes) 25 years ago. This impact is noteworthy because it stands in direct contrast to the Orwellian vision of the relationship between technology and the individual.[25] In George Orwell's *1984*, advancements in computational and communicative power enhanced the power of the state over the individual creating the 'Big Brother' effect.[26] There is no doubt that current technological advancement can increase surveillance capability and could support (to a degree) the ability of the authoritarian state to control its populace. However, the flow of events in Eastern Europe and the former Soviet Union at the end of the 1980s revealed that control of information resources was beyond the power of the communist state. In an ironic twist, it was an information supported domino effect that led in quick succession to the collapse of seven East European regimes and the Soviet Union itself.

While satellite television, radio, fax and telephony can be used with effect to undermine authoritarian structures, they also remain important sources of centralized information control.[27] The networked computer, particularly as a communicative tool, however, is the information age platform that to date seems most supportive of individual, rather than state empowerment. The empowerment of individuals gained through information technology spans across political, economic, and social realms.[28]

Revolution in Organization

While individual empowerment is important, revolutions are not made in isolation. Broader consequences, while related to and affected by individual empowerment, will appear to the degree to which the five characteristics of access, availability, speed, affordability and recursive simplicity bring about organizational re-structuring. The true revolution afoot is organizational in character. The key question is whether the network will become the superior form of organization for the information age. These five characteristics seem to hold such potential. The empowered individual can engage in organized activity without the costs, formality and, most importantly, attributable presence that tend to follow traditional bureaucratic organizations.

German sociologist Max Weber argued that organizational form can both define and be defined by the political, economic and social structures of society.[29] He felt that modern society, with its money economy as a foundation, was becoming increasingly affected by the emergence of bureaucracy as the dominant organizational structure. Weber argued that the advance of the bureaucratic form was tied to its superiority as an organizational type in meeting the demands of political, economic and social activities that required administration to be 'discharged precisely, unambiguously, continuously and with as much speed as possible'.[30] The ideal Weberian bureaucracy has five distinguishing characteristics: a focus on position rather than personality; hierarchy of rational–legal authority; written system of rules; division of labour (specialization); and, a career system tied to the organizational chart. The visualization of bureaucracy is the step-pyramid-shaped 'org chart', where power flows from the pinnacle down to the base. Weber asserted that bureaucracy profoundly affects social dynamics. Loyalty is directed toward the position rather than the occupant of the position. The goal is to rationalize the processing of information and decision flows. The consequence of this structure, according to Weber, is the creation of efficiency and the promotion of de-personalization. Although he viewed bureaucracy as a superior organizational form, Weber looked bleakly on its effect on individuals. He saw this organizational form spawning a 'narrowed professional, publicly certified and examined, and ready for tenure and career', who valued systemic consistency and coherence over the 'magical elements of thought'.[31]

Weber, of course, did not argue that bureaucracy was the ideal form of organization, but that it was relatively superior to other forms, particularly those associated with feudal, patrimonial and early plutocratic administrations.[32] One of the significant managerial dilemmas created by vesting authority in hierarchically demarcated functions is that some efficiencies do exist in de-centralizing decision-making power, particularly for implementation purposes. Weberian bureaucracy, at its core, rests on the principle of hierarchical control and thus is not well suited to grappling with situations that require dispersion of authority.

The progress of the Industrial Age (presumably the 'age' from which we are now transitioning), according to Weber, was supported by the routinization and rationalization created by bureaucratization. The market capitalist economy, in particular, thrives on business being conducted through reference to calculable rules and 'without reference to persons'. This is the goal of bureaucracy. But if we are moving toward a new 'age' in which social, economic, and political activities are dramatically altered might not a new organizational model begin to dominate. In line with Weberian logic, this organizational model will both produce and be produced by alterations in human practices across the spectrum of societal structures. The network stands in sharp contrast to bureaucracy and may represent the first effective challenger to this now 'traditional' form.

The *information technology network*, as organizational form, is distinguished structurally by its lack of centre (or put another way, the centre is not central) and its reliance on high technology. The network is nodal in structure, flat in visualization and essentially anarchical. In all, its characteristics might be counterpoised with those underlying Weberian bureaucracy (see table 1).[33]

The information technology network differs significantly from bureaucracy in organizational form. International relations theory defines an anarchical structure as one lacking centralized authority over the basic units of the system. The information technology network, in

FIGURE 1

COMPARISON OF BUREACRACY AND THE INFORMATION
TECHNOLOGY NETWORK

BUREAUCRACY	INFORMATION TECHNOLOGY NETWORK
Positional impersonality	Re-emerging personality (cloaked)*
Hierarchy of rational-legal authority	Modified anarchy of technical skill-based authority
Written code of rules	Norm-based action; reciprocity
Division of labour	Multi-tasking
Organizational chart advancement	Advancement through individual distinction

*The word 'cloaked' is used to capture the phenomenon reported on the Internet of people portraying themselves as different people, genders, ages etc.

its ideal form, approximates a modified anarchical structure;[34] that is, linkages between nodes may emanate from some centre, but the functioning of the information technology network is not dependent on that central node.

The original thinking behind the development of the communications network that led to the internet emphasized the need for *a structure without centre*. From a security standpoint, a hierarchically structured system offers the enemy a prized target – the centralized authority. Whether it is a communication system or a political structure, elimination of centralized authority can bring about the collapse of hierarchically based systems. During the Cold War, this was the logic behind first-strike nuclear attacks that sought to 'de-capitate' leadership either by the direct targeting of leaders or their means to communicate with their defence/retaliatory forces. It was determined that one could reduce the vulnerability of the communication system by replacing the 'Achilles heel' of a centralized command centre with, paradoxically, the absence of a centre.[35] The information technology network as an abstract organizational structure parallels the form envisioned in that original Defense Department program. The internet is currently the best example of this form. While it still relies on infrastructural support from government and large institutions (like universities and research centres) collapse of one node or set of nodes does not dramatically affect functions and processes across the entire information technology network.[36] The specific exploitation of information technologies by an individual or group no longer depends upon direct subsidy from a state apparatus.

In anarchical structures, authority is derived from the relative differences in power possessed by a system's units. Realist international relations theory holds that the distribution of territorial state power across the system impacts the functioning of the system. Similarly, in the information technology network, authority is not vested in hierarchically demarcated positions, but rather is derived from differences in the distribution of power. Power in the information technology network resides with those individuals that have *greater technical skill*, those who know how to manage and manipulate the technology best to achieve specified goals in the most efficient and effective manner. Leaders will be those who have ideas and the technical knowledge of how to spread and sustain those ideas through a network.[37]

In the information technology network, functional based positional authority is inconsequential (ideally it is non-existent). The anarchical nature of the information technology network creates a structural imperative to focus on technical skill. While a minimal level of skill is required for entry into the information technology network (on the internet it is quite minimal for basic functions like e-mail communication), continued access and advancement require personal initiative in maintaining and enhancing one's own level of technical skill. The nature of the technology, noted earlier, supports a trend of continual change. Survival and achievement in such an environment require consistent personal effort. Centralized functional controls will be taxed to keep up.

The information technology network is supported through *norm based regulation* that rests upon the principle of reciprocity, rather than a formal legal code of rule. This is necessitated by two factors. First, the absence of centrally designated authority inhibits the creation of law that is deemed legitimate by all units. Without a formal hierarchy of authority, the mechanism for establishing the regulation of the information technology network amounts to nothing more than what is ultimately most efficient. One begins to adopt or accept certain norms of behaviour because general consensus clusters around more efficient practices and avoids practices proven to be inefficient. The process is self-reinforcing as individuals reciprocate actions taken by others with cooperation based on the expectation that they will receive cooperation in return.[38] Second, since activity in the information technology network is dependent on personal skills (which are in flux) rather than bureaucratically designated job descriptions, regulation must be flexible.

Since the nature of information technology encourages rapid development, formal regulation will be constantly out of sync with the actual processes and dynamics of the information technology network. Informal norm based regulation is much more adaptive.[39]

The emphasis on individual technical skill in the context of a flat organizational chart promotes a fourth distinction between bureaucracy and the information technology network. To the degree that formal positions promote a division of labour and specialization, information technology networks promote 'multi-tasking'. For example, in the realm of information publication, the traditional division of labour between writer, editor, mass publisher is now combined in 'desk-top' publishing. While the information technology network does not eliminate the need for specialized expertise, it does formally organize itself to allow for individuals to function across specialities and efficiently produce the high quality once only ascribed to bureaucracies.

These characteristics add up to a most significant consequence. The information technology network can provide individuals with access to *shared global and local situational awareness*. In Weberian terms, one of the great advantages of the bureaucratic structure is the management of large enterprises through stepped supervisory power. In a bureaucracy, centralized authority provides strategic direction through its grasp of the whole; that is, its global situational awareness. Operational and tactical direction is funnelled through middle layers of authority and base production is conducted at the specialized local level, which only needs to be aware of its particular functions. The amount of time and effort required to provide everyone at the local level with strategic vision and the central authority with specialized local knowledge according to bureaucratic proponents made such a management approach unnecessarily inefficient. The bureaucratic structure, thus, serves as the means to disaggregate and disseminate knowledge. Information is distributed in parallel to bureaucratic functions. While this approach was a gain in efficiency over feudal or patrimonial organizations it does have its limitations. The bureaucratic reliance on standard operating procedures and the problem of centralized decisions/decentralized implementation ('the left hand does not know what the right hand is doing') are the most commonly noted problems with bureaucratic management.

The information technology network exploits the availability, accessibility, affordability and speed of modern information technology and organizes knowledge in a radically different fashion. In parallel with its flat structure, all individuals can effectively have their local situational awareness informed by a sense of the whole. It is technically possible to have the necessary amount of information traverse swiftly enough across a network in an organized fashion as to make shared situational awareness an efficient mode of operation. The emergence of this *shared* situational awareness is actually the key manifestation of a organizational revolution that could justify the designation of this period of human history as a definable 'age'.

What are the national security implications of empowered individuals working and organizing across networks? At a superficial level, the ability to organize more flexibly with less regard to geographical constraint means the potential for more actors in the security realm. This would not be a concern at the national security level, if it were not for the parallel trend in the ability to do great harm. The twentieth century saw a major leap forward in the capacity to destroy. In simple terms, it is requiring less and less effort in order to kill more and more people or disrupt greater levels of societal activity. The 'dual-use' nature of most technological advancement is what makes this trend so dire. Crude explosives can be developed from commercial products, but so too can chemical and biological agents. Base resources used for research in biomedicines (gene therapy, for example) or in energy production (nuclear waste) can be used for great harm. Network computers are vulnerable to disruptive attack and data is open to corruption or destruction by using computers themselves. Productive technologies can be used for destructive ends – the definition of the term 'weapon' is increasingly based on how you use something, rather than its specific design. Exploiting networks, it will become increasingly easier for a few individuals (small groups from the tens to hundreds) to organize and inflict damage (death and/or disruption) that at the beginning of the twentieth century would have required thousands of troops engaged in sustained aggressive action.

If individuals become serious national security threats, the pool of potential attackers becomes so wide as to make source identification extremely problematic. In theory, these trends in individual empowerment, network organizations, and destructive potential lead to the potential for great harm delivered anonymously. This opens an entirely new dimension of conflict.

MULTIDIMENSIONAL CONFLICT

The trends discussed above suggest that our conception of security must include several different dimensions of potential conflict that defy prioritization since each dimension has the potential for serious consequences. As with any conceptualization, the term multi-dimensional conflict is a simplification meant to illuminate certain important factors. As introduced here, the term suggests that conflict may be generated across three distinct but potentially related dimensions:

1. State
2. State proxies
3. Networks

State Dimension

Although some authors have suggested that great power conflict is less likely with the advent of weapons of mass destruction and increases in conventional firepower, conflict between states remains a possibility.[40] During the last decade, conflict between states has taken place even in regions with high degrees of integration and institutionalization.[41] Of all international actors, states retain the most significant potential for sustained conflict on a wide scale.

The most developed states are positioned to take advantage of anonymity and networked forms of organization, particularly in the area of intelligence gathering and surveillance, which can be combined with advances in precision weaponry for devastating effect when overt conflict is required. This state dimension of conflict will, over time, probably expand to competition (at least in the protection of economically important platforms) in outer space, which will come to have national security implications.[42]

Interestingly, however, the most developed states will also tend to be the international actors most susceptible to disruption and or destruction of information technology based assets. The more important such technologies and networked organizational forms become for economic and military activities, the more intriguing they become as specific targets.[43] The interconnectedness of these systems across developed states does produce an interdependent relationship that might constrain states from considering actions to disrupt or destroy another state's infrastructure, but such a constraining effect only encompasses a very narrow set of states (United States and Western Europe, perhaps) and it has been historically debatable as an approach to national security.

There is an unclear degree of risk associated with direct state activity in the specific realm of information warfare. The lines between intelligence gathering and establishing the basis for pre-emptive action is somewhat blurred and reliance on deterrence would require a clarification of the types of activity that would lead to major responses.[44] As part of the normal course of intelligence gathering, states will attempt to infiltrate important economic, communication, and perhaps military networked systems. The efforts needed to retrieve information are not much different from the activities that would be needed to provide sufficient access to enable more disruptive or destructive actions. The difference does not lie in the capabilities, or tactics, but rather the intentions of those engaged. The potential for anonymity combined with a lack of clear consequences if 'the cover is blown', could undermine deterrence between state actors at least in the area of information warfare. What helps sustain deterrence to some degree is the fact that if a state were discovered to be engaged in major information operations, it would have a wide set of values that could be held at risk to diplomatic, economic, and even military responses.

In a general sense, defence and deterrence are still relevant security models in the state-to-state dimension of conflict. Overt aggression can be handled through such models, although some concern must be directed to understanding how the potential for anonymity might embolden state action in certain types of aggressive behaviour, such as spying or information operations. States should be the most sophisticated actors in these types of operations. If, in fact, deterrence is effective in constraining overt aggression, a channelling of security competition toward information conflict is likely.

State Proxy Dimension

Such a channelling effect might also include reliance on proxies so that security competition is managed indirectly between states. This is one of the patterns of the Cold War. Locked in an intense political, economic and military competition, but constrained from direct action against each other, both superpowers used third-party proxies (both other states and non-state actors) to thwart, antagonize, and challenge each other.

While the Cold War is over, the logic of proxies remains a distinct security dimension.

What distinguishes proxies analytically is that their specific ability to disrupt or destroy on a significant enough scale to be a national security concern is dependent upon state subsidy. These security threats can be distinguished on the basis of their reliance on outside state support. States have continually used third parties as conduits for indirect security competition. Syrian, Iranian and Iraqi efforts against Israel have posed serious challenge without engendering direct Israeli action and the dispute over Kashmir has a proxy dimension to it as well.

This dimension is obviously not new and can be understood in the context of defence and deterrence models. However, the critical security trends noted in this paper suggest that proxies could become a more common agent of security competition, because the amount of state subsidy necessary to enable a proxy to be a significant security threat is declining. If it increasingly becomes easier for proxy forces to organize and sustain action, deep state involvement becomes less necessary. Groups asking for a little assistance from sympathetic client states may find those states more amenable to support. The potential for anonymous networked organizations empowered with increasing destructive potential could give states unable to compete directly against more powerful economic and military countries a promising option for security competition. Defence and deterrence strategies directed at client states will have to overcome the issue of deniability. Again, while this is not new, the frequency and severity of this type of threat might be taxing traditional security models. Deterrence failures may be less acceptable if the capability of proxies continues to increase.

Network Dimension

Throughout human history there have always been individuals and small groups completely unsatisfied with the current order of things, who sought to work around the system (crime) or completely overturn it (revolutionaries and anarchists). This has always been a very small percentage of the world's population, but in a world of billions of people it is not an insignificant number. From the perspective of national security, such individuals and groups on their own rarely achieved much beyond the level of nuisance. This is the dimension of conflict that is most profoundly affected by the information age. If there is anything new in terms of security threats, it is that individuals and groups are now potentially quite disruptive and destructive in their own right. These networks (sub-national, terror, criminal, or individual anarchists) are distinguishable analytically from proxies in that they do not require state subsidy to mount a serious security threat. In fact, it is the absence of state control and/or regulation (whether it is of territory, such as in Afghanistan or financial flows through a poorly regulated banking system) that provides the space for networks to take root and develop. The communication and transportation revolutions of the past century now give individuals and small groups an ability to organize in a sustained manner. While this would be an interesting development for security, it only becomes critical when such an ability links with the capacity to do great harm. There is a qualitative difference when a small group can listen to an individual rage against the system while sitting under a rock and when that individual can broadcast those rantings to millions of others some of whom may have the capacity to take serious action on those words.

The network dimension supports two security threats that must now be taken seriously. First, are the terrorist groups or other organizations that seek to use violence to create new political directions within the state system. The network dimension means that they are more capable and potent. Second, is the irreducible few who simply want to destroy the system. This historically marginalized segment of society will be able to do enormously disruptive and destructive things in the future. The 'problem of the few' is that size no longer matters, but their disaffection does.

Across all three dimensions, it is the network dimension in which the potential for anonymity is the highest and where the traditional models of security are completely inadequate.

Multidimensional Conflict and Defence

One way to organize national security policy is to focus on the concept of defence, where your primary objective is to deny opponents the potential to disrupt or destroy national assets. While defence can certainly be practised, its reliability is highly suspect when set against the consequences of individual empowerment, networks and increased destructive potential. There are at least two important factors that support the assertion that the ability to disrupt and destroy will outpace the ability to deny.

The Fractal Effect. The French understood where the Maginot Line ended. The conscious decision not to extend the line of defence to the sea was made for a number of reasons, including a determination that it was unnecessary. Although history revealed the poverty of that decision, the point is that the French could determine the geographical expanse that *needed* to be defended. Cyberspace when defined as the total universe of computer network connections, in an abstract sense may be considered a finite space at any given moment. And yet given the fact that an information technology network rests on access, there is a fractal quality to cyberspace. That is, while cyberspace maybe the sum total of all connections, the non-linear web-like organization of cyberspace suggests that there are an infinite number of access points. The problem this presents for defence is enormous. As connectivity broadens and deepens, the security of any particular system is only as good as its weakest access point. Since cyberspace disregards distinctions between national and international, private and public, simply *defining* the expanse to be defended becomes difficult, let alone developing the coordination that would be necessary for security. Isolation or segmentation can enhance the ability to defend. But the isolated information system borders on an oxymoron.[45] When traditional terrestrial space is considered, this effect is also relevant. As the number of people needed to inflict great harm declines, the relevant geographical space that must be defended expands. In Central Europe during the Cold War, there were a limited number of places (Fulda Gap) through which a major tank invasion could take place. This made defence more viable. In the information age, nineteen people can cross into a country from many access points, regroup, and inflict tremendous harm.

Too Many Actors. Under a defence model, security is found in limiting the number of people who have contact with information and access to capabilities that can produce harm. A conventional view of defence wishes to 'lock up' assets. The access points are identified, what is needed to get through the lock is the 'key'. Denial to the key becomes the objective of defence. The lock and key metaphor obscures the organizational change underlying the globalization of communication and technology transfers. Access and denial are better conceived as an issue of open portals, rather than locked doors. The portals can be large or narrow, but they are open. To close them is to opt out of the strength of a political, economic and military system increasingly reliant on networked computing and to move back into a pre-information age structure, where traditional dynamics rule. The issue is how do you defend when global interconnection exists. To attempt to defend by breaking the connection is to miss the point. In a general sense, if that is the option adopted, an opponent attempting to disrupt the advantages one gains from the information age has won. Since there are simply too many potential actors, little is gained on defining who has the keys and who doesn't. Traditional defence becomes unreliable and in some instances counterproductive.

Multidimensional Conflict and Deterrence

At the end of the Second World War, defence as a model was also viewed as insufficient. The turn toward deterrence was a response to that inadequacy. The requirements of deterrence include two basic points that could easily be overlooked in a nuclear-bipolar context, but are challenged by the existence of individuals empowered through networks. Deterrence assumes the scope of attack can be quickly determined and that the source of the attack will be recognized. In order to threaten costs that exceed the expected benefits of an attack, a state attempting to deter attack must be able to assess the likely damage from the offensive attack and what the opposing side hopes to gain. This assessment helps determine what to hold at risk that might persuade the opponent not to attack in the first place. Of course, a credible promise to retaliate (that inflicts the outweighing deterrent costs) rests on the presumption that the deterring state can identify the attacker.

The most significant problem of a 'retaliation in kind' model of deterrence in the context of information age trends is that attacks may not emanate from a state at all. The technology diffusion is such that small groups – terrorists, organized crime, hackers – now have a capability that once only belonged to states themselves. They can threaten societal-wide damage instantly or disrupt military operations. Deterrence requires that the opponent be identifiable. This may not be possible. Of course one can threaten to seek out opponents and promise great retribution, but there is a lot of room between threatening and *finding* them. The prospect of avoiding detection is at least high enough that most actors motivated enough to contemplate warfare will be unfazed by promises of future discovery. The difficulties with pursuing deterrence when source of attack can not be assessed should be obvious. What do you hold at risk prior to attack, if you are not sure who might attack you?[46] Blanket threats may lack credibility and cross-signals may not be obvious. Many analysts now see a link between American behaviour in the wake of losses in the Marine barracks attack in Lebanon, Somalia, and the Khobar towers even though each had distinct foreign policy goals directed at different states. US policy was not directed at Osama bin Laden in those deployments, but US behaviour may have sent certain signals to bin Laden that undermined strategic deterrence.

The difficulty with multidimensional conflict is that the signalling necessary for deterrence (about will and capability) is open to greater misinterpretation either because the threat is made too imprecisely or because it is directed too narrowly.

AN EXPANSION OF SECURITY MODELS

Defence and Deterrence must be supplemented and reinforced with other security approaches. This section discusses the three additions: preventive offence, pre-emption and recovery. The key to the notion of a strategy of IS, however, is to emphasize the interconnectedness between these security approaches. Multidimensional conflict requires a comprehensive strategic response, not a menu-list approach in which isolated strategies are chosen depending on contingencies. One of the fundamental reasons for this is the likelihood that such contingencies will defy easy source identification. The overall objective of IS is to move security competition toward more easily managed dimensions. In a relative sense, state competition is the dimension most susceptible to defence and deterrence. Source identification, signalling and value assessment are relatively easier at the state security dimension. The goal of IS should be to create overall incentives for states to limit networks and curtail proxies thus reducing the frequency and scope of these other security dimensions. In doing so, IS reinforces the state as primary security actor and the state based international system.

Preventive Offence

If one of the key conditions that undermines defence is the sheer multiplicity of potential threats, security can be enhanced (and defence made more reliable) through preventive action taken to reduce disaffection and access to destructive capability. I use the term preventive offence to emphasize the strategic nature of these activities, which can and are done for other reasons as well.

It is important to recognize that the reduction of disaffection and access must rely on non-military as well as military means. First, economic tools can be used to reform the financial system to make it more difficult to sustain networks and create a mix of economic incentives and disincentives for states considering the use of proxies. Second, developmental aid can be used to dry up some of the disenchantment that may lead to aggressive action. This is not humanitarian aid, but a long-term means that should be directed on stabilizing state authority as it relates to citizens. State structures based on mass support would find incentives in constraining networks and proxies. Third, democratic institutionalization and free marketization can be promoted again as long-term means. While there is some theoretical evidence to suggest that such domestic structures inhibit conflict between like-structured states, the broader rationale for such an approach is that such states in the twentieth century have tended to be the most stable forms of governance that tend to channel disaffection toward non-violent resolutions. Despite promoting individual freedoms, they also tend to maintain reasonable domestic order. At the systemic level, the development of more democratic states would mean a world of states more in line with the governance structures of the leading great powers in 2002, thus creating a 'buy-in' dynamic toward perpetuation of the current system. Fourth, the legal management of weapons and dual-purpose commodities is a critical security means for constraining access. This area requires great consideration, particularly in the area of bio- and information technologies which are driven by commercial incentives that tend to discount or overlook security implications. Such management will have to be contained in domestic legislation and international obligations. Fifth, diplomatic isolation and engagement are important means of preventive offence. Such tools must be applied to turn states into agents of greater control over networks and discourage state support of proxies. Reaching sufficient consensus for such diplomacy is unlikely in the absence of a common threat perception. The trends of individual empowerment and lethality, however, may prove sufficient over time to produce a consensus (a major destructive event may also prove, unfortunately, helpful in this regard). Finally, constant surveillance and intelligence leading to covert operations and overt military action against staging areas, bases, training and information systems must be considered viable means.

Such actions can enhance defence by physically reducing sources of threats and capabilities and creating incentives for states (particularly weak ones) to reduce support for proxies and reign in networks. Such actions reduce crisis stability and must be carefully chosen with consideration of the messages being sent to multiple actors.

Pre-emption

During the Cold War much attention was directed to the concept of crisis stability. The general argument from this literature recognized that preventive military tactics and pre-emptive strategies degraded crisis stability. That is, in environments in which the prospect of military conflict is increasing (crisis), strategies that put a premium on acting first would undermine attempts to manage military–diplomatic disputes short of actual war. When security rests on the need to avoid war (as it does in an environment of mutual assured destruction), pre-emption is a counterproductive strategy. However, where deterrence is not credible, defence not reliable, and the consequences of their failure is extensive damage, pre-emption must be considered. In this case, security may actually rest on the use of force.

Pre-emption can bolster defence through the disruption of enemy planning and destruction of enemy capabilities. The threat of pre-emption may have a suppression effect on the pursuit of certain banned capabilities (again, primarily more effective on weak states) making defence more viable.

Both preventive offence and pre-emption are primarily efforts to restore some viability to a strategy of defence. However, both can have an indirect deterrent effect, if incentives are created for buying into a state system (there are then costs for disrupting it which states might wish to avoid) and disincentives are created for being associated with proxies or not constraining networks. If the negative consequences of such associations or failure to constrain are significant enough, some deterrent effect could be created.

Recovery

The reality of a security environment in which defence is not reliable and deterrence not credible is that states will have to confront the consequences of serious destructive acts. Combined with other approaches, recovery will have to be seen as a security strategy. What I mean by recovery is the capability to regain lost assets in a swift and comprehensive manner – to be able to return to pre-attack political, economic and civil life quickly. The political goal of recovery – what makes it a security strategy, rather than a mere civil defence function – is to minimize the gains an attacker can expect. Although damage will have occurred, if recovery is comprehensive and viewed as well-managed, the attacked population is likely to rally around its competent government. Will to respond is likely to be hardened. In this sense recovery can be linked to deterrence. The key will be to leave open the possibility of a full range of responses that can be directed at states, state proxies and networks. Although source identification and cross-signalling will remain as problems, if expected gains from an attack can be minimized and retaliatory costs are high, the risk of action can be increased. Some deterrence leverage can be provided through a recovery approach, but only if the capability of recovery is revealed and the promised response is severe and perhaps not so precise.

Of course the balance between revealing recovery plans and undermining them can be complicated if such plans induce some sense of national peril. This could adversely affect economic behaviour (short-term versus long-term investing, for example). The presentation of recovery is thus a very significant element of its success. It must be established as positive preparation, pragmatic and in some areas involving a civic duty. To some extent, conceptualizing the qualitatively different security challenge of anonymous destruction as the problem of the few not only has the utility of removing politically charged debates about terrorism, but it conveys the double meaning that this is serious, but not incapacitating (in the sense that the majority of the world's population do not and will not engage in destruction).

The resources and organizational structures for recovery can and should be designed to support defence as well. The implementation of recovery will require a re-conceptualization of the divide between the military battlefield and a crime scene. This may prove, for many democratic countries in particular, a difficult re-conceptualization to make. Since disruptive and destructive anonymity is a real possibility, organizing security strategies primarily around the notion of source identification will prove problematic. From a bureaucratic perspective, if who responds to an attack is dependent upon who initiated the attack, recovery as a strategy will fail (it will also provide little support for deterrence and perhaps even defence). Rather than defining threat in terms of sources (states, state proxies, networks), which is necessary although problematic for preventive offence, pre-emption, defence and deterrence, threat will have to be defined in terms of outcomes. Recovery (and to some extent defence) must be organized around the consequences of attacks, rather than the sources. The security question is how to minimize the costs associated with attacks. The analytical framework must be grounded on the types of costs to be minimized and the capabilities used in an attack. Protocols must be developed that analyse the potential costs of a range of attacks (what is being lost and what capability is causing the loss) against their likelihood so that a risk assessment to guide resource allocation and organizational response can be developed. The use of a chemical agent to cause urban casualties (an attack on a city's downtown) presents a different set of consequences from a chemical attack specifically targeted against economic assets (the trading floor of the NYSE) or one against government (the halls of Congress). Although the attacking capability may be the same, the recovery requirements will be significantly different. This holds true for information attacks and conventional forms of aggression as well.

The utility of thinking through consequences, rather than sources for the purposes of recovery is that it will enable assessments of priorities. Clearly, every contingency can not be anticipated nor met. National governments will have to determine what they can accomplish. In many cases, private corporations (particularly in the area of data recovery and business functionality) and individual citizens will have to play their own roles in developing recovery capabilities and plans. The problem of the few, in particular, will require individual citizens to be preventive, defensive and recovery assets.

INTEGRATED SECURITY AND THE UNITED STATES

The threat of disruptive and destructive anonymity is not country-specific. It represents a condition that will produce a global security environment qualitatively different from the past century. That said, over the next decade, one country is more likely than others to face the full brunt of multidimensional conflict and thus be in most need of a strategy of Integrated Security (IS). Although why the United States will face this challenge can be debated, I would submit that it has less to do with specific policies and more to do with its position in world politics. States will remain concerned with maintaining some security independence relative to Washington (this creates incentives for security competition, at least in terms of intelligence and information-gathering), proxies may be relevant, and certainly networks will have concern over US capabilities. This holds true in terms of economic power and competition and political–cultural competition as well.

The United States has the most significant potential for implementing a strategy of IS and there are some signs that the Bush administration is conducting its response to the September 2001 attacks on the assumption that the attacks represented a premature manifestation of the potential threat from networks (or their direct or indirect use by states) as well as the problem of the few. To date, the Bush administration has, in fact, engaged in a number of actions that would follow from the analysis in this paper.

President Bush's assertion that 'you are either with us or against us' was criticized as being overly simplistic and narrow. However, as a response to the problem of the few it, in fact, produces significant policy flexibility. The United States is incapable on its own to circumscribe access to capabilities sufficiently and it can not manage the problem of the few globally. The only actor that has a chance to intervene realistically is the strong state. The looming challenge is one not simply against the United States, but the state system itself. In this, there may be sufficient incentives for coordinated activity among states as well as important economic players. Corporations need free markets, which only thrive where states are stable.

The Bush administration seems to be following the contours of a strategy of IS. Preventive and pre-emptive means are being employed (in contrast to many years of inhibitions against such means) and deterrence has been down-played. Interestingly, Bush has moved toward less precise deterrent threats and has rested credibility on the notion of sweeping accountability. Although most viewed the administration's belligerent policy toward Iraq as revolving solely around the issue of regime change, from the perspective of IS, pressure on Iraq may also have been an attempt to leverage the Hussein regime, counter-intuitively, to work for US security objectives. As a security competitor, Hussein had significant incentive to rely on proxies, which his training and general support of certain groups attests. The problem for the Bush administration was that this training may have reached down to actors capable of independent action (networks). These groups, in fact, may not have been under the control of Iraq (or for that matter other noted 'rogue states'), but Hussein was likely to have better intelligence than the United States on who they were and their potential. The Bush administration seems to have broken with past practice in indicating that it will not wait for a 'smoking gun' legal evidentiary approach to determine exact source in the aftermath of the next attack, but rather hit back at states that are not doing enough to constrain proxy or network activity. In actually bringing about regime change in Iraq, the Bush administration has bolstered the credibility of this leverage approach. In the case of states like Syria, Iran and North Korea, a strategy of guilt by association may give those regimes sufficient cause to make attempts at curtailing proxies, and, more importantly, networks which the United States can not identify.[47]

Although the United States has tremendous potential to secure itself, across the continuum of IS, it faces an enormous organizational (and conceptual) challenge with regard to recovery. The creation of the Department of Homeland Security was a necessary response to the events of 11 September 2001, but it does not represent the adoption of a strategy of recovery. For the most part, it is an important initial step in coordinating civil defence and disaster relief. It still rests on a bureaucratic structure that organizes responses primarily around identification of source. Currently, it is focused on a coordinating effort. This, over time, will prove inadequate.

The last major shift in security capabilities and conceptualization (the nuclear age and bipolarity) prompted the United States toward a massive reorganization of its approach to security. What is remarkable about the National Security Act of 1947 is that it came on the heels of military victory, which typically does not induce innovation but creates an inclination to support current practices that seemingly have worked. The shift in organization, therefore, speaks of the degree to which the new security environment of nuclear weapons and bipolarity was recognized. The shift toward multidimensional conflict in a structural environment of unipolarity requires an equally profound organizational change. One advantage that existed in 1947 that does not in 2002 is that there was a minimal national security bureaucracy in place relative to today. It is easier to create new bureaucratic structures in the absence of entrenched practices. The success of the Bush administration with regard to improving the security of the United States will likely face as great a challenge domestically (bureaucratically) as internationally (building and holding coalitions).[48]

If the question over whether a new security environment is emerging remains open or is incorrectly defined, failure in both areas is likely. In this, paradoxically, the events of September 2001 may have set in motion a response to actual trends quicker and more comprehensively than if the trends had continued without a major incident. It is important, however, to recognize that the response to information age multidimensional conflict can not be a response to an event (11 September), but must be an answer to an inexorable emergence of a new dimension of security competition. Conceiving of threats as outcomes produced from multiple dimensions is a critical step in developing an integrated continuum of security strategies that respond to twenty-first-century realities.

NOTES

1. Globalization is an often-used, but ill-defined term. For an overview, see Robert Keohane and Joseph Nye, 'Globalization: What's New? What's Not? (And So What?)', *Foreign Policy*, 118 (Spring 2000), pp.104–19. For the purposes of this essay, I understand globalization as a trend of reducing costs in the movement of information, goods, services, financial capital and people across wider expanses of geography. I specify the term *lethal globalization* as an accelerating trend in the diffusion of information, financial capital, goods, services and people which can support disruption and destruction.
2. Richard K. Betts, 'Is Strategy an Illusion?', *International Security*, Vol. 25, No. 2 (Fall 2000), pp.5–50.
3. See in particular Colin S. Gray, 'Nuclear Weapons and the Revolution in Military Affairs', in T.V. Paul *et al.*, *The Absolute Weapon Revisited: Nuclear Arms and the Emerging International Order* (Ann Arbor: University of Michigan Press, 1998), pp.99–136. Gray attributes the notion of what he calls the 'crystal ball effect' to my arguments contained in the same volume.
4. To note constraints such as inhibitions on direct attack against the adversary's home territory or the territory of principle allies is not to suggest that the competition was not intense, nor that either side was confident in the maintenance of those limits.
5. The greatest hurdle to new conceptual thinking, particularly in the United States, is the fact of 11 September and the pervasive use of the term 'terrorism' in its aftermath. The problem is much broader. Terrorism understood as a political use of violence is a problem that needs serious attention. However, the more fundamentally new aspect to twenty-first century conflict is the addition of rejectionism as a real national security threat. There have always been a small minority in every society that completely rejects the current system and seeks nothing else but to destroy it. These relative few have never had the capacity to be more than mere nuisance. This has changed. The term terrorism is, therefore, too encompassing since it still assumes a coercive bargaining environment. The 'problem of the few' is that some capable individuals and groups have no interest in bargaining across a table (or getting a seat at the table), but rather seek to overturn the table. This is where the most 'new' thinking needs to be directed.
6. This section is adapted from a previous essay, 'Threat as Outcome: The Security Challenge of Information Technology', ITIS Working Paper No.1, Joint Center For International and Security Studies (Spring 2000), <jciss.ucdavis.edu>.
7. William McNeill, *The Pursuit of Power: Technology, Armed Force and Society* (Chicago: University of Chicago Press, 1982); Martin van Creveld, *The Transformation of War* (New York: Free Press, 1991); Geoffrey Parker, *The Military Revolution: Military Innovation and the Rise of the West, 1500–1800* (Cambridge: Cambridge University Press, 1988).
8. Martin van Creveld, *Technology and War* (New York: The Free Press, 1989); Stephen Rosen, 'New Ways of War: Understanding Military Innovation', *International Security*, Vol. 13, No. 1 (Summer 1988).
9. For a brief overview of the lack of consensus over the basic definition of information warfare itself, see Martin C. Libicki, 'What is Information Warfare?', *Strategic Forum*, No. 28, May 1995 (Washington, DC: National Defense University, 1995). An extremely helpful bibliography on information warfare is included in Matthew J. Littleton, *Information Age*

Terrorism: Toward Cyberterror (unpublished Master's thesis, Naval Postgraduate School, December 1995).

10. The original US Defense Department plan created what was known as the ARPENET. Its basic goal was to create a communication system that was both redundant and independent. For background see Katie Hafner and John Markoff, *CyberPunk: Outlaws and Hackers on the Computer Frontier* (New York: Simon and Schuster, 1991), pp.263–82 The link between innovation, warfare and societal organization again seems apparent.

11. The idea that information warfare is fundamentally new is contested by many who point to the emphasis that has always been placed on knowing where your enemy was, what his plans were, and the capabilities that supported his plans as well as the importance of denying the same information to your enemy. Authors have pointed to the writings of Sun Tzu as an example. John Arquilla points to the Mongol approach to war as another example. See Arquilla and David Ronfeldt, 'Cyberwar is Coming', *Comparative Strategy*, 12 (April–June 1993), pp.141–65.

12. The computer supports, of course, text, pictorial, verbal, as well as real-time and taped full-motion video forms of information. The ubiquity of computers by the late Twentieth Century in most of the developed world was such that most people had little recognition that they were interacting with these machines.

13. One recent advance that highlights the break with dependence on geographic proximity is in the field of medicine. Real-time access to the expertise of specialists has traditionally required travel to where they are. Rural inhabitants, in particular, have either had to live without such expertise or make significant efforts to get to particular urban centres. The use of video computer connections between specialists in cities and local community doctors have allowed patients to be examined by and interact with a doctor hundreds of miles away.

14. This extends to information held by individuals as well. If the 'depository' of information is an individual, one has typically needed access to that individual. While the telephone removed the access obstacle of geographic proximity, the person still was required to be on the other end. The advancement in e-mail communication, which promotes efficient asynchronous retrieval and dissemination of information will be dealt with later.

15. Hafner and Markoff, *CyberPunk*, p.265.

16. Spring Tech Guide, 'Taming the Internet', *U.S. News and World Report* (29 April 1995).

17. James Glieck, *Chaos: Making a New Science* (New York: Penguin, 1987), p.103.

18. David Gelernter, *Mirror Worlds: or the Day Software Puts the Universe in a Shoebox...How It Will Happen and What It Will Mean* (New York: Oxford University Press, 1991), p.54.

19. Glieck, *Chaos*, pp.98–103.

20. Data from Dataquest cited in *U.S. News and World Report*, pp.60, 68; 'The Web Keeps Spreading', *Business Week*, (8 Jan. 1995), pp.92–3.

21. Norman Davis, 'An Information-based Revolution in Military Affairs', *Strategic Review*, Vol. 24, No. 1 (Winter 1996), pp.43–53; Pat Cooper, 'Information Warfare Sparks Security Affairs Revolution', *Defense News* (June 12–18, 1995); Andrew Krepinevich, 'Cavalry to Computer: The Pattern of Military Revolutions', *The National Interest*, 37 (Fall 1992), pp.30–42; William Odom, *America's Military Revolution: Strategy and Structure after the Cold War* (Washington, DC: American University Press, 1993).

22. I tend to ascribe to Thomas Kuhn's sense of revolution as a conceptual shift that requires the 'reconstruction of prior theory and the re-evaluation of prior fact'. Kuhn, *The Structure of Scientific Revolutions* (2nd edn) (Chicago: University of Chicago Press, 1970), p.7.

23. For an overview of the impact of information technology on individuals see Lee Sproull and Sara Kiesler, *Connections: New Ways of Working in the Networked Organization*, (Cambridge, MA: MIT Press, 1991).

24. The ENIAC (electronic numerical integrator and computer) first demonstrated in 1946 required 1,500 square feet of space and 17,468 vacuum tubes to operate. It could make 5,000 additions per second. *U.S. News and World Report*, 19 Feb. 1996, p.22.

25. The connection between futurist science fiction writing and technological development is an interesting one. Many advances in technology that have actually emerged can be found referenced in early sci-fi literature. However, the general vision of the technological society has been rather bleak. The Orwellian nightmare is a predominant theme. See, Charles Waugh and

Martin Greenberg, *Battlefields Beyond Tomorrow: Science Fiction War Stories* (New York: Bonanza Books, 1987).

26. Orwell's narrative was greatly influenced by his perceptions of the Soviet Union and the growing power of the totalitarian state.

27. Note that in the counter-coup attempt by Soviet communist hardliners in 1991, it was Moscow television and radio stations that remained key targets.

28. Attention is now being directed toward assessing the impact the Information Age will have on the relationship between individuals and their governments, particularly in modern democracies, how business practices are shifting, and how 'virtual reality' will redefine human to human contact. See Sproull and Kiesler, *Connections*; Robert Anderson, Tora Bikson, Sally Law and Bridger Mitchell, *Universal Access to Email: Feasibility and Societal Implications* (Santa Monica, CA: Rand Center for Information Revolution Analyses, 1995), pp.119–21. On this point also see J.D. Eveland and T.K. Bikson, 'Evolving Electronic Communication Networks', *Office: Technology and People*, Vol.3 (1987), pp.103–28.

29. Weber concluded that with regard to growing emphasis on bureaucratization, the 'economy leads, it is not led'. H.H. Gerth and C. Wright Mills (eds), *From Max Weber: Essays in Sociology* (New York: Oxford University Press, 1946), p.54.

30. Weber, 'Wirtschaft un Geseltschaft', part III, ch.6 translated in Gerth and Mills, *From Max Weber*, p.215.

31. Gerth and Mills, *From Max Weber*, pp.50, 54.

32. These other forms rested primarily on 'inherited avocational administration by notables' instead of 'paid professionals'. Weber in Gerth and Mills, *From Max Weber*, pp.224–5.

33. This is an idealized form of the information technology network set against Weber's bureaucracy. It is not suggested that this organizational form exists now, but its characteristics do seem in line with the features discussed earlier concerning the Information Age. The internet is used as an illustration of an early iteration of this idealized alternative structure, but the information technology network is theoretically applicable to many levels of social interaction.

34. Stephen Krasner, *Structural Conflict: The Third World Against Global Liberalism* (Berkeley: University of California Press, 1985).

35. The vulnerability of leaders themselves, could never be removed entirely. The solution practised by the superpowers during the Cold War was to have processes of pre-delegation of authority within their command and control system in case the leadership was lost. This reduced the gain to be achieved by eliminating leaders. In fact, since there were significant costs associated with decapitation (who would negotiate a peace, or might this lead to a massive spasm of retaliation) the incentive became negligible.

36. This is not to suggest that such disruptions are unimportant or that the entire net could not be attacked. The 60,000 computer system was disrupted on 2 November 1988 by a Trojan horse designed by Cornell graduate student Robert Morris. See Hafner and Markoff, *CyberPunk*, p.253–346.

37. One rather benign, but illustrative example of this phenomenon was experienced by my colleagues at the University of Cincinnati. As social science survey researchers, they attempted to assess the development of civic life in cyberspace, but ran afoul of a number of internet users, who felt that the posting of a research questionnaire was inappropriate. Because of their technical skill, these individuals were able to regulate the communication traffic and suppress the survey, essentially deleting it from many of the usenet groups to which it was forwarded. This authority derived not from any formally granted position as regulators, but from their individual technical capacity. Bonnie Fisher, Michael Margolis and David Resnick, 'Surveying the Internet: Democratic Theory and Civic Life in Cyberspace', *Southeastern Political Review* (1996).

38. Kenneth Oye, *Cooperations Under Anarchy* (Princeton: Princeton University Press, 1986); Stephen Krasner (ed.) *Regimes* (Ithaca, NY: Cornell University Press, 1983).

39. As in all anarchical systems, enforcement of regulations is dependent on the distribution of power. On the internet, the technical 'gods' have the power 'to censure and to censor those who offend them, and some of them may even rain flame down upon those who violate their netiquette'. However it is important to note that ordinary users have the opportunity 'to

improve their status. If they master the arcana and practice netiquette, there appears to be nothing that formally forbids them from ascending Mount Olympus and joining the deities.' Fisher, *et al.*, 'Surveying the Internet'.

40. See Harknett, John Mueller and T.V. Paul chapters in particular in Paul *et al.*, *The Absolute Weapon Revisited*.

41. NATO was forced into action in the Balkans during the 1990s despite the presence of a number of conflict prevention and management organizations. In their confrontation with NATO in 1999, Serbian leaders did not seem to place much faith in regional or international institutions constraining what they saw as an interventionist United States. See, 'Ultimatum at Ramboulliet', in Richard J. Harknett, *Lenses of Analysis: A Visual Framework for the Study of International Relations* (New York: WW Norton, 2002) <www.wnorton.com/lenses> visited 1 Feb. 2002.

42. For related literature and argument see Richard J. Harknett and David Butler, 'The Revolution Beyond Control: The Coming Clash of Profit and Security in Outer Space', *National Security Studies Quarterly*, Vol. 7 (Winter 2001), pp.27–49.

43. For related literature and argument see Richard J. Harknett and the JCISS Study Group, 'The Risks of a Networked Military', *Orbis*, 44 (Winter 1999/2000), pp.127–43.

44. For related literature and argument see Richard J. Harknett, 'Information Warfare and Deterrence', *Parameters*, 26 (Autumn 1996), pp.93–107.

45. Note that when the military uses civilian communication lines for 90 per cent of its traffic, segmentation of even Cyberwar may prove difficult.

46. Different country perceptions only complicate this issue further. Over 90 per cent of the US public believed that Arabs were responsible for the 11 September 2001 attacks in New York and Washington and thus approved overwhelmingly of the Bush administration's retaliation. However a Gallup poll taken in early 2002 revealed that many people in Muslim countries doubted that Arabs were responsible. Most surprising, 89 per cent of those polled in Kuwait did not believe Arabs committed the attack and less than a majority in Turkey (46 per cent) believed that Arabs were responsible. <http://www.usatoday.com/news/attack/2002/03/04/poll-results-full.htm> visited 1 April 2002. Much of this doubt was sowed through internet conspiracy theories and Arab regional television coverage. To the degree that states may need to rely on allies for deterrence, differing perceptions of ambiguous (if not anonymous) attacks undermine the credibility of deterrence – allies may dispute source identification and thus not support retaliation. The fact that al-Qaeda leaders never publicly trumpeted their responsibility may have been an attempt to encourage such disputes.

47. This logic may apply to the most extreme of asymmetric adversaries – those willing to sacrifice their own lives for a greater cause. If value prioritization places a value above life than it is that value that must be placed at risk. Suicide bombers individually can not be deterred, but those who organize the missions and order them can, if the value they hold (wish to achieve through violence) is placed at risk through a credible response. The counterintuitive notion is that use of WMD would likely allow the attacked state greater freedom to respond widely and strongly and more quickly with more international cooperation against groups (whether clearly involved or not) than incidents involving conventional explosives. In fact some groups might sell out other groups to avoid getting caught in the such a wide-scale internationally supported response, which could be sustained, conventional, as well as covert.

48. At the time of this writing, the Bush administration announced plans for a Department of Homeland Security. Although the contours of the proposed department are unclear, the reasoning of this essay suggests that a distinctive organizational break from current structures will be necessary for long-term success.

Revolution's End: Information Technology and Crisis Management

DAMON COLETTA

A study of security in the information age would be incomplete without a section devoted to crisis management. The stage before war often determines the advantages or handicaps under which opening campaigns are fought. In December 1941, few Americans believed the Japanese would risk a direct attack on Pearl Harbor. The United States, when fully mobilized, could field far more forces; it did not make sense for Japan to arouse a 'sleeping giant'. Nevertheless, poor crisis management on the part of the United States meant that the giant spent its first six months at war scrambling to catch up and desperately trying to anticipate where Japan would attack next. The situation would have been even worse had the Japanese bombers managed to catch US aircraft carriers in port, or if they had destroyed more fuel depots. Mishandling crisis management leaves even the most powerful states dependent upon fragile twists of fate.

With the advent of nuclear weapons, leaders became much more self-conscious about crisis management. Secretary of Defense Robert McNamara may have exaggerated after the Cuban Missile Crisis when he declared that 'there is no longer any such thing as strategy; there is only crisis management'.[1] Yet, given that any grave damage to the superpowers could draw a nuclear response, manufactured crises such as Hitler made with Poland and the Soviet Union before attacking them became much less likely. Any regime going up against the potential striking power of the United States after 1945 had to consider sincerely both the potential for disastrous escalation and the possibilities for a negotiated solution to the crisis.[2]

This remains true after the Cold War and into the Information Age. Additional countries such as China, India, Pakistan – perhaps Iraq and North Korea – are expanding arsenals that include weapons of mass destruction. Despite US military superiority, the nuclear, biological or chemical capability of several potential adversaries and the competing demands from America's global range of interests reinforce the need for allied cooperation and limited force in conflict resolution. Though it received more academic attention during the Cold War, crisis management is still crucial to US national security, and it is becoming more important to European countries that are seeking more autonomous defence capacities.[3]

Perhaps because of the Cold War victory and the demonstration of American technological prowess in the Gulf War, the continuing challenges of crisis management are being overlooked. Satellites and computers will not so easily conquer the dilemmas involved in pushing for the best agreement without tumbling into war. A typical textbook on International Relations lists 'improved crisis management' and 'greater difficulty of strategic surprise' among the likely benefits of mastering high technology. Just as advocates of greater investment for the Revolution in Military Affairs (RMA) highlight the role of information technology in identifying and eliminating threats before they can respond, the textbook explains how modern telecommunications and monitoring capabilities make failed communication, as occurred between Tsar Nicholas and Kaiser Wilhelm before the First World War, 'more difficult to imagine'.[4]

Will improved capacity for the collection, analysis and distribution of information reduce unnecessary wars and make crises easier to resolve? Before answering this question in the affirmative, optimists should note some important differences between the RMA argument and the case for crisis management.[5] With respect to combat, the great advantage of RMA technologies accrues to the party that acquires them first. Technological *asymmetry* allows one side to manipulate the decision loop of its adversary. The RMA works because the adversary cannot respond in kind.

In the example using the July Crisis before the First World War, the peaceful resolution would obtain if only the Tsar and the Kaiser *both* had more information.[6] This implies that information technologies for improving crisis management work differently from technologies for improving combat effectiveness though these differences are rarely analysed.

Once they are examined, the transfer of advantage from combat to crisis management seems much less automatic. A powerful country like the United States will be reluctant to share sophisticated technology that could raise an adversary to a level of information symmetry because such a development could reduce the RMA advantage should the crisis escalate to war. It may be the case that with complete information, states in a crisis could find an agreement that both sides prefer to war. Unfortunately, sharing again becomes more difficult if a range of such agreements exist and states care deeply about where within that range they finally settle.[7] In a crisis, states will guard their threshold for war; they will not wish to reveal how far an adversary can push them and still avoid the costs of fighting. Without a certain amount of cooperation at the human level, technical devices – even if both sides enjoy access to them – are unlikely to uncover foolproof solutions to international crises. Furthermore, if one side enjoys a clear information advantage due to RMA-type technologies, nurturing the cooperation necessary to sustain an agreement may actually become more difficult.

The importance of cooperation in successful crisis management points up a major difference in end-use for crisis technologies versus combat technologies. In principle, the purpose of war is to resolve a political test of wills by destroying an adversary's capacity to resist. On the other hand, persuasion, rather than elimination, drives crisis management. Coercion is certainly part of the crisis mix; threatened force and limited force are frequently involved. Yet, an enemy need not decide anything in order to be eliminated. The effectiveness of the RMA, in fact, is predicated upon denying the opponent any opportunity for decision before he is incapacitated. To resolve a conflict without full-scale war, though, enemies must cooperate by choosing peace and fulfilling their part of the bargain. Reaching a favourable decision – under conditions of information symmetry or asymmetry – presents a more formidable challenge for new technologies than simply destroying a foe's personnel and equipment.

One way to gain a sober appreciation of the challenges involved in applying data manipulation techniques to crisis management is to compare how leaders handled crisis dilemmas before and after the development of major information technologies. It so happens that in Central Europe, two crisis sequences occurred, involving many of the same state-actors some 30 to 50 years apart. During the Berlin series of crises between 1948 and 1961 there were no satellite communications, no digital imaging devices, and no fibre-optic cables to transfer high-density information packages across extended computer networks. By the end of the Kosovo crisis in 1999 – the most recent conflict over the break up of Yugoslavia – all of these devices for the collection, analysis and distribution of information were in use.

Certainly, more than technology changed in the decades between the Berlin and Yugoslavia crises. The Russian threat in the form of the Soviet Union was on the rise in the 1950s and 1960s, but by the late 1990s, the Soviet Union had disappeared, and Russian power was in decline. Greater difficulty in unifying the Allies on Bosnia or Kosovo could stem from the lack of a common threat rather than a failure of information technology.

Nevertheless, new information technologies still failed to compensate for the more difficult crisis management assignment in Yugoslavia. Furthermore, the difference in the level of challenge was one of degree rather than kind. Even against the more intense threat posed by the Soviets in Berlin, the Allies – France, Britain and later, West Germany – were not entirely unified. None wanted the communists to destroy the oasis of Western freedom and prosperity in the midst of East German territory, but they disagreed on the best way to keep that from happening. Especially in the later crises, for some allies, concessions to Soviet leader Nikita Khrushchev seemed prudent to lower the risk of nuclear war in Europe. Under Eisenhower and Kennedy, the United States managed an intra-alliance negotiation between the French and West Germans, who felt that firmness would best deter expansion in Soviet demands, and the British who felt that some compromises would make the Soviets more satisfied with the *status quo* and less willing to run risks that could lead to war.[8] It may be true that the immediacy of the Soviet threat made it less likely that an ally would permanently sever ties with the United States, but the seriousness of the threat made finding the right answer – flexibility or firmness – worth a genuine intra-alliance debate. Collection, communication and sharing of information among allies were vital functions in the crises of 1958 and 1961 as they were in discussions of how to respond in Bosnia or Kosovo in the 1990s.

Other changes complicating crisis management were the greater institutionalization and expansion of NATO between 1960 and 1999. Marshalling a greater number of allies, enmeshed in a thicker bureaucracy and less impressed by an out-of-area threat, was bound to be more difficult in the 1990s. That may be true, but before throwing out the Berlin–Yugoslavia comparison, other factors should come into play. Part of the institutionalization of NATO over the years was designed to make it easier for NATO to consult, decide and act as a unit. By the mid-

1990s, NATO already had experience operating out of area since several members contributed forces to the Gulf War coalition against Iraq.

Furthermore, in both that war and the bombing of Kosovo, the United States supplied the dominant air power that led to lopsided military victories. Largely due to its massive defence budget relative to both its foes and its European allies, the United States operated far ahead on the RMA curve. In previous crises, particularly the Cuban Missile Crisis, which some view as the last serious showdown over Berlin, conventional dominance has usually been viewed as a trump card. In the Cuban case, the Russians negotiated from a disadvantage because their far-flung troops would most likely succumb to the US invasion force assembled in Florida unless they resorted to nuclear weapons. If they went nuclear and prevented the American conquest of Cuba, the cost of a missile or bomber exchange involving Russian cities would still dramatically exceed that for a conventional defeat overseas. Not wanting to incur nuclear damage and not wanting to lose conventionally, the Russians had greater incentive than the Americans to avoid escalation and find a tolerable settlement short of war.

By comparison, the key to resolving the Kosovo Crisis also involved Russian and American cooperation. Again, the United States enjoyed conventional dominance in the area of operations, but this time, Russian interests in driving a hard bargain were less than they were during the 1962 missile crisis. Even if a more complex NATO bureaucracy and greater diversity of views among members hampered crisis management relative to the Berlin cases, US conventional dominance – in Cuba and the former Yugoslavia but not around Cold War Berlin – and greater Russian flexibility with respect to its post-Cold War goals in the Balkans both compensated.

The outcome of US crisis management in Kosovo should send a warning to unabashed technology optimists. The job in the former Yugoslavia was not much more difficult than the challenges over Berlin, and information assets for the United States were much more capable in the 1990s than they had been three or four decades earlier. The problem lies with a mismatch between the new high-tech capabilities and crisis management tasks. While the Revolution in Military Affairs has focused on detecting, identifying and killing foes, crisis resolution concentrates more on cultivating cooperation rather than eliminating the need for it.

The following section provides a richer description of the tasks that characterize crisis management. In order to show the imperfect match between these tasks and the RMA technologies, a second section explains how new systems have improved the US capacity for collection, analysis and distribution of information. The mismatch in theory plays out in practice. In the final section, a case comparison shows how certain difficulties recurred in the Berlin and Yugoslavia crises. It may still be possible that improvements in crisis management techniques could result from new information technology applications, but a wholesale transfer of RMA concepts to a very different end-use will bring a disappointing return on investment and may even poison the United States or European countries with false confidence as they attempt to manage new threats to their interests.

THE TASKS OF CRISIS MANAGEMENT

For the purpose of distinguishing crises from combat operations, the elements of crisis may occur before events anywhere on the spectrum of conflict, from displays of force or humanitarian operations to general nuclear war.[9] Crisis conditions also continue within conflicts if dramatic escalation is still a possibility. In their well-known, *Study of Crisis*, a massive data collection and analysis project that has generated several research articles, Michael Brecher and Jonathan Wilkenfeld (2000) offer a three-point definition: A crisis involves (1) a threat to one or more basic values; (2) finite time for response to the value threat; and (3) a heightened probability of involvement in military hostilities.[10]

This definition serves well for assembling a large sample of twentieth-century crises that can be used for statistical analysis, but for the purposes of exploring crisis management, it makes sense to recall why Secretary of Defense McNamara coined the term after the Cuban Missile crisis. He discounted 'strategy' in favour of more reactive crisis management techniques partly out of exasperation. Given the clarity of the Cold War competition at the strategic level, the tactical surprises came in stark contrast. Not only is it difficult to plan strategy for unanticipated circumstances but adversaries, particularly those manoeuvring from a position of military inferiority, have incentives to catch the United States off guard, to force it into scenarios where it does not have an appropriate strategy in place. Authors in previous studies have included the element of surprise as part of what makes a crisis, and it seems fitting to do so, again, in order to focus on crisis management.[11]

A second modification to Brecher and Wilkenfeld focuses on the criterion of 'a heightened probability of military hostilities'. As previously mentioned, quasi-crises, ginned up to justify an attack, do involve a high likelihood of military action, but they do not engage both parties in true crisis management since the possibility of a peaceful settlement is negligible. Given threats like those posed by Hitler against the Soviet Union in 1941 or by Saddam Hussein against Kuwait in 1990, the victim's best response eschews crisis management and prepares for war as efficiently as possible. Management becomes far more important if both sides believe that a peaceful settlement is available and preferable to dramatic escalation. While this preference ordering probably characterizes most day-to-day operations, a crisis is distinguished by an *ultima ratio*, a destructive final arbiter that both sides fear and that bears down on them like an onrushing train – unless they can find an agreement before it smashes home.

If we define a crisis as involving (1) a threat to important values; (2) elements of surprise; and (3) the approach of an *ultima ratio* that all actors seek to avoid, then certain policy dilemmas follow. These challenges come in combination and degree that is unique to crisis management as opposed to combat or non-crisis diplomacy. In order to evaluate the value of information technology – especially the types currently under consideration by NATO and the European Union – the distinctive mix of pressures in crisis management missions needs to be taken into account.[12]

As one moves across the spectrum of crisis response options, from the humanitarian relief aspects of operations in Northern Iraq to the peacekeeping missions in Bosnia and onto the combat missions in Kosovo, crisis management shifts from pure optimization to problems involving strategic equilibrium. If the mission is saving a population from flooding or starvation, crisis managers try to anticipate the disaster: When will the consequences begin? Who will be affected first? How severe will injuries and diseases be, and how long will they last? Such relief operations are more static compared to the mission of peace enforcement in the sense that the act of deploying information technology to answer critical questions will not provoke a response from the disaster. Natural hazards will come just the same regardless of rescuers' efforts to probe their dimensions.

This is not to say that actual humanitarian relief operations have been completely devoid of strategy. Deploying a US unmanned aerial vehicle

(UAV) to track the progress of flooding in Mozambique initially triggered a negative reaction from the host government there.[13] Victimized populations can respond in ways that alter the effectiveness of measures taken during humanitarian crises, so the distinction is one of degree. For the purpose of exploring the role of information technology in crisis management though, the difference between optimizing relief measures and outmanoeuvring a dangerous adversary matters.[14] Compared to 'rescue', 'peacemaking' or 'peace enforcement' include much more intense strategic aspects for crisis managers.

Pure optimists might argue that, while strategic decision-making differs from elementary decision analysis, information technology enhances the performance of either function. New devices for collection, analysis, command and control permit state-of-the-art forces to identify, target and kill threats before they can respond.[15] During strategic competition for the highest-stakes, reconnaissance and signal intelligence technologies dramatically reduce the fog of war and provide their possessor with lower-risk ways to eliminate another's capacity for resistance.

This may explain why EU descriptions of its new capabilities catalogue and NATO's Defense Capabilities Initiative both read as if European forces seek information dominance over potential non-Western foes. Still, dominance in combat, or collective defence, does not translate directly into superior crisis management.[16] The looming potential of an *ultima ratio* that all sides seek to avoid creates a policy dilemma for crisis actors distinct from the problem presented by combat.[17] Pressure against an adversary helps protect the national interest, but combat-level pressure in a crisis situation, rather than disarming or subjugating the enemy, instead drives him to greater ferocity. A huge price must then be paid to decide the conflict of interest. During the Cold War, that huge price was the mutual destruction involved in a large nuclear exchange. If more recent experiences in Iraq, Somalia and the former Yugoslavia are any indication, today that price involves victimization of entire state populations already under high economic stress, and the resort to a ground war by an American or European democracy that has not been fully mobilized or prepared to accept casualties.

Democratic publics' lack of tolerance for casualties on behalf of humanitarian causes or foreign regime change has further complicated the risks for Western powers.[18] Military strategy suggests that the safest and quickest way to intervene militarily is to strike decisively at the adversary's leadership and command structure, but organizations such as NATO and the UN fear they would lose legitimacy and create even more instability if they extracted a leader and assumed responsibility for setting up a 'friendly' government.[19]

Furthermore, as one-sided as casualty figures were when the West intervened in Iraq and the former Yugoslavia, information inferior leaders in both cases had opportunities to target civilian populations before their forces surrendered. Greater investment in information technologies to widen the military gap still further will not necessarily reduce the risk of a scorched earth response to Western intervention. Potential targets are likely to recognize that their information deficit is growing, and they can compensate through command and control arrangements, moving their military and police forces toward a hair-trigger mode, so the least provocation, with no time allowed for verification, sets off a humanitarian disaster.[20]

The expectation that escalation would bring unacceptable costs to all players encourages self-conscious limitation of objectives and means.[21] This is especially acute for militarily superior states that fear a Pyrrhic victory if a crisis situation should deteriorate to all-out war. Military leaders within the state might seek to minimize the risk to forces by employing decisive action. They are likely to be opposed, often by civilian elites in the cases of the United States and Western Europe, who fear that a clear tactical victory would push an opponent to exit crisis bargaining and call upon the *ultima ratio* for resolving conflict. While the clash of interests is not a true crisis unless all sides dread the final arbiter, it is often the case that a state can fare better by preparing secretly and transitioning to war first. In classic cases such as the Japanese–American crisis leading to Pearl Harbor and the Cuban Missile crisis, the United States laboured under a control dilemma.[22]

On the one hand, in the midst of escalation, the US sought to centralize control and constrain defence procedures in order to avoid signalling that war was certain. On the other hand, the US searched for ways to protect against an early shift by its opponent from crisis bargaining to war. It is difficult to provide such protection without mobilizing forces and loosening rules of engagement. Under crisis conditions, protection measures thus enter a positive feedback cycle. Even as they promise to make the damage of the *ultima ratio* less severe, they also encourage the other side to take similar precautions. As the adversary prepares, the *ultima ratio* appears even more likely: requirements for confirming an attack before responding are reduced, and more provocative protection measures seem justified. An inadvertent engagement of forces under these conditions has a high probability of triggering war because a crisis manager desperately trying to gain control and an attacker who has given up on the crisis both have incentive to make the very same claims about what has happened.[23] While state-of-the-art information technologies promise forces that retain their agility even as they are placed under tight, centralized control, it is less clear whether these technologies can reassure an inferior adversary as crisis conditions deteriorate and the *ultima ratio* looms ever closer.

THE FUNCTIONS OF INFORMATION TECHNOLOGY

The word technology conjures images of sophisticated hardware. Satellites, fibre-optic cables, and liquid crystal displays are just a few examples from the diverse array of devices that do not lend themselves to a simple classification scheme. Either a crisis actor possesses a particular machine or he does not. Rather than attempt to examine specific products one at a time, we may consider that information technology improves the performance of a smaller set of enduring functions. Once these improvements are described, it is easier to see why they do not ameliorate some of the serious challenges facing crisis managers. More data at a faster rate, compared against more signatures, and distributed to a wider array of users still cannot distinguish an elaborate bluff from the initial stages of a sudden attack even though these scenarios have very different implications for the crisis manager.

In general, information technology facilitates the accomplishment of three tasks: collection, analysis and distribution.[24] These functions are mission critical for specialized bureaucracies within the government. Intelligence agencies are organized along these lines. A military officer recognizes these activities as elements of command and control. During crises, presidents and their top advisers become intensely involved in these functions as part of crisis management.

All these functions involve the manipulation of information. Information itself, the *raison d'etre* for RMA technologies, exists when one state of the world is distinguishable from another.[25] So far, the quickest and cheapest way to record, compare and report the details of each change has been to shift electrons or to perturb the progress of electromagnetic waves. The primary product of telephony consists of mechanical compression waves formed by the human voice, but it is the translation of that energy into electrical signals that permits near instantaneous global communications. The same reliance on electrical charges and the electromagnetic spectrum also holds for collection and analysis functions. In the information field, the history of technological development is largely about the vast increase in the number of shifts that may be executed and stored by a single, transportable device and in the sensitivity with which electromagnetic disturbances may be detected.[26]

Though the specific details of NATO's Defense Capabilities Initiative and the EU's Capability Catalogue are not publicly available, we can survey the three functions of information technology to gain a sense of the systems that appear on the shopping lists of Western defence ministries.

Going on to predict the effectiveness of these technologies for improving crisis management is an imprecise art. Even researchers in the business world who benefit from economic data on information technology expenditures and who can reference income versus corporate assets over time still have difficulty nailing down a figure for return on investment.[27] On the pessimistic end of a range of estimates, G.W. Loveman (1994) concluded after his review of corporate studies that scant evidence exists for *any* increase in productivity due to information technology investment.

This analysis avoids the disagreement on how to measure the benefits of new technology and exploits the consensus recommendation on identifying end-use before installing an information system.[28] As new technologies for collection, analysis and distribution are described, it becomes clearer that they are insufficient for resolving the escalation decisions comprised by crisis management. In the oft-discussed context of the European Union, asking publics to provide increased defence budgets for the development and purchase of technologies designed for combat but intended for use in new crisis missions courts disaster. The shift in end-use translates into increased risk for the technologies that has so far been ignored. If Europeans decided, today, to spend more for their security, acquiring NATO-type information technology, they would in all likelihood be bitterly disappointed at how little the investment would help them succeed at their new crisis management tasks.

Collection

With respect to collection, the objective is to capture variations in electromagnetic emissions across the infrared and optical frequency ranges, as well as in the frequency ranges used for communications and radar. Right now, the US has the most expansive fleet of air-breathing and aerospace sensors, but even this array is not infallible as was demonstrated by the surprise nuclear explosions orchestrated by India in May 1998.[29]

Europe's new intelligence and satellite reconnaissance teams will face the same trade-offs as the Americans. Detailed coverage of smaller amplitude emissions requires moving in closer, but lowering the orbit of imaging satellites reduces both the area and timeframe for coverage. An expensive, multi-spectral suite on a high-flying aircraft could ameliorate the time-window problem and allow for greater focus on a suspicious area, but cloud cover will block the optical-range take just as it did in the 1960s.[30] The new $32 million unmanned aerial vehicles (UAVs) provide flexible and focused, multi-spectral imaging with 40 hour hover capability, but even these technical marvels, which can 'see' in all weather, are difficult to fly during a storm.[31]

The laws of nature do not impose this last limitation, but it does point up a second set of complicating factors. UAVs could be constructed as larger and more stable platforms, but at some point this would make them vulnerable to radar detection by the targeted forces. All of these technical systems for international crisis management are not just unobtrusively observing phenomena like weather patterns or deforestation; their targets have the capacity to react. In the fall of 1962, Premier Khrushchev nearly beat the U-2 by installing surface-to-air missiles in Cuba before deploying his intermediate-range nuclear weapons. The appearance of air defences persuaded the Kennedy administration to adjust the flight path of the U-2s so that they had to photograph the Russian sites at a more oblique angle. The resulting delay in detection nearly allowed Khrushchev to make his nuclear missiles operational before Kennedy began crisis bargaining.[32] In setting up a system architecture and in explaining the expected return on investment to the publics who will foot the bill, policy-makers should take platform vulnerability seriously. So far, however, capabilities have weighed much heavier in the public discussion than vulnerabilities.[33]

Vulnerabilities of information technology have special significance in the stage before combat. In war, the loss of a collection platform is regretted but expected. In crisis, the wilful destruction of a platform is tantamount to escalation. The defending state finds itself with less room to manoeuvre in the crisis bargaining. Its three options are to make a concession by discontinuing that form of collection, continue as before and risk the loss of additional systems, or move closer to the *ultima ratio* in an effort to make the other side stand down. In war, vulnerability can be compensated by a proliferation of expendable platforms: a fleet rather than a suite-based system architecture.[34] In crisis, large numbers of vulnerable sensors, even if they are relatively cheap, could make controlling crisis dynamics more difficult.[35]

Analysis

Computer-based analysis takes collected signals and compares them against a database of known signatures. The pre-set codes can be used to sort the incoming signal or to highlight particular portions of it. A complex input can also be analysed against itself in a 'factor analysis' to find if some subset of signals from multiple sources tends to run together. Thus, software tools and computer memory can be used to find the proverbial needle in a haystack of electromagnetic emissions, as long as the operator knows beforehand some special characteristics about the needle. By detecting mathematical relationships between previously unconnected variables, information age analysis can also inspire new hypotheses about previously unconnected events.

The limitation, here, is related to the constraints on collection technology. Electronic analysis works much more effectively if the operators already know what to expect, but crises always contain elements of the unexpected. Tactical surprise was prevalent throughout the series of crises over Berlin in the 1950s and 60s as Premier Khrushchev attempted to design his threats around the deterrent posture presented by the West. The Soviet blockade of 1948–49, the six-month ultimatum of November 1958 threatening to turn Berlin into a free city, the renewal of this threat against John Kennedy at Vienna in 1961, and the construction of the Wall later that year all came as a surprise.[36] Despite strategic warning in each case, US analysts missed diplomatic and physical clues because they expected the Soviet challenge to come some other way.

The advent of sophisticated software and fast computers has failed to eliminate the element of surprise from crisis. In the case of Kosovo during the spring of 1999, the NATO allies, and especially the US, equipped with the finest intelligence systems, still failed to anticipate the swiftness and effectiveness of Yugoslav ethnic cleansing tactics on Albanian civilians as well as the resilience of Yugoslav forces to Allied air attack once they had blended into Kosovo's population centres.[37]

Analysis can identify patterns among collected signals, but these patterns relate to physical movements or communications that, during crises, are ambiguous with respect to intent. In fact, throughout the history of NATO crisis management, leaders have not placed great stock in analysis software. Instead, they have sought meetings face-to-face, relying on human instinct rather than technology to take the measure of their adversary as well as other members of the alliance.[38]

Distribution

Distribution of information connects the other two functions of collection and analysis, and it links centres of political authority with diplomatic, military and intelligence agents in the field. As communications technologies have moved from copper wire to fibre-optic networks and wireless systems, the speed and bandwidth of information flow has increased.

That is not to say that the distribution function somehow escapes trade-offs founded in physical principles and strategic concerns. High-bandwidth, wireless communications require relatively large amounts of power. That requirement typically translates into an accompanying ground station, a large, immobile target that must be protected from attack. Large networks with two-way and conference communications require sophisticated switching and encryption devices, so smaller coalition members must still pay a large bill to maintain interoperability with the most advanced systems.

NATO's response to ameliorate the interoperability problem has been to fund common infrastructure projects.[39] Their existence is a major incentive for EU-members such as Britain, France and Germany to negotiate for automatic access to NATO assets. These include headquarters facilities and satellites for communications and navigation in the event Europeans should take on a crisis without US participation.[40]

This institutional shortcut to interoperability for EU crisis management must still pass over daunting political hurdles. It is unclear how the EU will maintain truly autonomous crisis management capability if it relies on distribution systems partially funded by the United States. Even if the United States agrees to automatically relinquish control of these systems to the EU under emergency circumstances, Turkey – a member of NATO but not of the EU – may veto the arrangement. If a way is found to address Turkey's concerns and the EU does obtain NATO systems, serious interoperability problems will remain because EU crisis management will emphasize European multilateralism. Many missions will base their legitimacy in the involvement of non-EU members, the so-called 15+15 arrangement.[41] Even if the EU manages to acquire state-of-the-art headquarters and communications systems, a gap will still obtain with respect to important non-EU participants in crisis management.

FROM BERLIN TO PRISTINA: THE PERSISTENCE OF CRISIS MANAGEMENT DILEMMAS IN THE INFORMATION AGE

Despite the technological progress in the collection, analysis and distribution of information, certain challenges of crisis management remain as acute today as they were three or four decades ago. The historical persistence of three particular difficulties from the Berlin crises of the 1950s–1960s through to the end of the Kosovo crisis in 1999 offers a sign that crisis management may represent 'revolution's end', an arena where new information systems do not wield the transformational capacities that they have already demonstrated in commerce and war. In genuine crises, the competition always possesses enough leverage to protect against an all-out elimination strategy. Even more vexing, it enjoys the opportunity to signal in ways that are empirically consistent with an actual attack. Knowing in finer detail that certain weapons are deployed or that certain ministers are angry often will not provide more precise conclusions about when or how the adversary's weapons will be used.

Advocates of the Revolution in Military Affairs can point to the increased variety of targets that can be identified or destroyed and the reduced risks to US forces armed with smart weapons.[42] Crisis managers, however, still face the dilemma of protecting their country from the enemy while attempting to elicit his cooperation for a settlement. Divining the enemy's intentions and crafting proposals or diplomatic signals to maximize the chances of their success still requires a personal touch. No machine yet manufactures negotiating presence or connects observed actions to the true psychological state of an adversary.

Time pressure and the importance of avoiding the *ultima ratio* create a second enduring challenge. They put top authorities under almost irresistible pressure to grasp for greater control and centralize decision-making even as intelligence probes and consultation networks fan out to ensure that escalation decisions are made on the basis of the best information possible. Advances in telecommunications and monitoring techniques permit more detailed intelligence, wider consultation and closer micromanagement under crisis conditions, but the two effects work against each other: a greater variety and amount of inputs tend to stimulate a more demanding response cycle in terms of timing and complexity. Higher expectations for both input and output bump up against the cognitive limitations of a central authority. While RMA technology has dramatically improved the process of applying force on target, the staple of crisis management is judging political risk. Automation must contend with the trade-off between overloading the central decision-maker and excessively filtering the information that shapes how that person balances protection of interests against avoidance of war.

A third aspect of crisis management that has persisted despite advances in information technology is the ability of militarily inferior adversaries to catch the United States in a tactical surprise. The number of unanticipated twists in the Kosovo Crisis point to the significant limitations of detection technologies. They cannot translate the signal streams they gather into an accurate assessment of how risk acceptant the adversary will become as the crisis intensifies. Also, an inferior opponent can exploit the dominant state's own fear of escalation to reduce the coercive power of advanced technologies and preserve freedom of action for itself.

The Personal Touch

A number of remarkable themes run through the series of Berlin crises. Quite dramatically, at a time when international relations were structured by two superpowers with awesome militaries and huge landmasses, the fate of the entire world seemed on several occasions to hang on the resilience of a single half-city protected by a small number of troops. Given the precariousness of the situation, it is also intriguing how much the force of personalities influenced critical decisions. Certainly, personal characteristics had something to do with why President Truman accepted the long odds of a sustained airlift after the Soviets severed road and rail routes to 2 million West Berliners in June 1948.[43] The same could be said for explaining John Kennedy's nonchalance after the Soviets, in August 1961, established a physical barrier against both the four-power status of Berlin and the eventual unification of Germany.[44] Crisis conditions force presidents to exercise their own judgement about whether and how to escalate. More data at a faster rate will not eliminate ambiguity as to an opponent's ultimate intention. A leader's response to uncertainty – the essence of crisis management – will draw upon personal attitudes toward risk.[45]

Not surprisingly, leaders realize how much rides on their judgement, and they seek to supplement it. They stimulate the bureaucracy and employ technology to collect information and formulate options, but once the crisis hits, there is also a tendency toward nominating a point person, someone to weigh the options with them and speak for them if necessary. For the Cuban Missile Crisis, Robert Kennedy took that trusted role, unofficially chairing Executive Committee meetings in his brother's absence and conveying secret terms of what became the final bargain to Russian Ambassador Dobrynin.[46] For the deadline crises of 1958–59 when Nikita Khrushchev threatened to sign a peace treaty with Walter Ulbricht's regime in East Germany if the US did not begin the process of ending its temporary occupation of West Berlin, President Eisenhower's second pair of eyes belonged to his Secretary of State, John Foster Dulles.[47]

For the two barricade crises over Berlin, blocking of the ground access routes through West Germany in 1948–49 and construction of the wall in 1961, General Lucius Clay became the point man. As American Military Governor for Germany during the first crisis, Clay's official portfolio did not extend to central foreign policy questions on whether to wage war with the Soviet Union. However, the wide latitude granted to him within Germany put him in a position to time and control the initial American response for the first Berlin crisis. His order to override Soviet intransigence and extend currency reform to all three Western sectors within Germany precipitated the Soviet blockade one day later, and Clay authorized the airlift to ferry in essential supplies before President Truman had the opportunity to react from Washington.[48]

The fact that President Truman retained General Clay through the end of the airlift in 1949, and the fact that John Kennedy called him back from retirement to rejuvenate the spirits of isolated Berliners twelve years later, speaks to the valuable service he performed for US Presidents in crisis. Bureaucratically outside the President's inner circle and affiliated with the Republicans, Clay nevertheless had demonstrated his willingness to stand firm for a continued Western presence in the face of Soviet harassment and intimidation. The alacrity with which he ordered troops and equipment nominally under other commanders to counter Soviet moves disturbed soldiers and civilian officials in the Kennedy administration, but the President stuck with him because Berliners were sticking with him.[49]

One might imagine that the development of satellite communications would reduce the need for a special representative during crises. The Berlin blockade and the Berlin wall both achieved tactical surprise, at least in the sense that the timing was unexpected and no appropriate contingency plans existed.[50] For the first 12 to 72 hours, inadequate information flow back to Washington essentially forced local authorities to take important initial decisions.[51] Although communication capabilities, in speed and volume, improved dramatically between 1962 and 1998, President Clinton still found it advantageous to call the star diplomat of the 1995 Dayton agreements on Bosnia out of retirement in order to salvage the situation in Kosovo.[52]

Richard Holbrooke knew the political conflict in the Balkans as General Clay had understood the local dynamics tearing at Berlin. Like Clay, Holbrooke was an outsider to the administration he served. While he did use a cell phone to keep his government informed, he also believed that diplomacy mimicked improvisational jazz more than a classical chess match.[53] Basic themes were necessary, but in the heat of crisis, conventional strategies designed at some other time and place gave way to spontaneous rifts. Not unlike Clay, Holbrooke took personal responsibility for successful crisis management, and he sought fine control over the timing and type of information presented to his opponent.

Holbrooke's freedom to delay a meeting or re-format a proposal was not always appreciated in Washington. In October 1998, Holbrooke personally convinced nationalist Serbian leader Slobodan Milosevic to halt his offensive against Albanian Kosovars and begin discussions with the Albanian peace faction on future autonomy. However, as the agreement unravelled in the beginning of 1999, Holbrooke was not invited to the last ditch Rambouillet negotiations.[54] It is not clear that Holbrooke could have achieved any different results, but he must have been frustrated on the last day before NATO's Operation Allied Force began. He was sent once again to negotiate personally with Milosevic, but this time he merely delivered a message with no room for improvisation to make sure the Serbian leader fully understood the consequences of rejecting the Rambouillet terms.[55]

Persuading an adversary to relinquish the leverage of potential escalation and compromise lies at the heart of successful crisis management. In addition, a leader must accomplish this feat under conditions of high threat and limited time to decide. Assuming Holbrooke is right to compare crisis management skill with the talent required for improvisational jazz, presidents will want to seek out these gifted negotiators in order to apply the personal touch during crises in the information age as they have done in the past. Furthermore, for crucial decisions on escalation or concession, the jet plane rather than the video teleconferencing system will supply the key technology. To enhance their judgement, to acquire the best possible sense of the crisis opponent's calculations and intentions, presidents will want their special representative to meet the adversary and, if possible, return to deliver any advice face-to-face.[56]

Micro-management and Filtering Dilemmas

Of course, crisis managers do not always find it expedient to wait for a trusted agent to come back from the field and personally report on their impressions of an adversary's intentions. In his study of the Berlin Blockade, Avi Shlaim detects a pattern where leaders in crises simultaneously expand the number of channels for information input while restricting decisional forums to smaller, *ad hoc* groups.[57] After the closing of the ground routes into Berlin on June 24, 1948, President Truman and particularly Secretary of State Marshall demanded more frequent and more detailed reports from a wider circle of government advisers. During the Berlin Wall crisis of 1961 and the Cuban Missile crisis a year later, John Kennedy also reached out for information inputs though he is better known for his willingness to go outside as well as within the government. The special reports of Dean Acheson and General Clay were quite salient in the weeks and months surrounding the first barbed wire barriers blocking access to West Berlin, and the Cuban crisis included attempts to use news reporters and businessmen as back channels for communication and intelligence on Khrushchev.[58]

Among the series of decisions taken during the Berlin crises, there are also plenty of examples where one individual or a small group made key choices. These critical decision points often approached with little advanced warning. Fluid reactions and counter-reactions made it difficult to know far ahead of time what information would matter or who would be likely to have it. General Clay and President Truman staked American prestige on an extended airlift strategy within days of the Russian blockade. In a situation that was even more perilous, the American decision to risk war on Russian willingness to respect a US naval blockade was developed over six days by a relative few members of the President's specially created Executive Committee.

The combination of a broad information search and a narrow decision hierarchy recurs in information age crises. It seems logical that more efficient technologies for data transfer would ameliorate the constraints in this situation. Yet, a wider and faster information net has not automatically translated into easier decisions or smoother crisis operations. With new methods of collection and communication, demands on crisis managers have increased. This kind of compensation played out in the targeting debates during the Kosovo air campaign.

While it is true that Richard Holbrooke's efforts in Belgrade to avert NATO air strikes failed, the Kosovo crisis continued after 24 March 1999 in the sense that the first bombing sorties constituted another step, albeit a dramatic step, on the escalation ladder with the United States. If the first phase of bombing did not convince Slobodan Milosevic to allow NATO troops on Serbian soil, the Alliance could move on to targets tied to the civilian economy. If neither Phase II nor Phase III sufficed, ground troops, despite President Clinton's early statement ruling them out, still represented a type of *ultima ratio* for both sides, lurking somewhere in the not–so–distant future.[59] That meant that crisis needs (persuading the Serbs to cooperate without pushing too hard) and combat needs (eliminating the Serbs' capacity to hit back) competed to shape the design of US military missions in Kosovo.

Under these circumstances, the Chief of the US European Command, General Wesley Clark, experienced some of the most challenging side-effects of voluminous information flows combining with concentrated crisis management authority.[60] General Clark often felt sandwiched between the concerns of his subordinates executing military missions and the interests of his political masters both in Washington and Europe. With the new information technologies, top civilian or military leaders could access details and insert themselves into operations at the micro-level. President Clinton or Secretary of Defense Cohen could review justifications and set priorities on target lists. Even within Clarke's own command, generals attuned to high-level political concerns could talk live to pilots as they executed a strike on a hotly debated target.[61] A naïve application of collection and communications technology made this intense involvement between crisis managers and their agents possible. However, additional skill at high decision-making levels is required in order to know when enough of the right details have been digested, so that real-time countermanding of orders at the level of execution makes sense. General Clark and his deputy for air operations, US Air Force General Michael Short, both came away from their crisis management experience concerned that political interference limited the effectiveness of the Allies' escalation in Kosovo, at times to the point of endangering the larger objectives that motivated strikes in the first place.[62]

On the other hand, while cabinet secretaries and high-level commanders need to discipline themselves from reacting too quickly to gun camera footage or near real-time digital imagery, they cannot exactly remain aloof from crisis operations either. A pure *laissez faire* approach would place too much trust in filtering mechanisms – both human and technological – that supply authorities with more easily interpreted but less detailed decision memos.

General Clark's worst day during Operation Allied Force occurred when American planes, working off neatly packaged target folders, mistakenly bombed the Chinese Embassy in Belgrade.[63] The American information system for selecting targets passed information up the military and political decision hierarchies as designed. The problem came in the updating cycle for certain maps controlled by the Central Intelligence Agency: lower level officials plugged old information into the system and sent it along with hundreds of other thick portfolios for prioritization. This seemingly small mistake created major difficulties for the Clinton Administration, which by the month of May was struggling to hold the anti-Milosevic coalition together, largely based on the propositions that US forces were closely integrated with Allied nations and that their precise control minimized the chances of collateral damage.

After the Embassy bombing happened, the glitch in the US information system was quickly corrected.[64] Nevertheless, the larger point is that new technologies drive expansion in the already broad information searches conducted during crises, and in the future it will be difficult to anticipate all of the flaws that could lead to disaster. The much greater salience of political constraints on the use of force during crises as opposed to all-out combat implies that breakdowns in the information age will be significantly more costly than conventional RMA analyses depict. A political embarrassment during total war is tolerable for the information dominant force as long as it retains the ability to react faster than its opponent's defences, but the same sort of flap could easily ruin a crisis management team's attempts to reach favourable settlement of a conflict through signalling and negotiation.

The Persistence of Tactical Surprise

Although one reason for continued system breakdowns in the information age relates to the growing demands as technology evolves, a second source of problems lies in the element of tactical surprise that accompanies international crises. As previously noted, recent scholars have downplayed the importance of surprise in the definition of crisis conditions. In hindsight, to be sure, the June 1948 Berlin Blockade and the August 1961 construction of the wall appear as predictable moves preceded by unmistakable public signals. Yet, part of what gives crisis management its unique character is the common desire to avoid the *ultima ratio* and the numbing effect this has on both sides' ability to foresee the timing and nature of escalation. Despite Russian resort to a mini-blockade in April 1948, General Clay and President Truman had to scramble for a coherent response when the real one came in June. Despite the growing number of refugees crossing into West Berlin in the summer of 1961 and the public warnings by the East German Communist party leader Walter Ubrecht as well as Nikita Khrushchev, President Kennedy reacted to the wall with amazement and some anger because none of the many reports he had requested on Berlin addressed the contingency he faced on August 13.[65]

In their report on early-warning in the information age, Alexander George and Jane Holl describe how the difficulty lies not in detecting signals but in interpreting them correctly before the threat has materialized. Keeping in mind that crises are situations in which neither side wants to provoke drastic escalation, deteriorating situations are sometimes wilfully ignored – held on the back burner until it is too late. George and Holl were writing in the context of catching failing states before they have deteriorated too far.[66] Interpretation of evidence becomes even more complex in direct conflict situations like Berlin or Kosovo.[67] Nikita Khrushchev and Slobodan Milosevic were not simply operating in isolation, they tailored their moves to catch the United States off balance, improve the likely terms of settlement for themselves, and still leave the United States without a clear mandate for action.

In the information age case of Kosovo, new US technology did not prevent Milosevic from achieving surprise on several occasions: his ability to plan systematic cleansing of Albanian Kosovars during the peace talks at Rambouillet; the speed with which he was able to execute these plans after rejecting the Rambouillet plan; his ability to accelerate the expulsion of Albanian refugees and add a new high card to his bargaining hand *after* the first phase of NATO bombing began; and finally, his ability to protect Yugoslav Army forces for the better part of 78 days under a sustained Allied air campaign.[68] Milosevic still lost the war, but because both sides wanted to avoid the consequences that would follow the insertion of NATO ground troops, he was able to alter the zone of agreement from Rambouillet. Fewer guarantees were given with respect to the political future of Kosovo and fewer rights were accorded NATO forces in areas of Yugoslavia outside Kosovo.[69]

The bureaucratic and psychological barriers to fully appreciating early warning signs and the incentive for opponents to devise innovative moves that create an escalation dilemma for the US make it difficult for RMA-type technologies to eliminate the problem of tactical surprise in crisis management. Surprise, in turn, prompts leaders to stress crisis information systems by asking them to function for *ad hoc* users and in ways for which they were not designed. Novel end-uses increase the chance of failures, especially in the delicate stages of a conflict when negotiation and cooperation are paramount, before the objective has deteriorated to all-out elimination of the opponent.

CONCLUSION

Policy-makers who are looking to reap a windfall from RMA technologies in the area of crisis management should beware the sanguine textbook estimates. Crisis management involves different decision dilemmas, which centre on persuasion and cooperation rather than efficiency in disabling the other side. RMA successes in combat as demonstrated in the Gulf War and Kosovo will not carry over directly to deterrence and coercion during crises. In some sense, the limited utility of information dominance for crisis management was also demonstrated before Operations Desert Storm and Allied Force.

This article attempts to identify key features of crisis management that distinguish it from combat as an end-use for new information technologies. In order to address the trajectory of technological development, the focus, here, has been on the projected impact of functional improvements in collection, analysis, and distribution rather than the design details of specific systems. The sober prediction that greater investment in RMA-type information technologies will not bring a high return in the area of crisis management also has some historical foundation.

A comparison of US crisis management during the Berlin crises of the 1950s versus the Yugoslavia crises of the 1990s shows that three ingredients for success in crises have remained elusive despite the dramatic advances in the collection, analysis, and distribution of information. In Kosovo as in Berlin, protecting the national interest while avoiding escalation to the crisis *ultima ratio* depended on key personalities. Representatives like General Clay in Berlin and Richard Holbrooke in Yugoslavia were not just officials applying fungible skills to resolve generic international conflicts; they established personal reputations and rapport with other important crisis participants. 1990s technology has not altered this part of the process from the 1950s, nor is there reason to believe that new information systems will do so in the foreseeable future.

Regarding the second and third ingredients that are hard to reproduce, there may be a larger role for new information systems, but it differs from the textbook application of RMA-type devices to crisis management. In both the Berlin and Yugoslavia crises, leaders sought to expand their sources of information while centralizing control over decisions on how and when to escalate. The speed and volume of information flow over official networks has dramatically expanded over four decades, but the advantages of these developments for crisis management are limited by the fact that a crisis leader must make a choice between attempting to digest overwhelming amounts of raw information or relying on layers of filtering agents that lack a big-picture perspective on the crisis. New information technology probably will not make this dilemma much easier, especially when the third ingredient, adapting to tactical surprise, is taken into account. The difficulty of interpreting available indicators, coupled with the desire not to escalate crises unnecessarily, leaves opportunities for adversaries to surprise the United States, even in the information age and even if they are information inferior. The persistence of tactical surprise means that leaders will have to make decisions about how to filter their information networks even as they attempt to employ them under unanticipated constraints.

Though new information age devices will not eliminate the filtering dilemma created by the combination of broad searches with centralized control, the added stress of tactical surprise might be alleviated somewhat by constructing more flexible links between military and commercial systems. Instead of trying to anticipate specifics about the locations and types of information needed in the next crisis and rushing toward *ad hoc* networks after tactical surprise, why not plan ahead of time to switch significant portions of crisis management operations over to commercial technology? Information security is, of course, a concern, but it may be overrated in the early stages of a crisis. If both sides truly fear the *ultima ratio*, having the United States capable of demonstrating its resolve – both to protect its interests and to avoid war – on commercial networks may actually work to the crisis managers' advantage.

Again, planning to make better use of commercial collection and communication technologies is not what many experts have in mind when referring to crisis management in the information age. At least in its public stance, the European Union, as it prepares for its expanded crisis management mission, seems focused on acquiring RMA technologies in precision strike and satellite reconnaissance that have already augmented NATO combat power. Before making large information technology investments with the expectation of improving crisis management, both the EU and the United States should note explicitly how crisis management differs from previous war-fighting applications. Doing so would encourage policy-makers to build a better match between expensive new information systems and their projected end-use.

ACKNOWLEDGEMENTS

This essay in no way reflects the opinions, standards, or policy of the United States Air Force Academy or the United States Government.

NOTES

1. Alexander George, *Avoiding War: Problems of Crisis Management* (Boulder, CO: Westview Press, 1991), p.377.
2. Some might question whether this logic applied to the terrorist attacks against the United

States on 11 September. Al-Qaeda is not a regime in the sense of accepting responsibility for order within a demarcated territory. The Taliban's status on 11 September fit the logic somewhat better. Despite the absence of formal recognition, the US had dealt with the regime before. After the attacks, there emerged a series of proposals and counterproposals on the arrest and extradition of Osama bin Laden before the American strikes of 7 October. Even in this case, there was some opportunity for crisis management.

3. Antonio Missiroli, *CFSP, Defence and Flexibility*, Chaillot Paper No.38 (Paris: Institute for Security Studies – Western European Union, 2000); Martin Ortega, *Military Intervention and the European Union*, Chaillot Paper No.45 (Paris: Institute for Security Studies – Western European Union, 2001). More information and additional Chaillot papers are available at <http://www.weu.int/institute/>.

4. Donald Snow and Eugene Brown, *International Relations: The Changing Contours of Power* (Boston, MA: Addison Wesley Longman and Pearson Custom Publishing, 2001), p.314.

5. For a recent version of the argument supporting greater investment toward the Revolution in Military Affairs, see Admiral Bill Owens with Ed Offley, *Lifting the Fog of War* (NY: Farrar, Strauss, Giroux, 2000). Two works for the general audience are Joseph Nye and William Owens, 'America's Information Edge', *Foreign Affairs* Vol.75, No.2 (March/April 1996), pp.20–36 and Eliot Cohen, 'A Revolution in Warfare', *Foreign Affairs* Vol.75, No.2 (March/April 1996), pp.37–54.

6. Snow and Brown, *International Relations*, media also involved in monitoring function. Jessica Mathews, 'Power Shift', *Foreign Affairs* Vol.76, No.1 (1997), pp.50–66 on informed NGOs and Chiapas.

7. General conditions under which two states will prefer at least one division of the spoils to the expected outcome for war are spelled out in James Fearon, 'A Rationalist Explanation for War', *International Organization*, 1995. Fearon discusses how states will have incentives to hide their true positions, even when full information would allow them to find a peaceful resolution to their conflict. Harrison Wagner, building on Fearon's work, shows the logic behind a state actually waging limited war in order to improve its outcome along the range of possible settlements that might be achieved in negotiations. Harrison Wagner, 'Bargaining and War', *American Journal of Political Science*, 2000.

8. Intra-alliance positions and negotiations are described in Jack Schick, *The Berlin Crisis, 1958–1962* (Philadelphia: University of Pennsylvania Press, 1971).

9. As part of the European Union's process for increasing its crisis management capabilities, it has described a range of future missions known as the Petersberg tasks, covering humanitarian and rescue tasks to the tasks of combat forces in peacemaking (Treaty of the European Union (1992), Article 17.2).

10. Michael Brecher and Jonathan Wilkenfeld, *A Study of Crisis* (Ann Arbor, MI: University of Michigan Press, 2000), p.3, note 16 – Part I.

11. Ole Holsti, *Crisis, Escalation, War* (Montreal, Canada: McGill-Queens University Press, 1972). Jonathan Roberts, *Decision-Making During International Crisis* (NY: St Martin's Press, 1988).

12. A general description of future crisis management missions for the EU can be found in language set down by the Treaty on European Union (1992). [Article 17.2: Questions referred to in this Article shall include humanitarian and rescue tasks, peacekeeping tasks and tasks of combat forces in crisis management, including peacemaking.] These missions have come to be known as the Petersberg tasks, and the language has been reiterated at various meetings of the EU's European Council, including that which produced the recent Treaty of Nice (2000).

13. Lt General Joseph Wehrle, Jr, USAF, 'The Changing Nature of US National Security: Joint Task Force Atlas Response', lecture at the United States Air Force Academy, 26 October 2000.

14. Drew Fudenberg and Jean Tirole, *Game Theory* (Cambridge, MA: MIT Press, 1991); James Morrow, *Game Theory for Political Scientists* (Princeton, NJ: Princeton University Press, 1994).

15. Nye and Owens, 'America's Information Edge', Cohen, 'A Revolution in Warfare'.

16. David Yost, *NATO Transformed: The Alliance's New Roles in International Security* (Washington, DC: US Institute of Peace Press, 1998).

17. George, *Avoiding War*, p.22.

18. John Oneal, Brad Lian and James Joyner, Jr, 'Are the American People "Pretty Prudent"? Public Responses to US Uses of Force, 1950–1988', *International Studies Quarterly*, Vol.40,

No.2 (June 1996), pp.261–80. Bruce Jentleson and Rebecca Britton, 'Still Pretty Prudent: Post-Cold War American Public Opinion on the Use of Military Force', *Journal of Conflict Resolution*, Vol.42, No.4 (Aug. 1998), pp.395–417.

19. The international legitimacy and stability criterion afforded substantial protection to Farah Aidid in Somalia, Saddam Hussein in Iraq, and Slobodan Milosevic in Yugoslavia. However today's *ultima ratio* is not as crystal clear as it was during the Cold War. Legitimacy and stability concerns did not constrain the United States when it unilaterally took down Manuel Noriega's regime in Panama. Bob Woodward, *The Commanders* (NY: Simon and Schuster, 1991). Jentleson and Britton, 'Still Pretty Prudent'.

20. Robert Keohane and Joseph Nye, 'Power and Interdependence in the Information Age', *Foreign Affairs*, Vol.77, No.5 (Sept./Oct. 1998), pp.81–94 make a similar claim when they discuss 'discounting' to compensate for a disadvantage in information. Peter Feaver, 'Blowback: Information Warfare and the Dynamics of Coercion', *Security Studies*, Vol.7, No.4 (Summer 1998), pp.88–120 also argues that information dominance may cause unintended effects that make successful deterrence more difficult.

21. George, *Avoiding War*.

22. George, *Avoiding War*; Holsti, *Crisis, Escalation, War*; Gordon Prange, *At Dawn We Slept* (NY: McGraw-Hill, 1981).

23. See Chapter 8, 'Perceptions of Centralization', in Robert Jervis, *Perception and Misperception in International Politics* (Princeton, NJ: Princeton University Press, 1976); For applications to the command and control of strategic forces, see Paul Bracken, *The Command and Control of Nuclear Forces* (New Haven, CT: Yale University Press, 1983); Peter Feaver, *Guarding the Guardians: Civilian Control of Nuclear Weapons in the United States* (Ithaca, NY: Cornell University Press, 1992); Peter Feaver and Emerson Niou, 'Managing Nuclear Proliferation: Condemn, Strike, or Assist?' *International Studies Quarterly*, Vol.40, No.2 (June 1996).

24. Robert Keohane and Joseph Nye, 'International Relations in the Information Age', p.88, list five functions characteristic of the new technologies: gather, sort, process, transfer and disseminate. A list of the functions performed in knowledge management includes collection, integration, organization, analysis and distribution. See Jan Van den Hoven, 'The Data Warehouse: If You Build It With the Users, They Will Come', *Information Strategy*, Vol.17, No.3 (2001), pp.29–35. For the purposes of describing the impact of technological development in this paper, integration and organization are subsumed under analysis.

25. A lost treasure by John Mills, *Signals and Speech in Electrical Communication* (NY: Harcourt, Brace and Company, 1934), explains the concept of information in modern telecommunications systems.

26. Two signals may share the same carrier frequency without becoming garbled. Lay descriptions liken the process to imposing different languages on simultaneous streams of human voices; see *SPECTRUM Magazine*, 'Technology 1998: Analysis and Forecast, (NY: IEEE, 1997). This technique could some day bring a quantum leap in the available bandwidth for information distribution. Last year, physicists announced a breakthrough in the manipulation of light. Light waves were, for practical purposes, arrested by a specially prepared medium; James Glanz, 'Scientists Bring Light to Full Stop, Hold It, Then Send It On It's Way', *New York Times*, 18 Jan. 2001, p.A1. The practical effect could be a quantum decrease in the already low amounts of time, space and energy it takes to operate computer memory.

27. Mingfang Li and L. Richard Ye, 'Information Technology and Firm Performance: Linking with Environmental, Strategic and Managerial Contexts', *Information and Management*, Vol.35, No.1 (1999), pp.43–52.

28. Richard Lanza, 'Does Your Project Risk Management System Do the Job?' *Information Strategy*, Vol.17, No.1 (2000), p.8, cites a study of 650 NASA projects between 1960 and 1970. Among six of the most common risks leading to project failure, the authors listed 'poorly defined objective' and 'inadequately defined tasks'. See also John Murray, 'Finding the Right Level of IT Expense', *Information Strategy*, Vol.17, No.2 (2001), pp.29–35 and Van den Hoven, 'The Data Warehouse'.

29. Craig Covault, 'Eavesdropping Satellite Parked Over Crisis Zone', *Aviation Week & Space Technology*, Vol.148, No.20 (1998), p.30.

30. Angelo Codevilla, *Informing Statecraft* (NY: Free Press, 1992), pp.313–24.

31. Linda Shiner, 'Predator Hunting Evil in the Balkans', *Air & Space* (May 2001), pp.49–57.
32. George, *Avoiding War*, pp.434–6.
33. See, for example, Ministry of Defense, France, *Premiers Enseignements de la Crise du Kosovo – Evaluations Techniques et Operationnelles* (Sept. 1999).
34. Codevilla, *Informing Statecraft*.
35. Two other popular collection systems that might be acquired in greater numbers by EU members are the AWACS and JSTARS aircraft. These radar-based systems record electromagnetic returns from the movement of forces, but in a crisis the signals for communicating resolve resemble those for preparing an imminent attack. For more on the limitations of high technology systems for early warning, see Roberta Wohlstetter, 'Cuba and Pearl Harbor', *Foreign Affairs*, Vol.43, No.4 (1965), pp.691–707 and Alexander George and Jane Holl, *The Warning-Response Problem and Missed Opportunities in Preventive Diplomacy* (Washington, D.C.: Carnegie Commission on Preventing Deadly Conflict, 1997).
36. Schick, *The Berlin Crisis*; Alexander George and Richard Smoke, *Deterrence and American Foreign Policy: Theory and Practice* (NY: Columbia University Press, 1974); Roberts, *Decision-Making During International Crises*.
37. Independent International Commission on Kosovo, *The Kosovo Report* (Oxford: Oxford University Press, 2000), pp.4, 85–91.
38. For the enduring importance of a personal approach to crisis management even in the information age, see Richard Holbrooke, *To End a War* (NY: Random House, 1998) and General Wesley Clark, USA (ret.), *Waging Modern War* (NY: Public Affairs, 2001).
39. NATO, *50 Years of Infrastructure: NATO Security Investment Programme Is the Sharing of Roles, Risks, Responsibilities, Costs and Benefits* (Brussels, Belgium: NATO Infrastructure Committee, 2001).
40. Rutten, *From St. Malo to Nice*, pp.203–08.
41. Yost, 'The NATO Capabilities Gap and the European Union'.
42. See note 5.
43. In his intensive case study of the Berlin Blockade, Avi Shlaim claimed that 'as all President-watchers have emphasized, the incumbent's personality will shape the formal structure of the policy-making system that he creates around himself and, even more importantly, it will influence the ways in which he encourages and permits that system to operate in practice'. Avi Shlaim, *The United States and the Berlin Blockade, 1948–1949* (Berkeley, CA: University of California Press, 1983), p.69.
44. The four powers represented the victorious Allies after the Second World War: The United States, the Soviet Union, Great Britain and France. Schick, *Berlin Crisis*. Norman Gelb, *The Berlin Wall: Kennedy, Khrushchev, and a Showdown in the Heart of Europe* (NY: Times Books, 1986).
45. An entire school of thought rejects rational deterrence theory on similar grounds. Classic works linking psychology and deterrence include George and Smoke, *Deterrence and American Foreign Policy*; Richard Ned Lebow, *Beyond Peace and War: The Nature of International Crisis* (Baltimore, Md.: Johns Hopkins University Press, 1981); and Robert Jervis, Richard Ned Lebow and Janice Gross Stein, *Psychology and Deterrence* (Baltimore, Md.: Johns Hopkins University Press, 1989).
46. Graham Allison, *Essence of Decision: Explaining the Cuban Missile Crisis* (NY: HarperCollins, 1971); Graham Allison and Philip Zelikow, *Essence of Decision*, second edition (NY: Longman, 1999).
47. Schick, *Berlin Crisis*, Ch. 2, esp. pp.53–6.
48. Shlaim, *United States and Berlin Blockade*.
49. Gelb, *Berlin Wall*, 245–69.
50. Shlaim, *United States and Berlin Blockade*; Schick, *Berlin Crisis*.
51. Shlaim, *United States and Berlin Blockade*, pp.180, 417.
52. Michael Ignatief, *Virtual War: Kosovo and Beyond* (NY: Metropolitan Books, 2000).
53. Ibid.
54. Ibid.
55. Ibid. and Clark, *Waging Modern War*, p.179.
56. Shlaim, *United States and Berlin Blockade*, p.275.

74   National Security in the Information Age

57. Ibid., pp.272–80, 410–23.
58. Gelb, *Berlin Wall*, 105, 245–48; Allison, *Essence*, 134.
59. Ivo Daalder and Michael O'Hanlon, *Winning Ugly: NATO's War to Save Kosovo* (Washington, D.C.: Brookings Institution Press, 2000), p.142.
60. Clark, *Waging Modern War*.
61. Ignatieff, *Virtual War*, p.101.
62. Ibid., pp.91–114; Clark, *Waging Modern War*, e.g. pp.224–6.
63. Ignatieff, *Virtual War*, p.103.
64. Here, information system is used in the broad sense to include the human interface as well as acquired hardware and software.
65. Schick, *Berlin Crisis*, pp.158–73.
66. See note 35.
67. Roberta Wohlstetter famously made a similar point with respect to Pearl Harbor. See, for example her article, Roberta Wohlstetter, 'Cuba and Pearl Harbor', *Foreign Affairs*, Vol.43, No.4 (1965) pp.691–707.
68. See note 37; Ignatieff, *Virtual War*; Daalder and O'Hanlon, *Winning Ugly*, pp.88, 89–96, 101–24.
69. Vojin Joksimovich, *Kosovo Crisis: A Study in Foreign Policy Mismanagement* (Los Angeles, CA: Graphics Management Press, 1999), pp.273, 326.

Note Added in Proof

The analysis in this volume precedes Operation Enduring Freedom in Afghanistan and the most recent war in Iraq. Although the timescale for escalation and potential disaster in nationbuilding extends beyond that in classic crisis management, similarities between the two operations may help explain some current difficulties. Despite wielding clear advantages in information technology, US forces on nation-building missions are still struggling to control Afghanistan and especially Iraq.

Wars of Disruption:
International Competition and Information
Technology-Driven Military Organizations

CHRIS C. DEMCHAK

AFTER THE COLD WAR,
THE INFORMATION AGE WAR BECKONS

Organizations fight wars and how they do so is heavily influenced by the military organization's internal evolutionary paths. Over the 1990s, despite a decade of internal rhetorical support for new information age technologies and ambitious conceptual developments, the US military clung to its traditional approach to war. Despite observations to the contrary, the 2001 US-led operations in Afghanistan continued a historically comfortable bias towards lethality and state-level targets.

This is surprising given that the Cold War ended with a bow wave of new technological developments in flexible scale, rapid networks, and long-range capabilities originally developed to meet larger Soviet conventional forces. Over the 1980s, promoters of these new capabilities emphasized precision in the application of force and in disrupting the organizational processes of an opponent, advantaging smaller forces by producing a 'levelling' effect with the use of advances in computerized equipment. By the end of the 1980s, this was taken for granted as the strength and province of the West. The precision associated with these new technologies also promised to maintain societal support for military operations by avoiding innocent or arbitrary casualties.

The end of the Cold War was also associated with the possibly unpredictable actions of a multitude of mid-level states and non-state actors no longer constrained by the Soviet Union. Individually and corporately, they added a dimension of great unknown to the security environment of the Western world, especially to its biggest player, the US. The computerized capabilities developed to track, plumb and correctly interpret the actions of the former Soviet Union and its proxies, massive networks that could move information instantaneously across heretofore-unprecedented distances, were now heralded as the answer to a confusing globe. They could provide the rapidity of response necessary to deter, mitigate or negate security challenges before they rippled through the international system to harm Western nations.

The need was apparent, and the stage set, for the emergence of a newer form of warfare by the early 1990s. The scale up or down aspects of these developments meant that 'less than full scale war' operations could be legitimate in the eyes of Western societies if designed, targeted, and employed so as to succeed in their mission while minimizing casualties on either side. These exquisitely targeted operations required a shift in future evolutionary paths for Western militaries, of their organizational structures, acquisition plans and leadership vision. A great debate emerged in the US military community outlining a new model of a military able to meet these requirements, the Revolution in Military Affairs (RMA) model. In principle, it was to employ the precision capabilities of advanced information systems to rapidly disrupt an organizational opponent at or below the state before extensive damage occurred to all participants. This model need not focus on lethality.

Unfortunately the internal debates of the leading Western military, the US, channelled the wider community's conceptual understanding of new IT-enabled operations. To maintain the uniqueness of the military in budget debates, American senior leaders appealed to the enhanced lethality available from the speed and accuracy of new integrating technologies. Information moving at lightening speed from a 'sensor' to a 'shooter' became the shorthand concept of adequate tests of effectiveness. In addition, the lack of understanding of complex information systems among senior defence leaders produced statements with unrealistic operational expectations for the emergent RMA model.

The underlying military structure struggled to meet these expectations simultaneously and fragmented into battles to upgrade and connect existing systems. By the end of the 1990s, many legacy systems were linked into networks and more capably exchanging data but the overarching military was not close to the vision of the exceptionally integrated RMA military. As a result, when the US's strategic depth was violated by a sub-state actor in the Al Qaeda network, military planners fell back upon tradition in their response – the use of highly lethal blast technologies on a territorially bound state actor.

This piece explores the shortcomings of the RMA model, its unrealistic integration expectations, its inadequate support for operations involving non-state organizations, its overemphasis on lethality, and its under appreciation for knowledge as a critical policy tool. Moving the US military onto a new evolutionary path, away from lethality and state-level opponents, will prove difficult. Better conceptual developments in understanding IT-enabled military organizations and the appropriate targeting of their operations are required. Charting future research directions, this article offers a different model of a modern information-enabled military and of the role of lethal coercion in a more targeted policy approach to globally emergent non-state opponents.

COLD WAR'S LEGACY: PROMISING TECHNOLOGIES, ORGANIZATIONAL CONUNDRUMS

Until the mid-1980s, war among the major powers – the Soviet Union, the United States and (in geostrategic terms) China – still seemed possible. Defence organizational and technological choices tended to be relatively focused on the threats of specific nations or alliances. Military organizations argued for increased conventional capabilities but these were expensive – resulting in large personnel and maintenance budgets. In technological developments, the US turned to meeting the conventional and nuclear threat with renewed nuclear deterrence. Major scientific and engineering advances were justified in the US in the name of meeting Cold War nuclear force-on-force targeting requirements and Star Wars defence plans during this period. The beneficiaries were the rising field of precision-guided munitions and rapid telemetry and communications, all needed if an overwhelming conventional army was to be stopped in its tracks *en route* to Bonn or Seoul.[1]

In the process, however, the groundwork was laid for new technological paths. By the beginning of the 1980s, the Western nations were particularly concerned about a rapidly increasing Soviet quantitative edge that Western nations were unwilling to meet financially in funding standing forces. It was well recognized that a smaller NATO force would have trouble stopping the momentum of a massive Warsaw Pact attack without equally credible lethality. To meet and stop a Soviet attack would require unprecedented, even heroic, reach and resupply operations. In particular, the ability to reach well into the Warsaw Pact to head off a losing conventional exchange had to be exceptionally accurate and rapid.[2] Since such actions were likely to invoke a response with nuclear weapons, the public debate on the legitimacy of high-lethality nuclear technologies emerged, especially in Germany.[3]

By the middle of the decade of the 1980s, the blast power of the deterrent weapons of choice – nuclear weapons – had become dismaying rather than reassuring.[4] Unable to rely on simply overwhelming the opposing force with its blast capabilities, the US turned segments of its defence research communities to seeking non-nuclear alternatives to large conventional standing forces.[5] The goal was explicitly to scale up smaller conventional forces to be able to deter, meet and defeat larger Soviet-style mass assaults. That involved being more agile, integrated and knowledgeable in real-time about what the enemy was about to do. By the end of the decade, the push to make everything faster and more accurate – as major additions to merely hitting harder on target – to meet the Soviet threat had developed a life of its own in the US defence industry.[6] This new emphasis was enhanced by the experiences with limited war in which the inability to find the enemy accurately and with enough time to act determined the outcome of these wars.[7]

The 1980s and the Cold War ended with this bow wave of new Western technological developments in flexible scale, rapid networks, and long range destruct capabilities developed to meet larger Soviet conventional forces. The dawn of the final decade of this past century did not, however, bring the peace dividend in military technologies anticipated with the fall of the Soviet Union. Instead, the loss of the other superpower complicated the threat spectrum enormously with respect to large- and mid-sized nations, making a focused response in technologies difficult at best.[8] For leading military leaders, organizational and technological choices in assuring security became ever more complicated by the broadening contingencies.

The demise of the Cold War, along with the obvious complexification of the global threat environment, posed a tough conceptual challenge to Western militaries whose core competency was lethal operations in 'war'. For the West, 'war' has had general characteristics; it is not random or occasional unpremeditated small group violence. It involves direction by a governmental structure, implementation by a military, premeditation and willingness to engage in destruction for some societal issue, and permanency in the results.[9] Furthermore, the West's experiences with the Second World War suggested that 'war' has a scale involving national mobilizations and fights whose outcomes involve the survival of whole systems of government. The competition with a large single governmental actor, the former Soviet Union, permitted the intermediate conceptual step between peace and war, called the 'Cold War'. While the major actors did not engage in institutionalized application of mass lethality, the overarching threat of mutually assured destruction and lethal 'proxy' wars on the periphery justified war-like military forces in the West.

Over the course of the 1980s, however, Western legislatures were already vigorously seeking budget savings or 'peace dividends' by cutting the Cold War-sized military budgets. Early in the 1990s – the immediate post-Cold War period, scholars even seriously discussed the possible 'end' of total war as traditionally seen between states.[10] Senior US officers vigorously fought the force downsizing in order to retain what was considered a safe level of military capabilities.[11] They argued that it was likely that Western powers, specifically the US, would need to be able to rapidly and coercively respond to external challenges in the near future.[12] Military practitioners moved to portray military operations less as major wars and more as varying scales of deployments made possible and successful by the incorporation of expensive new computerized technologies.

The development of new concepts of future operations was further complicated by changing notions of what kinds of casualties were legitimate in any operation involving military force. Under Western notions, lethality is the fundamental characteristic of war. Lethality is legitimated in part by war's society-wide scale. When whole societies are mobilized to fight, it is recognized as inevitable that mass assaults and accidents will inflict heavy casualties. However, with the rising wealth and expectations in the West, operations below total war were increasingly expected to have greater accuracy in their conduct.[13] The deliberate or arbitrary killing of innocents was, by the late 1990s, increasingly seen as illegitimate, even in wartime.[14] For example, in 2002–2003 one of the chief objections to a US-dominated attack on Iraq – as stated by many Middle Eastern leaders – was the likely plight of the Iraqi people, presented widely as innocents in their cruel leader's games. This argument played well in Western nations, despite the fact that the leaders themselves had human rights violations in their own nations. Nonetheless, it was echoed, perhaps more sincerely, by Western European leaders as well.

As a result, senior leaders have over this period needed to justify to their key legislative audiences a military role in a future without major wars and to demonstrate their modernizing efforts towards a military capability that met all challenges with minimal death or destruction. For those needs they turned to the information technologies developed during the Cold War to meet any challenge at any scale as rapidly and accurately as possible. The result was enthusiastic endorsement of the concept of 'Operations Other Than War' (OOTW),[15] and widespread promotion of a new kind of highly integrated information-enabled army – referred to as the RMA model.[16]

In developing this model, non-technically skilled US senior officers anchored their argument in the ways that newer technologies made lethality – the military's traditional domain –faster and more accurate.[17] The Gulf War occurred just when military leaders needed to show legislatures a continuing need for their services. This conflict was marketed as the first highly technical and accurate 'information age' war.[18] The operation's enormous use of traditional blast technologies such as B-52 bombers was downplayed to the public, while the speed of its conclusion was used as proof that the US was on the correct path to conducting casualty-free, almost sanitary war.[19]

After 1991, the literature on the US-defined RMA model ballooned, even as the US community struggled with what this military actually looked like or was able to do. In subsequent years, the nascent RMA model's scaling potential explicitly linked the smallness and integrated speed of the modern force (with its smaller personnel budgets) to the successful use of force-multiplying, computer-enhanced equipment to ensure preparedness for any surprise in the complex post-Cold War environment. By the mid 1990s, lethality dominated as the core competency of the US's plans for a highly networked, 'tailored precision military' capable of moving information rapidly to apply force on a target. Knowledge pursuit and refinement – the great advantage of integrated computerized systems – was characterized as valuable and even critical but relegated to a secondary support function.[20]

MODERNIZATION DETOURED BY RMA DEVELOPMENT

The US military's steady coupling of complex technologies to lethality produced acquisition fragmentation. Achieving an all-purpose, highly scalable, fully informed, tightly networked human machine of unprecedented range, accuracy, speed and lethality requires extraordinary geographical reach, rapid absorptive capacity, and surprise-mitigation in a social system. These are exceptional expectations and the transition to this new organization was poorly coordinated. First, the priorities stated by senior US defence officials in their four year (quadrennial) reviews (QDR) of national defence forces contributed to decisions by lower level managers to focus on existing systems emphasizing lethality over innovative knowledge processes.[21] Second, the operational goals of the emerging RMA model were unrealistically described so lower level managers inserted their own preferences given a lack of reality checks by senior officer statements.

QDR Statements and Acquisition Realities

By the 1993 quadrennial defence review, senior defence leaders addressed scenarios far removed from the former Soviet threat and based on a much smaller total force structure than the Cold War force.[22] This review modelled its recommendations after Operation *Desert Storm* and a hypothetical North Korean invasion of South Korea. Not only were both scenarios considered unlikely and undoable by lower level managers in the defence agencies, but the document also made ambitious and optimistic estimates of future US capabilities. Knowledge-development capabilities were assumed to be available in the reserves or automatically to emerge in the active forces.[23] The latter would prove particularly problematic for the future development of an organizational concept of wars of disruption as opposed to lethal destruction. The review's authors reinforced the notion that the same general purpose forces intended for highly lethal actions in major wars would be effective when simply scaled down all the way to small peacekeeping missions, as long they received some specialized training. The net effect was to channel the managers of the newer technologies away from serious organizational consideration of novel IT-enabled policy options and constrain them to more traditional paths emphasizing lethality.

This pattern continued through the next review. The 1997 QDR noted military service efforts already underway to develop innovations in operations – while still being highly lethal.[24] Behind the scenes, peacekeeping was disdained by senior US military leaders, an unpleasant costly operation beneath the skill levels of US military personnel. The exception was the use of lethal force in quick get-in-and-get-out operations. The 1997 QDR did attempt to further develop an RMA military by recommending more funds for C4ISR[25] through reductions in force structure and base closures.[26] All the major weapons systems already on the drawing board, including controversial budget busters like the F-22 Raptor, RAH-66 Comanche helicopter, and Crusader howitzer were retained.[27]

By the time the latest QDR was rewritten by the incoming Bush administration barely months before the Afghanistan operation, the 'modern' military model behind the discussion had become interlaced with a focus on accurate and rapid lethality using computer systems.[28] The document acknowledges the great uncertainty about future operations but retains an emphasis on traditional notions of deploying armed forces to, for example, meet asymmetrical, lethal warfare. The dominating vision is strikingly combat-oriented. In this new military, massive pipelines of information are constantly, seamlessly and intensely active, linking sources from overhead unmanned aerial and satellite sensors to the infrared night vision device of the individual soldier, from the massive data maps in the Pentagon to the full colour near-real-time battle map display of the rugged laptop of the tank commander, to the deployed US streamlined IW forces which will operate quickly, accurately, lethally and effectively.[29] Emphasizing 'synchrony', i.e., the elements moving in tightly coupled closely coordinated, extremely rapid operations, this vision of an invincible human machine has only seemed possible now with massive computerization and the 'death of distance' through networks allowing organizations to know enough to make the vision real.[30] Despite all the novel language such as 'transformation' and 'fundamental changes', traditional personnel and force mix recommendations remained virtually unchanged.[31]

Under this guidance throughout the 1990s, lower level defence managers had no incentive to alter their established path of acquisitions. Policies did not clarify paths towards novel concepts of knowledge-based militaries. The poorly directed concept of modernization made for piecemeal guidance, making it unlikely that an alternative to the lethality theme would emerge. Upgrading legacy systems focused on traditional lethal operations under the rubric of RMA-like modernization. In keeping with prior reviews, the Rumsfeld 2001 QDR recommended funding selective upgrades to existing legacy systems such as Abrams tanks and B-1 bombers.[32]

Only the creation of a new DOD position (Director, Force Transformation) suggests a better understanding of the enormity of organizational changes in the RMA process. This position, directly accountable to the Deputy Secretary of Defense, in principle, has an impressive mission to 'evaluate the transformation efforts of the Military Departments and promote synergy by recommending steps to integrate ongoing transformation activities'.[33] Its bureaucratic impotence, however, is apparent. The position has an overly large mandate without the budget or decision–making authorities to act. As a result, there is no senior leader push to alter existing evolutionary paths and traditional preferences flourish at lower levels.[34]

RMA System Architecture and Design Flaws

The situation is compounded by the unrealistic organizational expectations of the new 'modern' RMA military that senior leaders had spent a decade promoting. Networked information technologies are the foundation elements of the RMA model but less clear in senior leader statements are clear understandings that intricate technical and social systems are inherent in this model. 'Digitized data networks ... allow commanders at all levels to visualize the battle more clearly and to control its pace.' and 'As was the case in Desert Storm, victory will be determined in many cases by which side has the best electronics.'[35] Defence leaders' expectations of the organizational structures that will use these technologies are often stated in technologically related terms. The RMA force is one that is presumed to be: 'rapidly tailorable, rapidly expansible, strategically deployable and effectively employable ...in all operational environments. ... defined by five characteristics: doctrinal flexibility, strategic mobility, *tailorability* and modularity, joint and multinational connectivity, and the versatility to function in War and OOTW (Operations Other Than War).'[36]

> We will be able to do more with less. Battle command based on real-time, shared, situational awareness, hierarchical responsibility, nontraditional hierarchical organizations, – capabilities-based designs, – smaller, more lethal, more versatile, more effective building blocks, – top-to-bottom force congruence, – electronic connectivity instead of geographic/physical connectivity, – increased strategic deployability with a full range of early entry capabilities *tailorable* to a full range of missions.[37]

The language seems excessive but the promises of the IT revolution suggested a whole new kind of warfare, information war (IW), from which the American military was drawing its images of the future RMA military 'managing' the battlespace faster, more accurately, and more predictably than previously possible. Unfortunately, the model is at its base highly problematical. First, a fully implemented RMA requires large-scale technical systems (LTSs) that are exceptionally difficult to manage reliably and inexpensively. Second, these LTSs tend to pose huge organizational knowledge burdens on their managers.

RMA as Surprise Prone Large-scale Technical System (LTS.) This language describes an organizational structure similar to that of a large technical system (LTS) with all the rigidities and surprises that have been revealed and explored in civilian organizations by LTS scholars over the last ten years. The central attributes of an LTS are as follows. First, an identifiable social system with boundaries and internal coherence emerges when heterogeneous small to mid-scale organizational activities (linked at their core by interdependencies among machine elements) expand, possibly compete, and then consolidate into a highly interdependent and spatially wide-ranging network of essential relations.[38] Second, the scale of these phenomena is such that they are extraordinarily complex and hence difficult to comprehend by average non-expert individuals, a situation affording the system considerable insulation from normal mechanisms of social control other than costly concerted efforts in times of crisis.[39]

Third, the system's inherent complexity and spatial reach increase the likely opportunity costs of predicting, mitigating, protecting against, or surviving the surprising outcomes of complex systems. LTSs have, among large organizations, a particular potential for the deleterious surprises inherent in complex systems.[40] In any system, some outcomes will always remain unknown ('unknowable unknowns') while others are knowable with sufficient research but not currently known ('knowable unknowns'). This set of undesirable unknowns, called here the 'rogue' set, produces the unpleasant surprises for users of highly complex equipment. These unexpected negative events are more likely to be disruptive because any complex system is more tightly coupled and prone to experience ripple effects from shortcomings in key nodes along lengthy contingent chains of operationally necessary actions.

It is extremely difficult to discern in advance the actual dynamic capabilities of large organizations inextricably intertwined with complex electronic equipment.[41] Both machines and organizations can be such complex systems with rogue sets. The rogue set can be reduced by 'accommodating the knowledge burden'.[42] Accommodation involves having the right knowledge available when and where surprises occur. For militaries or any organization, accommodation is the ability correctly to diagnose a surprising problem quickly and then fix it on the spot with the right process, data, trained person, mission, additional equipment and amount of time. Given the nature of these surprises, such systems quickly channel human individual and group behaviours in directions often not anticipated by the designers or purchasers of the technical systems.[43] Such large systems can manifest 'artifactual success combined with system failure', i.e., costly and or catastrophic surprises developing inexplicably.[44] The RMA model as it developed over the 1990s was at best flawed in complex systems terms.

RMA and Inherent Organizational Knowledge Burden. Five presumptions in particular made the RMA system likely to be organizationally difficult to implement successfully. Each suggests the size of the large knowledge burden for organizational leaders to manage.

Comprehensive information flows. With the RMA model in place, senior military staff expect that operational leaders throughout the military organization will automatically know more through the massive increase in access to information networks with high-volume bandwidth, super-large storage capabilities and very rapid retrieval rates. According to the general definition of effectiveness, greater knowledge is indeed positively associated with greater effectiveness. Militaries have traditionally *not* known enough at critical moments; much of military history is about organizing in order to compensate for what they cannot know about the enemy.[45] Hence, if the computerized systems could immediately provide the missing information throughout the organization, it is difficult for military officers not to see this outcome as an unalloyed benefit.

The difficulty for organizations is that increased internal information flows must be met or exceeded by rising abilities to process the information into knowledge.[46] Note that knowledge is more than mere provision of data or the thousands of linked data sets comprising information flows; for any given surprise or uncertainty, knowledge is the right bit at the right time, place and mode – whether it is relevant analysis concerning enemy approaches, imagery of intervisibility obstructions not on maps, or a critically needed spare part.[47] The mere provision of information does not mean knowledge for the recipients. Nor does knowing where the missing component is in the pipeline provide that knowledge item to the needy user when needed

If compensation for information overload is not explicitly acknowledged by senior leaders and designed into the organization, usually with slack resources, the organization's processes will slow down commensurate with the need of local nodes to individually figure out how to screen information for their local needs.[48] As individual nodes make their own decisions about what is important, mistakes and confusion can ripple through the rest of the highly integrated, precision-based organization.[49] For example, public discussions of the future military structure by leaders and industry promoters have not focused on the processing that will be necessary for subordinate leaders to sift through large quantities of electronic data.[50] One of the difficulties encountered during actual hostilities during the 1991 Gulf War was the inability by operational staff to process the volume of messages being pumped forward.[51] This shortcoming continues today. In 1999 a US Marine Corps simulated exercise revealed that troops had a 15 per cent higher casualty rate due to the inability to input and process the data on which their success depended.[52]

Exceptionally rapid. Senior leaders expected that the RMA organization will act more quickly than any hostile force as well as faster than militaries using any previous force design. Flexibility is a key component of effectiveness for most organizations. However, speed alone is a worthless criterion if the accuracy of response is misdirected or inaccurate. In organizations generally, the more quickly each must act, the clearer the cause–effect, ends–means and fact–value tradeoffs must be.[53] But the new RMA's focus is largely on gathering all available data and pushing it to the front line leaders who, it is reasoned, will then be able to act faster.

Speed conflicts with accuracy in machines as well as organizations if the circumstances surrounding their use or the inputs they are given change in unexpected and intolerable ways. It often requires considerable human knowledge and skill to overcome protocols or boundary conditions embedded in hardware or software. Similarly, highly complex fast machines often demonstrate transient errors in processing that are particularly disrupting and frustrating because they are so difficult to diagnose.[54] At a minimum the user needs to constantly check output against other known indicators to verify accuracy. Often users in a hurry will mistake precision for accuracy. For example, in escaping from the US forces in Afghanistan in fall 2001, Osama bin Laden sent his bodyguard in a different direction while using bin Laden's personal satellite cell phone continuously. The US forces precisely located the phone and captured the bodyguard. They did not accurately discern who was on the phone, however, and that was arguably the more important information. Bin Laden escaped.[55]

Throughout the 1990s, senior leaders focused more on flowing data rapidly than on the contents. But the latter is what will actively determine the organization's ability to change rapidly in response to surprise. Designers have responded, in some cases, by making assumptions or restricting user options in order to reduce user-introduced deviations that could slow down processing. Often the data provided or input required is in response to questions the designers assumed the local commander would ask, not the ones he or she may need to ask at that moment. In the 2001 Afghanistan operation, for example, US troops were killed by friendly fire because of designer assumptions built into the default mechanisms of the global positioning equipment being used by ground troops to direct aircraft bombing runs. In the heat of an operation, a soldier changed a battery which died while he was sending enemy coordinates to incoming aircraft, unaware that a new battery automatically reverted to the *user's own coordinates* when inserted. The new battery completed the transmission giving the aircraft not enemy locations, but the location of the friendly unit using the equipment, resulting in three deaths and twenty casualties.[56] In Afghanistan, as in the decade long record of senior leaders' preferences, speed is emphasized over knowledge. Recently advances in 'sensor to shooter' cycles have been used to declare the Afghanistan operation an innovative success.[57]

Central control. Senior leaders anticipate being able to more closely control the action-reaction-counteraction flows of the battle through their unprecedented connectiveness to all their organizational elements. Few leaders can resist seeking more control when the apparent means of doing so are present.[58] Decades of studies on organizations of all types suggest that the more centralized the control, the more stable and homogeneous both the environment and the organization must be in order to provide consistent outcomes.[59] If the conditions of homogeneity and stability are met, then alternate sets of rules of operations can be developed in advance. That is, if internal operations or the environment's demands are predictable in form, if not in frequency, then central control could well be effective. Central decision-makers identify the range of acceptable alternatives for subordinate leaders, who then chose predetermined options.

The reality of military operations, however, is far from having either stability or homogeneity in operating environments. The range of alternative operational options offered to subordinate leaders must be large indeed to accommodate all possible local instabilities and surprises. And such a large latitude for subordinate commanders can rapidly become inconsistent with senior leaders' command and control preferences, even if they are reinforced electronically. The 2001 Afghanistan operation offers some striking examples of this expectation. First, the commander of the US operations in Afghanistan kept his headquarters in the US state of Florida. Traditionally commanders move to be as close as possible to the actual operation in order to see what is happening, to acquire systemic knowledge on the ground. The considerable physical distance from the reality on the ground encouraged a great initial willingness to use local Afghani soldiers in the frontlines, thereby sparing US soldiers from risk and US budgets from expenditures. Later in the operation, the US-based senior leaders were surprised that the local fighters were letting Taliban and Al Qaeda fighters escape through the frontlines of the US-backed Afghani forces. Such behaviour was unanticipated by US senior leaders and planners accustomed to the professionalism of volunteer Western soldiers. This unexpected outcome forced US solders back into harm's way on the frontlines. Similarly, air units faced surprises in the difference between the very current and urgent mission orders by the Tampa, Florida headquarters and the ground forces' reality in Afghanistan. Heavy use was made of Air Force bombers operating from bases far from the ground operations with generally poor battle damage assessment and several largely avoidable incidents of friendly fire casualties as well.[60]

Precise predictions. Senior leaders expected IW sensor systems and automated analytical programs to offer widespread, multilevel and near-blanket coverage of the area of operations, permitting precise predictions of future and real-time organizational needs in all operations. With such information in advance, for example, just-in-time (JIT) supply lines can respond accurately and efficiently to needs. However, apart from post offices with state monopolies and auto manufacturers with standard models, few other organizations have done as well with the just-in-time arrangement. Even auto manufacturers have suffered when surprises disrupt an otherwise robust just-in-time setup. The 1995 earthquake in Kobe, Japan disrupted and shut down manufacturers miles to the south because suppliers key to the just-in-time strategy became non-operational.

The difficulty is that, the larger the organization and the more stringent the demands on its operations, every increase in complexity makes surprises more inevitable and routine and the whole system less predictable.[61] Military organizations may be shrinking in comparison with their sizes during the era of the superpower competition, but they are still large organizations and therefore subject to the surprises of complexity. Add sophisticated machines whose needs, uses and channelling of human behaviour increases complexity as well, and the potential disruption of surprise magnifies. Under these conditions, the apparently trivial event may have enormous consequences, and the ability to predict outcomes commensurately falls.

In the Afghanistan operations, much was made of the sensor capability of the US forces, to include air dropped motion detectors possibly scattered all over the mountains separating Afghanistan and Pakistan. The goal was to use motion and heat sensors in the winter passes to indicate the presence of Al Qaeda slipping through the noose of Afghanistan into Pakistan. 'If he moves, we spot him', a Pentagon official told *Time*. 'If he doesn't move, we close in on him, cave by cave'.[62] But it seems ten years of promoting the precision of the information systems being acquired has not solved the basic military problem of having enough appropriate knowledge on the ground in a time frame relevant for the local commander. According to a US senior commander two months after the start of the Afghanistan operation, 'if you see one (Taliban fighter), you don't know how many others are getting away'.[63]

Furthermore, US commanders were consistently surprised by how few bodies they uncovered in the caves after the Shah-I-Kot battle of early 2002. They had confidently predicted an enemy bloodbath given the ordnance the US was laying on known locations of enemy soldiers.[64] It could be that the rate of fire of these dedicated fighters may have been high enough to fool the US troops into thinking more fighters were in these caves than there actually were.[65] Or it may be that the sensors, however well designed in the abstract, never alerted the US troops to the use of back doors out of the caves into Pakistan because they were visible to fleeing soldiers and destroyed, buried too deeply in snow, or merely not scattered thickly enough for good coverage. Predictions have not been operationally as robust as the decade of promotion of the new military capabilities in an RMA-like military would suggest, even in relatively traditional blast technology operations.[66]

Just-in-time substitutes for slack. Senior leaders expected that expensive support mechanisms such as logistics, intelligence, and training can be optimized to a just-in-time strategy, saving money by eliminating the need to overproduce or overstock in advance.[67] This desire on the part of senior leaders is understandable in an era of declining budgets but it is far from what studies of organizations employing complex technologies would suggest as an appropriate strategy. Just-in-time operations first developed among large volume manufacturers having long-term stable relationships with reliable suppliers and relatively predictable market demand for their products. Automobile manufacturers are perhaps the best example. A just-in-time (JIT) war is predicated on minimal (hence cheaper) on-site slack, and relies on the raw speed of communication to move material to meet shortfalls as needed.

For militaries, however, the greater the uncertainty, or the lower the predictability, of the task environment or operational systems, the more slack must be built into the system so as to assure robust operations, especially at the points of critical use.[68] JIT warfare visions of the RMA model neglect critical considerations such as the content of transmissions, the coordination requirements of responses, the distortion potentials of differing priorities and local needs along widely spread nodes, and finally the surprises inherent in such operations. In particular, logistics realities of organizational operations with IW are lost in this RMA transformation. Contemporary senior leader attitudes towards logistics seemed to be based more on hopes for savings than reality. Lieutenant General Pagonis (now retired), wrote in his 1992 book based on his 1991 Gulf War experiences as the senior officer in charge of logistics: 'We in the military must....stockpile a little or a lot, just in case'.[69] Even expert civilians suggested reducing the logistics 'tail', the connection to distant depots and the complexity of new technologies.[70] And yet, barely four years after the 1991 Gulf War, the US Army's Digitization Master Plan of 1995 had only one paragraph on logistics across roughly 56 pages of discussion.[71] The situation was, in these terms, hardly better in 2002. Indeed, after years of building towards an RMA model and the associated information systems, the chief of the Defense Department's Office of Transformation stated in fall 2002, 'The question is not how far can you shoot, but how close can I sense ... We have never thought in those terms before ... So we do not have a holistic concept for how one goes about gaining information superiority.'[72] Without this understanding of the interdependent uncertainties of JIT operations, knowledge is unlikely to be available on the spot but delayed in the also surprising large pipeline.

This last point is an especially critical issue for expeditionary forces. Although logistics is generally neglected in traditional military discussions, shortfalls in this arena have often historically been the chief reason a military was defeated.[73] In a military organization, despite the cultural images, myths, and experiences that highlight combat, internal interdependencies in the role and robustness of the logistics support are critical for survival and effectiveness. In fact, evaluations of 'systems fit' for any identified military operation can profitably begin with an inspection of (1) the organization's logistic systems and (2) propensity to be vulnerable to surprise.[74] It is in these areas that the promises of information warfare in the RMA have proven most extravagant. Despite the acknowledged escalating complexity of the new technologies, senior leaders spent the 1990s echoing the downsizing credo absorbed from the business world: 'we no longer can afford to have specialists ... Soldiers on the battlefield will have to get used to just-in-time logistics support'.[75] 'support troops can provide just-in-time logistics with fewer resources ... The mathematics prove that you can do the same job.'[76]

The envisioned logistics system of the RMA model developed attributes never before achieved in so complex and challenged an institution: close control of a complex large-scale organization, avoidance of error in just-in-time deliveries, and extraordinary requirements for highly trained personnel. The digitization objective had the underlying vision of the entire organization as one large synchronized machine, a truly massive rapid large-scale technical system. Senior leaders focused on the artefacts' potential rather than on the human behaviour channelled by and responding to the artefact's reliability and appropriateness for the situation at hand, with all of its unavoidable uncertainties. The difficulty is that this kind of organizational precision is not achievable in a complex organization facing the inevitable uncertainties of ground warfare or any kind of risky long distance operations. In view of these realities, the following statement by a contemporary senior military leader seems simply extraordinary: 'We will know what we need, when we need it and where it is. Rather than building up huge stockpiles just in case, information technology will allow us to anticipate and respond just in time to sustainment requirements.'[77]

In both systems design and organizational terms then, operational effectiveness would have been elusive when the RMA organization was deployed and employed. Over the 1990s and even well into the Afghanistan operation, senior leaders' expectations appear to be unmodified by what is currently known about large organizations that critically rely on complex technologies. The late 2002 and early 2003 build-up to an assault on Iraq took months, not weeks, not days and certainly not hours, just as it did ten years earlier in 1991. Yet this enduring reality of complex organizations continues unacknowledged officially.

In sum then, leaders of the largest information-enabled force in the world may still plan on acquiring maximizing information technology benefits while avoiding major costs with a flawed concept of what an information-enabled military facing such environmental instability and heterogeneity might, or might not, be able to do. And other nations follow in these developments in their own modernization plan.[78] A better concept is needed.

WARS OF DISRUPTION – A DIFFERENT CONCEPTUAL PATH

Beliefs about technology strongly influence the institution of war, especially the less frequent the opportunities to test these convictions.[79] An understanding of the surprise inherent in complex organizational systems would help re-orient this military model. Understood properly, modern information technology offers a significant reduction in opportunity costs in long term monitoring of potentially hostile organizations and their critical nodes. An appropriately focused IT-enabled military can create the conditions for a third policy option beyond deterrence and destruction, that of systemic disruption. A 'war of disruption' is both doable in today's world of not-quite-war conflicts and desirable because of its coercive potential which is not directly lethal to non-combatants.[80]

Searching for this option is important because, as Waltz notes, 'The Cold War militarized international politics.' And the US military has become the embedded fist enforcing the rules of a civil global behaviour. Hence changes in the perspectives of the US military drive what the international community thinks are the proper roles and techniques of military organizations. Lots of new actors are learning how to scale down highly lethal operations using smaller delivery packages and how many access points there are into open, free, flexible, globalizing, wealthy societies. Furthermore, many of these new actors have more reasons than before to be bitter about the increasingly more evident unequal international distribution of global resources. It behooves the US military to develop concepts of operations that are successful without contributing to the greater proliferation of small highly lethal easily deliverable packages drifting into the hands of the very large, young, increasingly resentful populations in the developing world.

Operations at a scale between total war and mere peacekeeping are a logical development in a world with few superpowers and lots of intermediate military capabilities scattered among nations. Such operations benefit significantly from using information technologies if seen as an alternative to highly lethal, major war. If the new force accommodates knowledge requirements and inevitable surprises through tested and sustained organizational slack, information technologies can provide interesting and unprecedented advantages. Such a force – more redundant and more knowledgeable – would focus on the opponent as an organization with critical information flows and thereby provide new national security policy possibilities. A major state can push the development of non-lethal military capabilities much further than destructive force applications.[81]

Such a force can robustly implement 'organization-oriented operations' (O3) continuously, not just during war, and take advantage of the interdependencies of any opposing forces, be they state level actors or not. Successes in peacetime could indirectly bolster the deterrence capabilities of major Western powers. A successful military organization implementing such wars of disruption does not have to be either intricately and systemically tightly integrated or particularly lethal.

As a logical development of the defensive and even pre-emptive use of information technologies, such low key on-going 'wars' can be useful as components of information-oriented operational strategies. For this situation, an organization-oriented IW force using knowledge management, not the lethality-oriented LTS-like force that is presently emerging in the US's RMA process, offers the best possibility of management of the disturbance in the international system before armed, costly deployments become the only option.

Disruption does not mean destruction if the target of the force is an organization's coordination capacity. Focusing on disrupting the coordination allows for a wider range of options in international system management. This policy option has always been present in military actions but never as a main policy option on its own. Historically it was used as a corollary source of pressure on an enemy, almost always followed by destruction. For example, during the Cold War, the US military's use of disruption was mainly in electronic warfare such as jamming incoming hostile forces and in deep strikes by air and missile attacks that 'disrupted' by destroying rearward located forces. Even the putatively highly electronic Gulf War 'disrupted' the Iraqi communications by massive destruction in the form of multiple B-52 blasts on telecommunications bunkers and land wires. However, the comprehensive organizational data collection that precedes any disruption operations will benefit a wide range of actions involving non-state organizations, even if they are not reasonable electronic targets. Effectively demonstrated, disruption itself could become a form of effective coercion as a threat, and a destructive blow would not necessarily have to follow. Although this policy option becomes a much more reasonable threat once states become more modernised and dependent on electronic communications, today's terrorists are global in their operations.[82] For example, it requires some cross national coordination, but their movements can be tracked intensively long before action is envisaged and they can be made aware of the surveillance as part of the process. Recent arrests and subsequent revelations show that capturing or intimidating lower level actors in non-state terrorist organizations can disrupt or permanently derail near and midterm planned operations. Whilst this sort of disruption operation may channel them to other alternative targets, a consistent policy of continuously similarly disrupting easier plans forces a resort to ultimately riskier plans and more vulnerability over the long run.[83]

Research into such new conceptual approaches is critical now. When the occasion to use a new form of operations emerged as a result of a non-state attack on the US in 2001, the underlying themes of lethality and state-centric deployments surfaced too soon despite decade-long developments in US thinking about knowledge-enabled conflicts. The stated search for a non-state but largely Arab network that attacked the territory of the US resulted in combat operations against a state deemed guilty by association, not by direct action. Other actions against, for example, non-state financial networks, were implemented long after the combat assaults.[84] If the US military's focus in 'modern' operations remains on the technical systems to physically destroy opponents, the longer-term outcome may be to simply delay a continuing set of future, equally lethal, conflicts. For example, the build-up to a war with Iraq after the terrorist events of 2001 was notable for the rapid turn of senior US leader interest in, and public support for, physical destruction of the Iraqi hierarchy. A newer concept of the disruptive potential of these systems would have first attempted a longer-term strategy involving the exceptionally aggressive employment of considerable technical resources to aid UN inspectors in a less lethal disruption of Iraq's banned weapons programs.

Furthermore physical coercion itself may only be useful as a small part of the major power's response to destabilizing actors. To construct such a disruption-oriented military and to conduct appropriately structured operations requires a different approach to risk–response calculations when an undesirable actor has initiated challenges to global civil society. If terrorism is societal churn, not opportunism, then coercion is clearly an inappropriate policy emphasis. The military forces of the world's remaining hegemon need more options.

The scope of this work does not allow more than a brief overview of two suggested paths for future research. The first is a new form for a knowledge-oriented military force, and the second, a new midrange theory aimed at explaining the mix of policy levers – including this new military – which are appropriate for responding to security challenges in the new complex international system.

The Atrium Model as an Alternative to the RMA Military

To meet these aims in today's national security environment, an alternate model to the RMA must be explicitly knowledge-based, compatible broadly with some existing structures and most contingencies, and accommodate a basic understanding of the surprises in operations. In this brief overview, I propose a variant of the 'hypertext' organization described by Nonaka and Takeuchi.[85] Labelled the 'Atrium' model of an information based organization, this refinement is a design that treats knowledge as the new element in the modern military organization, a partner rather than just the content of a pipeline or a database. Knowledge is developed through the whole process of sophisticated and rapid collection and massive accessible archiving of data, then data mining it into information and, finally, integrating and displaying knowledge for local decisions, long term thinking out of the box, or reorienting future paths. People with their individual explicit and implicit inventories of knowledge cycle assignments between task forces and central organizational operations, pausing to contribute to or draw upon the whole institution's inventory of that knowledge. The result is the computerized ingathering of the implicit knowledge of the organization and an incredible wealth of information about that firm's inner workings and responses to contingencies, constraints and opportunities.[86]

The model has three main organizational elements as shown in Figure 1. There is first the main core (or stem) of operations functionally divided as a military normally is today across functions such

FIGURE 1

THE ATRIUM MODEL OF A KNOWLEDGE-ORIENTED MILITARY

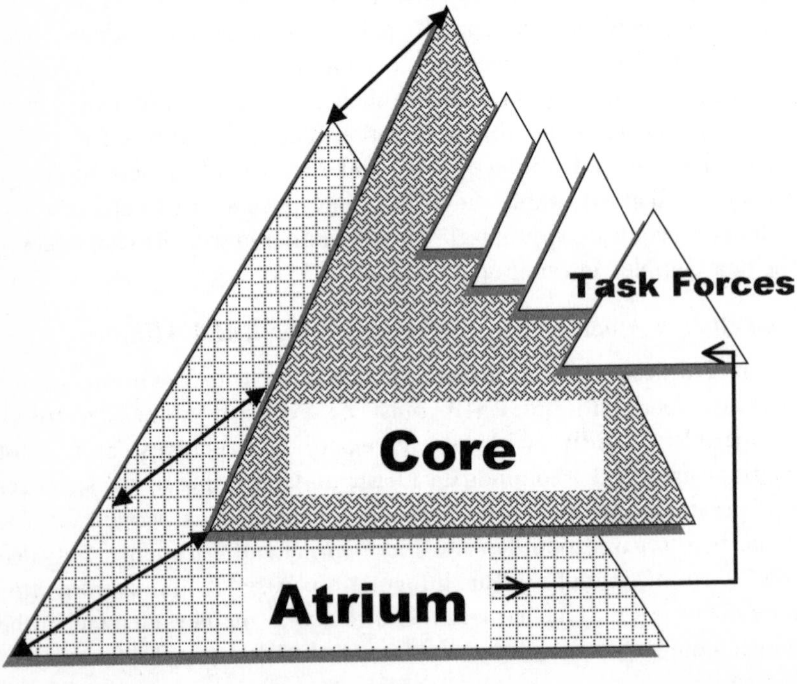

as finance, personnel, transportation, operations, logistics and recruitment elements that keep main systems functioning. Secondly, there is the Atrium – an underlying computerized database that is graphically accessible much like a 3D website. Military members interact with the Atrium in three ways: as consumers of knowledge from queries they inputted, as contributors providing explicit and implicit data to the underlying matrix, and as knowledge producers massaging the information into knowledge that is then available through various recall and query techniques to the consumers.

Finally, there are the task forces. These are specialized units that have existed for years in preparation for specialized missions that may or may not ever emerge. In the Atrium model, a small cadre of permanent support staff are left to provide continuity to the specialized task forces for as long as they or the mission are operative. But every mission or the task force is time limited, and the bulk of the members rotate in and out on six- to twelve-month assignments, developing specialized skills but staying connected with the needs and problems of the main stem of operations.

The Atrium model specifically recognizes the crucial role of the Atrium as a knowledge based partner, not merely a large computerized inventory. The periodic rotation of every member into the Atrium to be both a contributor of implicit knowledge and to learn or refresh his or her producer experiences keeps the Atrium a dynamic representation of what the overall organization is capable of learning. As a result of this churn, the structure and processes of the Atrium actively nurture the institutionally integrated knowledge base, reconciling the speed of a hierarchy with the innovation of a matrix. The result is to increase the accuracy of organizational responses to demands by the environment. This 'partnering' social construction of the knowledge base is integral to the success of processes and the survival of the institution. Hence my choice of the label, 'Atrium' serves to capture the sense of being a place to which a member of the organization can go, virtually or otherwise, to contribute and acquire essential knowledge, and that it is also a place of refuge to think out solutions. The Atrium is a player in the structure of the organization but one that supports, suggests and helps channel the actions of the others in the organization; it is not, however, a decision-maker. Over time, career soldiers will then be able to both use the Atrium but also to adapt its products to emerging needs. The goal is that the Atrium processes will not only gather implicit knowledge but that every organizational member, even part-time members or retired members on retainer, would be skilled enough to innovate in some way with or through this knowledge.[87]

Across nations allied with the US in its defence against terror, rudiments of such a database are being developed in response to the security surprises and shortcomings after the attack of 11 September 2001. Recently a senior US official said information gleaned worldwide that seemed relevant to the search for Al Qaeda terrorists is 'all going to go into a central place ... This is how we're going to proceed from now on'. US security agencies known for their struggle to share even basic data are attempting to support a joint computer centre to allow analysts, via web page technologies, to access across all organizational lines all information that is arriving. Presumably a military organization designed according to the Atrium model would be a major player in these other integrating events.[88] It is also possible, given the security focus of the knowledge sought and the military's access to a larger pool of skilled labour in its reserves, that an Atrium military would be the logical lead actor in maintaining and upgrading the Atrium for national leaders.

Much more work on this model is required. It is appropriate to note, however, what the advantages of such a knowledge-oriented military would have offered for the Afghanistan operation of 2001. Prior to the attack, more information from multiple sources on the breadth of the Al Qaeda network operations would have been crosslinked with data on other international groups including criminal, financial and ethnic nets to track movements and capabilities more closely. An Atrium mentality would have induced the kind of information sharing across agencies that proved so difficult in the months following the attack, as well as a greater capture of implicit knowledge by outgoing and incidental members of the defence community. This knowledge base expansion and innovative use would have continued throughout the operations.

A Midrange Theory of Latitude in Security Risk and Response Strategies – 'Mirror the Mix'

Knowledge-oriented operations require a systematic approach to the mix of incentives inducing the hostile actors to choose to act at a particular time in a violent way. A war of disruption requires a fairly accurate assessment of this mix of incentives to target practical short and long term policy responses. The knowledge developed by an Atrium military is particularly appropriate to this mission of correlating the incentives of hostile actors with appropriate policy levers.

A sensible explanation of planned violence must explain why it happens as well as why it does not. Actors can endure unpleasant conditions for some time while doing nothing organized or violent. To be able to act, violent opponents need three complementary elements that are present, to varying degrees, in a kind of societal churn equation. These elements are social constructions, cultural *predilections* that legitimize such actions, a perception of a *need* that is met by this action, and finally a *confidence* that the tools, plan, leader or opportunity are now available to ensure success. In this approach, all three elements – predilections, need, and confidence – must jointly supply sufficient catalysing influence on the actors to produce social violence. If one element, say predilections, does not contain a social construction legitimizing violent acts against a proposed target, it is more difficult to organize individuals into that violence. In that case, the influence of the other two elements must be commensurately much greater.

This work presumes that action is stimulated when, if you will, the circle is complete and the element of the equation that has been missing is provided. Perhaps it is a social construction that bombing civilians is legitimate because a senior cleric recently declared all of those kinds of civilians as combatants. Perhaps it is a demonstration of another clan's members appearing to be getting more resources than the actor perceived them to have had in the past or the actor now perceiving a longstanding distribution as unfair. Perhaps resentment has simmered for years but only with the arrival of a key leader or the demonstration of the power of riots by other groups does the actor perceive a way to obtain a more favourable outcome, a path that requires action by this actor. In all, however, there is usually a lag time between the elements coming together and the action, made longer by the complexity of the planned violence. The equation coming together can occur in a minute under riot circumstances where others demonstrate that looting can be successful (confidence). It takes considerably longer to set up something more complex like a successful bombing. Such things as suicide bombing, while easy to perform, take months to work on the predilections of individuals as well as their confidence.[89]

This work proposes a midrange theory of latitude in governance and security risk–response calculations that builds on explanations involving knowledge and perceptions as keys to action.[90] In the long run, this midrange theory outlines a way to integrate observations in international relations, organization, and psychological theories[91] under the lessons of surprise theory (knowledge burdens) and complexity theory (uncertainty). This approach begins with the presumptions of these latter theoretical approaches that, e.g., only broad trends are visible in advance and path dependence explains much of what actually emerges globally. Hence, disrupting plans for societal violence requires a coordinated view of intervening in the behaviours of opponents by channelling their social constructions, either in predilections, needs, or confidence in the long run whilst directly disturbing the trends in the shorter run.

This approach begins with knowledge, lots of it, that is then integrated into policy options. It is quite consistent with scholars of international relations who argue that a successful security policy requires understanding why any actor is willing to take risks to disturb the *status quo* and then identifying what can be done to change that actor's mix of incentives.[92] Similarly, work in political psychology and expectation theory strongly suggests that actors' perceptions of threat are particularly powerful in stimulating non-routine action. Actors will risk more in response to a threat to their illusion of control than they will for a benefit in general. In this regard, actors will desire to disturb the known *status quo* most when they can envision a more favourable outcome that mitigates or eliminates a threat to that set of environmental knowns.[93] This phenomenon is also known in the international security literature; historically populist leaders were better able to bring out the crowds if they posited a threat than if they offered a benefit.[94] Hunting for an attacker in order to consolidate local politics is a well hallowed political strategem. From the organizational theory literature, we know that organizations act in gross terms much like people once socialization of the organization's members is sufficiently advanced.[95] Understanding the relative weighting of incentives in a broad mix is the best a policy maker can do in responding to security threats if the policymaker is in a complex system.[96] The most likely strategy, then, is to act upon this knowledge of general trends in order to alter future paths of events.

The proposed theory of latitude in security strategies attempts to match policies aimed at changing social *constructions*, *capital* distributions, and *coercion* mechanisms with the general trends in predilections, needs and confidence of hostile actors. This basic one-to-one correspondence of incentive conditions and policy levers is presented in Figure 2. A war of disruption relies on knowledge to channel policies that may focus the intervention on, say, changing the *information* that sustains cultural predilections permitting violence. They could also intend to disrupt the directions of *capital* flows that sustain the perceptions of need in actors. Both can be disruptive but neither is necessarily lethal; nor do they necessarily involve military combat forces as lead players. One may also find the only effective way to derail planned violence is to use *coercion* to calm things down on the spot. But coercion itself may not require resort to lethality very often; in some cases, merely removing the tools of the violence physically reduces the confidence in their use. This is, after all, the point of strict gun laws in many European nations.

Unfortunately, disruption of the plan for or conduct of intended violence is not as simple as merely removing any one of these three elements. Recent work on networks shows that mere removal of a catalyzing leader may not close down the network.[97] Needs may be simmering in a cultural predilection permitting violence on and off for years before a leader or technology comes along to complete the equation. In that case, removing the newly arrived leader or technology merely removes the last contribution. It does not change the underlying conditions. Such a focus means one will have to keep removing new leaders or technologies as they pop up *ad infinitum*. In this case, coercion to remove the confidence only buys time rather than solving the underlying problem. For example, after invading in 1979, the Soviet Union hoped to win the Afghanistan war by 1980. The opposition was quiescent but simmering and could conceivably have remained so for many years. In the mid-1980s, however, the massive influx of foreign resources sent by the US and wealthy Gulf Arabs to buy military equipment enabled the impoverished mujahidin clans to mount the ultimately devastating war that ended with the Soviet withdrawal in 1989.[98]

With a knowledge-oriented approach and a well established Atrium military, the military community is less likely to recommend decision-

FIGURE 2

POLICY LEVERS IN A MIDRANGE THEORY OF LATITUDE AND CONTROL

	'Actors seek	latitude (control of key elements) to make	outcomes more favorable	if they think they can.'
Perceptions	Referent group associations	Perceptions of legitimate actions to control system components (PREDILECTIONS)	Perception of Conditions Necessary (NEED)	Perception of Actions Possible (CONFIDENCE)
Policy Levers	Presence in system	*Information* challenges PREDILECTIONS	*Capital* changes NEED	*Coercion* changes CONFIDENCE.

makers turn to physical coercion as a first choice. More likely would be a knowledge-oriented focus on closing the escapes from Afghanistan before physically emptying the caves, or even delaying blast-based operations some weeks until other operations such as freezing global financial assets were well underway. Coercion in Afghanistan removed from power the hosts of the Al Qaeda network, the governing coalition in the Taliban, but appears to have missed the central actors of the network itself such as Osama bin Laden. These escapes suggest the highly lethal American attacks delayed the targeted network's operations but did not succeed in destroying the network itself.[99]

The future of security in the emerging information and terrorism age involves disrupting continually emerging networks that promote violence. In complex mass global society, destroying a network requires understanding on what incentives it thrived. Osama bin Laden had been active for a number of years before he achieved any major terrorist successes. He was nearly ejected from Afghanistan by the Taliban in 1998 because of a local perception of his cultural arrogance. Without his and other Saudi funding streams, bin Laden would not even have had the attention of the alienated in the teeming poor populations of potential recruits. Hence, the two other elements of predilections and need perceptions are at play, perhaps more strongly than the emergence of bin Laden or the technology he can buy.

Due to the long-term view of global societal trends in this approach, the response to threatening undesirable societal churns such as terrorism is to mirror the mix and undermine the strongest catalyst rather than merely the most recent. The relative emphasis of policy levers of information, capital and coercion (in varying forms) must correctly match the relative weights of incentives motivating the initiating actor to change social constructions and co-opt the initiating actor into a more civil global society. It seems axiomatic that the poor and resentful are the seedbeds of dissent and yet security theories rarely are used to stimulate capital flow policies intended to directly change the need element of the equation.

In this application of sensitivity analysis, that one undermines the greatest contributors to the growth of the unwanted trend rather than continually focusing on a known tool such as coercion. If mirroring the mix does not occur and wars of disruption continue to emphasize lethal coercion, they may lead us to a more ancient kind of global environment, one littered with fortresses and badlands, and possibly a greatly reduced and threatened Western family of nations.[100]

Mirroring accurately involves continuously collecting relevant information and using knowledge to maintain critical levers available in policies – just the sort of ongoing cumulative analysis intrinsic to an Atrium military. With this approach and the resources of a knowledge-enabled military, senior policy-makers can accept that their longer term goal is to ensure that the nation 'mirrors the mix' continuously in a growing world. A more effective short and long-term policy response mix can be developed. For example, such a security approach to the Palestinian situation would start with the need element, using capital flows as a lever and followed closely by using information to challenge the predilections that are currently legitimizing suicide bombing in extant social constructions.[101] Only after these policies are in place, would physical disruption to coercively undermine the confidence the organization has in the new leader or tools be incorporated. This analysis could conceivably be applied to the Palestinian situation. Coercion might be the first choice, however, if the sudden arrival of a new leader ignites confidence in action although the attachment to better outcomes is weak and the cultural predilections do not fully support action. An example that fits this situation might be Milosevic's actions in Kosovo.

Finally, using information first to channel predilections might be a first choice for the following situation. A group of people always had a vision of better outcomes and knew how to make these a reality, even had the tools, but they did not act because they lacked the presumptions legitimizing violence. Slowly information from beyond this community undermines the cultural constraints against such action and destabilizing events emerge. The circumstances of most of Thailand's Muslims might fit this category. A policy response here is the most challenging since it involves using information to channel the social constructions that sustain cultural predilections.

Under this proposed midrange theory, lethal coercion is rarely acceptable as the default policy choice. As this approach underscores, the civil portions of the international system require more sublime responses than that proposed by Huntington in his famous 'Clash of Civilizations' argument: 'The principal responsibility of Western leaders, consequently, is not to attempt to reshape other civilizations in the image of the West, which is beyond their declining power, but to preserve, protect, and renew the unique qualities of Western civilization.'[102] It is not sufficient to attempt to simply physically suppress threats to Western civilization as a way to return to a relatively non-violent *status quo*.

Moving to strike too quickly, before integrating knowledge properly, can fail. For example, in terms of a growth of Muslim solidarity globally and new recruits for the Al Qaeda network, the US response to the jihadist challenge of 11 September 2001 focused too heavily and rapidly on coercion. For three weeks, Islamic officials worldwide were shocked and offered information and access we had never been able to achieve. But the US's RMA had not been developing its own understanding of the other two tools in the policy inventory to match the incentives mix – capital and information (to these Muslim populations). The US delayed in finding and freezing financial assets and, after the combat operations were unleashed, many of these information and aid portals in the wider Muslim world immediately closed. An Atrium military would have argued at least for a delay in the operations to permit other kinds of disruptions in financial networks to be in place. A 'mirror the mix' policy approach would not have forgotten to include any money to rebuild Afghanistan in the 2003 budget issued by the Bush administration a year later.

Further evidence in the relative neglect of the two other levers lies in the abysmal record of US policy makers in reaching the bulk of the moderate Muslim world.[103] Despite vocal senior-level interests in the third policy tool, using information to change social constructions, not until months after the ground deployment were efforts to provide credible information to moderate Arab states effectively a part of the war. This tool is so under-considered and poorly valued that an office devoted to this policy lever was clumsily and belatedly constructed and leaked by an insider offended at its existence.[104] The social construction of this policy tool itself needs considerable effort to legitimize it as a useful long-term deterrent tool events. Proper application of this approach would have encouraged much greater consideration of why jihadism is growing rapidly among the poorest Muslim populations or why Osama bin Laden found it fertile ground for his largely unionist organizing techniques.

In sum, this midrange theory integrates across several fields in response to a need to incorporate the new realities of security in a mass society surrounded by an even larger globalizing world. It suffices to note the comments of senior thinkers in international relations theory on the subject. In 1999, Kenneth Waltz noted that the 'main difference between international politics now and earlier is not found in the increased interdependence of states but in their growing inequality'.[105] Similarly, John Lewis Gaddis wrote 'A regime that must leave its people at the mercy of market forces is not likely to enhance its reputation in their eyes. And yet globalization requires placing national economies within an inherently unpredictable international marketplace ... A *laissez-faire* economic system is emerging at the global level a century after the invention of the welfare state limited *laissez-faire* economics at the national level. The social and political compromises that saved capitalism through an expansion of state authority early in the twentieth century no longer constrain it.'[106] Finally, the eminent military historian Martin van Creveld notes – but does not explain why some states are better than others at containing violence. 'From Japan to Taiwan, South Korea, and Singapore, some Asian states have been enormously successful in maintaining internal order and protecting the lives and property of their residents. Not so others such as Afghanistan, Burma, Cambodia, India, Iran, Iraq, the Philippines, Sri Lanka, Turkey, and, most recently, Pakistan; all of these are now confronted with a loss of control that ranges from riots and clashes between opposing gangs to full-scale civil war.'[107] Clearly there is a need to link violence, national security and demographics in ways that are policy-relevant and, in the modern world, offer choices other than coercion as a first choice for disrupting planned violence.

Actual deployment of combat forces should be a last option in a continuum of policy levers but, once undertaken, it can be pitted against organizations whose coordination elements have been studied and diagnosed as amenable to disruption by an Atrium military. This 'knowledge strategy' offers the best chance to manage the international system while its level of destructive violence is still amenable to being channelled.108 But such a strategy requires both a different model of a military and a more subtle understanding of the mix of incentives inducing violent behaviours among sub-state actors than those that emerged among senior Western defence leaders in the past decade. This work has presented a mid-range explanation that provides the basic elements on which future research will build towards a more general theory of security in the information and terrorist age.

NOTES

1. The situation was worse on the Soviet side. In 1983–1984, the aging leadership became convinced of an imminent US attack during the NATO annual exercise 'Able Archer'. Their mobilization actions puzzled and frightened US analysts. See Robert L. O'Connell, *Ride of the Second Horseman: Birth and Death of War* (New York: Oxford University Press, 1995), pp.224–5. For standard perspectives of the era, see Jonathan Alford, 'Perspectives on strategy', in John D. Steinbruner and Leon V. Sigal, *Alliance Security: NATO and the No-First-Use Question* (Washington D.C.: The Brookings Institution, 1983). See also Seymour Deitchman, *Military Power and the Advance of Technology: General Purpose Military Forces for the 1980s* (Boulder, CO: Westview Press, 1983).

2. Alford 'Perspectives on strategy'; Fred Ikle and Albert Wohlstetter, *Discriminate Deterrence Report of the Commission on Integrated Long-Term Strategy*, (Washington D.C.: US Government Printing Office, Jan. 1988).

3. Dieter Senghaas, *Europa 2000: Ein Friedensplan* (Frankfurt: Suhrkamp Verlag, 1990).

4. Colin S. Gray, *Weapons Don't Make War: Policy, Strategy and Military Technology* (Lawrence, KS: University Press of Kansas), p.85 and O'Connell, *Ride of the Second Horseman*, p.237.

5. For a contemporaneous and enthusiastic presentation of this view, see Barnaby, Frank and Marlies Ter Borg (eds) *Emerging Technologies and Military Doctrine* (New York: St, Martin's Press, 1986).

6. Gray (p.73) argues persuasively that this is a typical American approach to military technology. See also Thomas L. McNaugher, *New Weapons, Old Politics: America's Military Procurement Muddle* (Washington D.C.: The Brookings Institution, 1989) for an equivalent argument about the US weapon acquisition system.

7. 'The common theme in firepower case studies [of limited wars – First Indochina War, Second Indochina War, Afghanistan Intervention, Falklands War, Gulf War 1991] ... is the recurring inability of the side with the firepower advantage to find the enemy with sufficient timeliness/speed and accuracy to exploit that advantage fully and efficiently'. This quote is from Robert H.J. Scales *Firepower in a Limited War* (revised) (Novato, CA: Presidio Press, 1995), p.292.

8. For a discussion of the implications of these changes for the international system, see Barry R. Posen, 'Nationalism, the Mass Army and Military Power', *International Security*, Vol.18, No.2 (Fall 1993), pp.80–124.

9. This definition is from O'Connell, *Ride of the Second Horseman*, p.5.

10. See John Mueller, *Retreat from Doomsday: The Obsolescence of Major War* (New York: Basic Books, 1989). See Francis Fukuyama Fukuyama, *The End of History and the Last Man* (New York: Penguin, 1992).

11. Historically major powers have engaged in something like war about 10–20 per cent of the time. Britain was at war for 12 years in the past century – not including limited actions; since 1927, the former Soviet Union was at war for 22 years including Afghanistan; the US has averaged a major conflict every 25 years since its inception. Every decade since the Second World War has seen the major industrialized nations in an armed conflict of some kind – none of them a declared all-out war. See George Friedman and Meredith Friedman, *The Future of War: Power, Technology and American World Dominance in the Twenty-First Century* (New York: St. Martin's Griffin Press, 1996).

12. Military leaders were not alone in suggesting a less stable international environment. Mearsheimer is particularly noted for his ominous warning that the West would miss the organizing role played by the former Soviet Union. See John Mearsheimer 'Back to the Future: Instability in Europe after the Cold War', *International Security*,15 (Summer 1990), pp.5–56.

13. See O'Connell, *Ride of the Second Horseman*, p.233.

14. Michael Howard, George J. Andreopoulos and Mark R. Shulman (eds*) The Laws of War: Constraints on Warfare in the Western World* (New Haven: Yale University Press, 1994).

15. See Roger Allen, Leslie Lewis, Carl Dahlman and John Schank, *Assessing the Potential for Using Reserves in Operations Other Than War (MR-796-OSD)* (Santa Monica, CA: Rand Publications, 1997). See also JV2010, *Joint Vision 2010*, Joint Chiefs of Staff, Department of Defense, United States Government, US Government Printing Office, Washington DC, 1997.

16. There is a continuing debate on whether this is a revolution. See Earl H. Tilford, 'The Revolution in Military Affairs: Prospects and Cautions', *US Army War College Published Papers*

(Carlisle, PA: May 1995), p.1; Andrew R. Krepinevich, 'Cavalry to Computer: The Pattern of Military Revolutions', *The National Interest*, 37 (Fall 1994), pp.30–42; Robert L. Pfaltzgraff, Jr and Richard H. Shultz, Jr, eds, *War in the Information Age: New Challenges for US Security Policy* (Washington, DC: Brasseys, 1997). Others argue this is merely the next step in incremental technological changes. See Stephen Biddle, 'Assessing Theories of Future War' Paper presented at American Political Science Association annual conference. Washington DC: September 1997.

17. This is not necessarily new. Senior leaders of the US defence establishment have long had difficulty understanding the organizational implications of the new technologies they acquire. See Chris C. Demchak, *Military Organizations, Complex Machines: Modernization in the U.S. Armed Services* (Ithaca, NY: Cornell University Press, 1991); idem., 'Complexity, Rogue Outcomes and Weapon Systems' *Public Administration Review* Vol.52, No.3 (May–June 1992), pp.347–55; Russell F. Weigley, *The American Way of War: A History of United States Military Strategy and Policy* (New York: Macmillan Publishing Company, 1973)..

18. See Michael J. Mazarr, Don M. Snider and James A. Blackwell, *Desert Storm: The Gulf War and What We Learned* (San Francisco, CA: West View Press, 1993). See also Gene I. Rochlin and Chris C. Demchak, 'The Gulf War: Technological and Organizational Implications', *Survival* Journal of the International Institute of Strategic Studies, Vol.33 No.3 (1991), pp.260–73. See also Bruce W. Watson and Peter G. Tsouras (eds) *Military Lessons of the Gulf War* (Novato, CA: Presidio Press, 1993).

19. See James Adams, *The Next World War: Computers are the Weapons and the Front Line is Everywhere* (New York: Simon and Schuster, 1998), p.296 for a good discussion of the dominance of the idea that information warfare can produce a 'sanitary war' where no friendlies and few innocent enemies die. See also Michael Howard, George J. Andreopoulos and Mark R. Shulman (eds), *The Laws of War: Constraints on Warfare in the Western World* (New Haven: Yale University Press, 1994). For a discussion of this process in Israel, see Stuart Cohen, 'The Israel Defense Forces: from a "Peoples Army" to a "Professional military" – Causes and Implications', *Armed Forces and Society*, Vol.21, No.2 (Winter 1995), pp.237–54.

20. For the development of this term as a shorthand to describe the attributes of this new military, see Chris C. Demchak, 'Tailored Precision Armies in Fully Networked Battlespace: High Reliability Organizational Dilemmas in the "Information Age"', *Journal of Contingency and Crisis Management*, Vol.4 No.2 (June 1996).

21. QDRs are first mandated by the reform legislation of 1986, the Goldwater-Nichols Act.

22. See Les Aspin, Secretary of Defense Statement: 'The Bottom-Up Review: Forces for a New Era' US Department of Defense. Washington DC: US Government Printing Office (1 Sept. 1993), pp.10–13.

23. James Joyner, 'Back to the Future: The Rumsfeld Defense Strategy Review in Historical Perspective', paper presented at the annual International Security Studies Section conference of the International Studies Association, Whittier, California, October 2001.

24. See the following service documents. For the Army, see TRADOC, 1994, 'Force XXI Operations: A Concept for the Evolution of Full-Dimensional Operations for the Strategic Army of the Early Twenty-First Century', Pam 525–5, Washington, DC: US Army Training and Doctrine Command (TRADOC), Department of the Army. Washington DC: US Government Printing Office. For the Army After Next, see also USAv2010, 1996, 'Army Vision 2010', Department of the Army, Washington DC: United States Government Printing Office. For the Air Force see USAFGE, 1996, 'Global Engagement', Department of the Air Force, Washington DC: United States Government Printing Office. For the Navy and its emphasis on sea-based network-centric warfare see USNFFS, 1994, 'Forward From the Sea', Department of the Navy, Washington DC: United States Government Printing Office.

25. Command, Control, Communications, Computers, Intelligence, Surveillance and Reconnaissance

26. See Joyner.

27. See QDR1997, 1997, 'Report of the Quadrennial Defense Review (QDR) to William Cohen Secretary of Defense', US Government Department of Defense, Washington DC: US Government Printing Office (May), pp.7–6.

28. See QDR2001, 2001, 'Report of the Quadrennial Defense Review to Donald Rumsfeld Secretary of Defense', US Government Department of Defense, Washington DC: US

Government Printing Office (30 Sept.), pp.iii.

29. Formally, what was planned was a 'system of systems' linking four large networks for complete battlefield overview by the commander. The first is a sensor grid providing long range (up 300 km) real-time and detailed information streams. The second is an engagement grid with graphical real-time depiction of all elements of the battle (and refined trend analyses on the spot, presumably). The third is an enormous database grid providing query, drill down, summary and push information [AU?] in all directions of the command structure. The fourth is an offensive information operations network that enables the overt or covert destruction, disruption, diversion, intrusion, insertion and inspection of the targeted organization's use of information technologies. For elaboration of these concepts, see *Joint Vision 2010*. See also David C. Gompert, Richard L. Kugler and Martin C. Libicki, *Mind the Gap: Promoting a Transatlantic Revolution in Military Affairs* (Washington DC: National Defense University Press, 1999), p.34. See also Patrick D. Allen and Chris C. Demchak, 'An IO Conceptual Model and Application Framework', *Military Operations Research Journal*, Special Issue on Information Operations/Information Warfare, 2000.

30. See Frances Cairncross, *The Death of Distance: How the Communications Revolution Will Change Our Lives* (Cambridge, MA: Harvard Business School Press, 1996).

31. The only noteworthy changes were the accelerated introduction of the Interim Brigade Combat Team (IBCT) structure to the Army and the injunctions to the Air Force and Navy to increase the forces appropriate for Western Pacific and Indian Ocean contingencies. See Joyner.

32. See QDR2001.

33. Ibid.

34. For a detailed discussion of how this sort of leadership vacuum produces traditional outcomes, see Thomas L. McNaugher, *New Weapons, Old Politics: America's Military Procurement Muddle* (Washington DC: The Brookings Institution 1989).

35. See Paul E. Blackwell, 'Winning the Wars of the 21st Century' in *AUSA, Association of the United States Army* (AUSA Press, Washington DC, 1994), pp.121–34, 123. See Leon E. Salomon, 'At AMC, the future begins today', in Association of the United States Army Greenbook (Washington DC: AUSA Press, 1994), pp.69–76.

36. See TRADOC Pam 525–5, 3–1.

37. See Blackwell 'Winning the Wars of the 21st Century', p.132.

38. See Wiebe E. Bijker, Thomas P. Hughes and Trevor J. Pinch (eds), *The Social Construction of Technological Systems: New Directions in the Sociology and History of Technology* (Cambridge, MA: The MIT Press, 1987)

39. For seminal discussions of the concepts of complexity, see the following: Todd R. LaPorte (ed.), *Organized Social Complexity* (Princeton, NJ: Princeton University Press, 1975); Charles Perrow, *Normal Accidents: Living with High Risk Technologies* (New York: Basic Books, 1984); for applications to military systems, see Paul Bracken, *The Command and Control of Nuclear Forces* (New Haven: Yale University Press 1983); Chris C. Demchak, *Military Organizations, Complex Machines: Modernization in the U.S. Armed Services* (Ithaca, NY: Cornell University Press, 1991); Scott D. Sagan, *Moving Targets: Nuclear Strategy and National Security* (Princeton, NJ: Princeton University Press, 1989).

40. These are, for example, air traffic control organizations, US Navy nuclear carrier air operations, and nuclear power generating plants. See Todd R. LaPorte and Paula Consolini, 'Working in Practice but Not in Theory: Theoretical Challenges of "High Reliability" Organizations', *Journal of Public Administration Research and Theory*, 1 (Jan. 1991), pp.19–48.

41. Locus of control and the effects of machine requirements for formal rationality are central concerns of this field as well. For an introduction to the field and to further references see Sheila Jasanoff, Gerald E. Markle, James C. Peterson and Trevor Pinch *Handbook of Science and Technology Studies* (Thousand Oaks, CA: Sage Publications, 1995). See also Carl Mitcham, *Thinking Through Technology: The Path Between Engineering and Philosophy* (Chicago, IL: University of Chicago Press 1994); Jane Summerton (ed.), *Changing Large Technical Systems* (Boulder, Colorado: Westview Press, 1994). For a discussion of technology in organizations, explicitly, see Urs Gattiker, *Technology Management in Organizations* (Newbury Park, CA: Sage Publications, 1990).

42. One form of accommodation is extensive preparatory testing that reveals the form and frequency of previously unknown outcomes. Unfortunately this testing is normally

extraordinarily expensive and, as a result, rarely done. For a more extensive discussion with application to the US Army and for better discussion of organizations and various aspects of responses to technology, especially knowledge and information processing, as well as the validity of this method, see Demchak, *Military Organizations*.

43. For a discussion of how, in a complex system, the proportion of these unknowable outcomes will be high compared to a more simple system, see Joseph G. Wohl, *Diagnostic Behavior, Systems Complexity, and Repair Time: A Predictive Theory*, MITRE Note No M80-0008 (Bedford, MA: MITRE Corporation, 1980). For a discussion of how component reliability contributes to the system's overall ability to avoid errors, see Larry Heiman, 'Understanding the Challenger Disaster: Organizational Structure and the Design of Reliable Systems', *American Political Science Review*, Vol.87 No.2 (June 1993), pp.421–35.

44. For a discussion of this kind of outcome in the nuclear power industries of Europe, see Gene I. Rochlin, 'Broken Plowshare: System Failure and the Nuclear Power Industry', in J. Summerton (ed.), *Changing Large Technical Systems* (Boulder, CO: Westview Press, 1994), pp.231–61.

45. For discussions of military history and knowledge shortfalls, see Kenneth Macksey, *For Want of a Nail: The Impact on War of Logistics and Communications* (London: Brassey's, 1989). See also Martin Van Creveld, *Technology in War* (New York: The Free Press, 1989).

46. For the seminal work on this topic, see Jay R. Galbraith, *Organizational Design*, (Reading, MA: Addison-Wesley, 1977).

47. Knowledge is such an important distinction of information technology systems that senior leaders will need an explicit 'knowledge strategy' to enable the organization to succeed. See Alvin Toeffler and Heidi Toeffler, *War and Anti-War* (Boston, MA: Little, Brown and Company, 1993).

48. See: Galbraith, *Organizational Design*; James D. Thompson, *Organizations in Action* (New York: McGraw-Hill: 1967); both are seminal works on this issue.

49. An important development in social constructions of this technology is that it has become seen as way of conducting war while minimizing physical risks to soldiers. See Mazarr *et al.*, *Desert Storm*, p.166. It is open to question what happens to the positive social constructions of these military technologies if they do not actually save lives.

50. Curiously enough, after many 'experiments' with new organizations, the US Army has retained the functional heavy structure that has been standard for decades. See TRADOC, 'New Army division smaller but with more infantry, punch', News Release No.96-06-01 (Fort Monroe, VA: US Army Training and Doctrine Command. 1996).

51. See Rochlin and Demchak, 'The Gulf War'.

52. See David Freedman, 'Killed At Their Keyboards', *Business 2.0 Magazine*, Feb. 2002.

53. See Demchak, *Military Organizations*, LaPorte, *Organized Social Complexity*, Gareth Morgan, *Images of Organization* (Beverly Hills, CA: Sage Publications, 1996); Michael Harrison, *Organizations: Methods, Models and Processes* (Beverly Hills, CA: Sage Publications, 1997); Gareth Jones, *Organizational Theory* (Reading, MA: Addison-Wesley Publishing, 1995), for discussions of these rules of thumb in organizational literatures.

54. A transient error is an error that only occurs during actual operation, often intermittently. If the machine is turned off, nothing appears to be wrong with the system. For a discussion of transient errors in the Challenger I tank, see Chris C. Demchak, 'Colonies or Computers: Modernization and Organizational Challenges to the Future British Army', *Defence Analysis*, Vol.10, No.1 (April 1994).

55. See ABCNEWS online, 'Report: Bin Laden Dodged U.S.: Bodyguard Used Phone to Distract Intelligence Agencies at Tora Bora' (21 Jan. 2003).

56. See Vernon Loeb, '"Friendly Fire" Deaths Traced to Dead Battery', *Washington Post*, 24 March 2002, p.A21.

57. This test of effectiveness is called the sensor-to-shooter (STS) cycle and is the time duration beginning when a target is seen by a sensor to the moment a 'shooter' has it in his or her sights and shoots a lethal projectile. See Phillip S. Meilinger, 'Preparing For The Next Little War', *Armed Forces Journal International* (April 2003). Downloaded.

58. See Demchak, *Military Organizations* and 'Modernizing Militaries and Political Control in Central Europe' for a discussion of how difficult it is for senior managers to resist seeking increased control if they believe they have the technical means to do so. For similar discussions pertaining to civilian organizations, see Shoshana Zuboff, *In the Age of the Smart Machine* (New York: Basic Books, 1984). See also Johannes M. Pennings and Peter Buitendam

(eds) *New Technology as Organizational Innovation: The Development and Diffusion of Microelectronics* (Cambridge, Mass.: Ballinger, 1987).
59. For one of the seminal works on the notions of environmental stability and predictability in organizations, see Thompson, *Organizations in Action*.
60. See Phillip S. Meilinger, 'Preparing For The Next Little War', *Armed Forces Journal International* (April 2002). Downloaded.
61. See LaPorte, *Organized Social Complexity*. See also Dan S. Felsenthal, 'Applying the Redundancy Concept to Administrative Organizations', *Public Administration Review*, 40 (May–June, 1980), pp.247–52.
62. See David Windle and Damian Carrington 'Silent Sensors Wait for bin Laden', *New Scientist* (21 Nov. 2001). Downloaded.
63. See Linda D. Kozaryn *Stopping Escaping Al Qaeda, Taliban Like 'Catching Fleas'*, American Forces Press Service (17 Dec. 2001). Downloaded.
64. See Jim Garamone, *Gunning for Al Qaeda, Taliban Leaders*, American Forces Press Service (10 Dec. 2001). Downloaded.
65. In a dated but still interesting work, Marshall argues that armies associate the size of opposing units with a certain rate of fire. According to Marshall's Second World War research, normally only 25 per cent of soldiers actually fire their weapons. Hence if 100 per cent of a band of committed fighters fire, a standard military analysis would assume the opposing unit is four times its actual size. See S.L.A. Marshall, *Men Against Fire: The Problem of Battle Command in Future War* (Gloucester, MA: Peter Smith, 1978 (1947)).
66. See CNN, 'U.S. Commander: Enemy Forces "taking a beating"', CNN.com. (6 March 2001).
67. See Dennis J. Reimer, Address of the Army Chief of Staff at the Acquisition Reform Conference, Atlanta (23 April 1996).
68. See Perrow, *Normal Accidents: Living with High Risk Technologies*, and Thompson, *Organizations in Action*. See also Arthur L. Stinchcome, *Information and Organizations* (Berkeley, CA: University of California Press, 1990).
69. See, William G. Pagonis, *Moving Mountains: Lessons in Leadership* (Boston, MA: Harvard Business School Press, 1992), p.210.
70. See NRC, *Star 21: Strategic Technologies for the Army of the Twenty-First Century* (Washington D.C.: National Academic Press, 1992), pp.31,76.
71. See Gordon Sullivan, 'America's Army – Focusing on the Future', in Association of the United States Army, *Army Greenbook* (Washington DC: AUSA Press, 1994), pp.19–29. See also AMDP, *Army Digitization Master Plan*, US Government Department of the Army, HQDA, Army Digitization Office (30 Jan. 1995).
72. See OFT. 'Defense Trends Newsletter Online', Office of Transformation, Department of Defense, US Government (30 Sept. 2002.).
73. See William Seymour, *Decisive Factors in Twenty Great Battles of the World* (London: Sidgwick & Jackson, 1988).
74. See Demchak, *Military Organizations*; Perrow, *Normal Accidents: Living with High Risk Technologies*; LaPorte, *Organized Social Complexity*; and Rochlin, 'Broken Plowshare'.
75. Statements made by Brigadier General Joseph Kellogg, Assistant Deputy Chief of Staff for Combat Developments, TRADOC. See TRADOC, 'New Army division smaller but with more infantry, punch', News Release No.96-06-01 (Fort Monroe, VA: US Army Training and Doctrine Command, 1996).
76. Statements made by Col. Stephen Garrett, Chief of Staff of US Army Combined Arms Support Command. See TRADOC, 'New Army division smaller but with more infantry, punch'.
77. See Sullivan, p.23.
78. Elsewhere I argue that the worldwide military community is increasingly structurated such that what the US does with its military forces increasingly becomes the standard for other members of the worldwide military community, whether or not the changes desired appear rational for these nations. See Chris C. Demchak, 'Creating the Enemy: Worldwide Diffusion of an Electronic Military', in Emily O. Goldman and Leslie C. Eliason (eds), *The Diffusion of Military Technology and Ideas* (Stanford, CA: Stanford University Press, 2003). For a discussion of this process in Central Europe in particular, see Chris C. Demchak, 'Modernizing Militaries and Political Control in Central Europe', *Journal of Public Policy*, Vol.15, No.2 (1995), pp.111–52.

79. For a modern discussion of the causes of war, see Byman, Daniel and Stephen Van Evera, 'Why They Fight: Hypotheses on the Causes of Contemporary Deadly Conflict', *Security Studies Journal*, Vol.7, No.3 (spring 1998).

80. This piece was written long before two authors published a piece using the term 'disruption' as a strategy only for terrorists. It is interesting to see the development of concepts in parallel but with very different applications. See Stephen Gale and Lawrence Husick, 'From MAD (Mutual Assured Destruction) to MUD (Multilateral Unconstrained Disruption): Dealing with the New Terrorism', *Foreign Policy Research Institute Wire*, Vol.11, No.1 (Feb. 2003) online.

81. See Dan Reiter, 'Exploding the Powder Keg Myth: Preemptive Wars Almost Never Happen', *International Security*, Vol.20, No.2 (Fall, 1995), pp.3–34.

82. Against a backdrop of possible widespread or rolling disruptions in targeted infrastructures is clearly depicted, advanced nations are actually easier to subdue because people have to eat, and urban living does not allow for much self-sufficiency. This analysis explains the lack of actual resistance in the highly urbanized Western European lands occupied by the Nazis in the Second World War. See Peter Liberman, 'The Spoils of Conquest', *International Security*, Vol.18, No.2 (Fall, 1993), pp.125–53.

83. See Rohan Gunaratna, 'Al-Qaeda's Operational Ties with Allied Groups', *Jane's Intelligence Review* (1 Feb. 2003) online service.

84. Two months after the initial attack and a solid month after initial combat operations, suspected al-Qaeda assets were frozen. See AP News. 'U.S. Freezes Terror Network Assets', *Associated Press Online* (7 Nov. 2001).

85. In their original work on successful corporations innovating in this direction, Nonaka and Takeuchi describe the knowledge base (KB) as a third and equal partner in the organization. The other two are a central business operation that functions much like the previous firm, and a set of task forces answering to the CEO for innovative and problem-solving missions. Nonaka and Tageuchi have identified several Japanese corporations that seem to operate along these lines productively and view implicit knowledge developed by human interactions related to the job as not only viewed as a source of value by the corporation but also as key to long term survival and preparedness for surprise. See Ikujiro Nonaka and Hirotaka Takeuchi 'A New Organizational Structure' (HyperText Organization), in Laurence Prusak (ed.) *Knowledge in Organizations* (Boston: Butterworth-Heinemann, 1997), pp.99–133.

86. To carry this further, wisdom might be said to be the decisions based on this knowledge. In any event, I am grateful for Dennis A. Lowrey, a former senior MI officer and chief 'wirehead' who played a role in the sophistication advances of the US Army's military intelligence community in the 1990s.

87. In a manuscript presently under construction, 'The Atrium – Refining the HyperText Organizational Form', I more fully explain the mechanisms of integrating an Atrium into an organization. Meanwhile, for the application of this model to varying circumstances see Chris C. Demchak, 'Knowledge Burden Management and a Networked Israeli Defense Force: Partial RMA in "Hyper Text Organization"?', *Journal of Strategic Studies*, Vol.24, No.2 (June, 2001). See also Chris C. Demchak, 'Modernizing Defence in Small Nations: Israel, Taiwan and the "Atrium" Model of a Future Military', *Taiwan Defense Affairs*, (summer 2001), pp.6–33. See also Chris C. Demchak and Patrick D. Allen, 'Technology and Complexity: The Modern Military's Capacity for Change', US Army War College Annual Strategy Conference (April 17–20), *Proceedings of Annual Strategy Conference: Transforming Defense in an Era of Peace and Prosperity* (Carlisle, Pennsylvania, 2001).

88. A knowledge base as a partner requires more than the database itself; it requires the social construction and the organization required. For example, the Department of Defense's 'Total Information Awareness' program pursued after the 2001 World Trade Center Towers attack was closer to a static library of data, not the organizational knowledge base partner proposed here. See Dan Caterinicchia 'All eyes on Total Info Awareness', *Federal Computer Week* (16 Dec. 2002) online.

89. For an interesting case of how long this takes, see Peter Hermann, 'Recruited To Die: An Arab's Story,' *Baltimore Sun*, (20 Feb., 2003) online.

90. See Robert Jervis, *Perception and Misperception in International Politics*, (Princeton, NJ: Princeton University Press, 1976).

91. The theoretical approach is under development as part of a longer project.

92. See Kenneth N. Waltz, *Theory of International Politics*, (Reading, MA: Addison-Wesley,

1979). See also Hans J. Morgenthau, *Politics Among Nations: The Struggle for Power and Peace* (Fifth Edition, Revised) (New York: Alfred A. Knopf, 1978), pp.4–15.

93. This differs across cultures. Several authors investigated expectancy values in terms of an illusion of control or trust comparing the US and Japanese cultures. There were experimental differences but the resulting action was much the same: loss of either stimulated action. See Lin Ostrom Nahoko, James Walker and Toshio Yamagishi, 'Reciprocity, Trust, and the Illusion of Control: A Cross-Societal Study', *Rationality & Society*, Vol.11 No.1 (1999), pp.27–46. In situations where the individual can develop more social intelligence about another person or group, cooperative behaviour increases. See, Toshio Yamagishi, Masako Kikuchi and Motoko Kosugi. 'Trust, Gullibility and Social Intelligence', *Asian Journal of Social Psychology*, Vol.2 No.1 (1999), pp.145–61. A lack of knowledge 'in the absence of communication opportunities, individuals and groups decreased their cooperation'. In short, more communications dampens disruptive behaviours. See, Hein Lodewijkx, 'Individual Group Continuity in Cooperation and Competition Under Varying Communication Conditions', *Current Research in Social Psychology* (23 May, 2001), pp.166–81.

94. These statements reflect the work on prospect theory and, especially, framing. This research suggests individuals will value the probable over the possible, if either gains or losses, but they evaluate outcomes as gains or losses depending on how those outcomes are presented to them. Hence, of great importance in wars of disruption is to know when, where, and how to frame information in order to disrupt planned violence. See A. Tversky and D. Kahneman, 'The framing of decisions and the psychology of choice', *Science*, 211 (1981), pp.453–8.

95. See Thompson, *Organizations in Action*.

96. For an application of complexity theory to international relations, see Robert Jervis, *System Effects: Complexity in Political and Social Life* (Princeton: Princeton University Press 1997). See also David S. Alberts and Thomas J. Czerwinski (eds) *Complexity, Global Politics, and National Security* (Washington, D.C.: National Defense University, 1997).

97. See Vaiclia Krebs, 'Mapping Networks of Terrorist Cells', *Connections*, Vol.24, No.3 (2002), pp.43–52. See also Richard Rothenberg, 'From Whole Cloth – Making up the terrorist network', *Connections*, Vol.24, No.3 (2002), pp.36–42.

98. See Anthony H. Cordesman and A. R. Wagner, *Lessons of Modern War*, Vol.III (Boulder, Colorado: Westview Press, 1989). *See Chronological History of Afghanistan – Part IV* (1978–Present), Afghanistan Online (originally known as the Qazi Webpage on Afghanistan found at <http://www.afghan-web.com/history/chron/index4.html>).

99. See BBC 'Profile: Abu Zubaydah', BBC News Online (2 April 2002).

100. 'Western intervention in the affairs of other civilizations is probably the single most dangerous source of instability and potential global conflict in a multicivilizational world.' See Samuel P. Huntington, *The Clash of Civilizations: Remaking of the World Order* (New York: Simon and Schuster, 1996).

101. This is the most serious threat to Western societies whose entire legal systems are based on the presumption that the perpetrator wants to live. Weaken that presumption and add millions of possible perpetrators, and the legal systems will perforce become more pre-emptive, rolling up innocents as well as plotters. Under this approach, channeling the surrounding system to minimize the potential number of recruits is far better than the legal tightening alternative. Only the most brutal of empires has survived in the face of overwhelming social numbers in dissent and, historically, not for long. There is here a strong cautionary note for American defence planners in particular.

102. See Huntington, *The Clash of Civilizations*.

103. See Thomas L. Friedman, 'U.S. hasn't won hearts and minds of Arab–Muslim world', *New York Times*, 25 Jan. 2002.

104. See Eric Schmitt, 'Rumsfeld Formally Disbands Office of Strategic Influence', *New York Times*, 26 Feb. 2002.

105. See Kenneth N. Waltz, 'Globalization and Governance', PS Online (Dec. 1999).

106. See John Lewis Gaddis, 'Living in Candlestick Park', *Atlantic Monthly Online*, April 1999.

107. See Martin Van Creveld, *The Rise and Decline of the State* (Cambridge: Cambridge University Press, 1999).

108. See Toeffler and Toeffler, *War and Anti-War*, p.139.

The Strategy and Tactics of
Information Warfare

MATT BISHOP and EMILY O. GOLDMAN

Over the last decade, information technology has been championed by
policymakers, activists, international bureaucrats, business leaders and
intellectuals as a catalyst for social transformation – generating
economic growth and development, peace and global cosmopolitanism,
personal freedom and individual empowerment. Like the industrial
revolution before it, the information technology revolution appears to be
creating a new ruling class, a new economy and a new society. It should
come as no surprise that strategic thinkers and security experts have
become enamoured with the ways that information technology can
transform military operations and warfare. Information technology,
military leaders and intellectuals argue, can supplant the Clausewitzian
industrial-era model of destructive war with an information-era model
promising greater efficiency and flexibility, and fewer risks of casualties
through the use of more highly skilled troops and 'smart' technologies.
Just as the nuclear age elevated the logic of deterrence over destruction,
in the information age, the logic of disruption has the potential to rival
the logic of destruction. For these reasons, the information age in
warfare represents a significant disjuncture with the past.

Information technology, however, has always been central to warfare
and crucial for enhancing military effectiveness. The establishment of a
telegraph network considerably influenced the conduct of military
operations and enhanced the effectiveness of military forces during the
American Civil War and Wars of German Unification.[1] The
introduction of wireless around the turn of the twentieth century
represented an important aspect of the naval revolution that many
associated with the development of the all-big gun battleships powered
by turbine engines, and the development of extended-range submarines
and torpedoes. The wireless was also a means of providing greatly
enhanced strategic warning. During the interwar period, the rapid

growth in the application of radio and, later, the advent of radar, had an enormous influence on military operations. The German Army's development of *Blitzkrieg* depended as much on the ability of radio to coordinate large, fast-moving, highly dispersed forces as it did on mechanization and aviation.[2] Great Britain's integrated air defence network was also heavily reliant upon – indeed, held together by – a radio and radar infrastructure.[3] The continuity between these historical examples and the present are evident in efforts by the US military to employ emerging information systems, like space-based GPS, to inform terrestrial manoeuvre and precision targeting.

Information as 'content', as distinct from information as 'conduit', has also always been a critical dimension of strategy in combat and competition, whether due to its absence or presence.[4] It was Carl von Clausewitz's scepticism about the reliability of information and intelligence at the tactical and operational levels that led him to emphasize, in *On War*, the need to maximize and concentrate one's troops, maintain reserves, and ensure that leaders possessed intuition and experience. For Sun Tzu, on the other hand in *Art of War*, deception, disinformation and knowledge of the enemy's innermost thoughts and plans are the keys to surprise and victory, perhaps even a bloodless victory.

What makes the information age unique is the fact that information *as* warfare has become as important as information *in* warfare. Information is not just a means to boost the effectiveness of lethal technologies as has occurred often in the past, but opens up the possibility of non-lethal attacks that can incapacitate, defeat, deter or coerce an adversary. By expanding the tools and techniques of information attack, the information age has enlarged the domains of IW and its purveyors. Warfare now occurs on the battlefield, in the marketplace, and against the infrastructure of modern society. Attackers include individuals and private groups in addition to professional militaries, making warfare an activity no longer the exclusive province of the state.

Yet even though the repertoire of tools, domains and purveyors of war have changed in important ways, the logic of warfare remains the same. Warfare involves sequencing and coordinating attacks to achieve lower order technical or 'cyber' goals, that are part of a broader campaign to achieve higher order political, material and/or symbolic goals. Understanding how different types of technical goals can contribute to the achievement of higher order strategic goals requires bridging the worlds of the strategist and computer scientist. Only then can the techniques of information attack be effectively used in the service of strategy, and can strategic concepts like deterrence, escalation, retaliation and linkage, adapt to embrace the new contingencies presented by information warfare.

This essay examines the strategy and tactics of information warfare by showing how the tools of cyberwar present novel ways of achieving traditional political, material and symbolic objectives. We discuss how information capabilities have altered the current conflict environment: the nature of vulnerabilities and threats. We provide an overview of how to think about information warfare and discuss the underlying logic and technical prerequisites of various types of information attacks. We conclude by discussing some of the most important continuities and discontinuities between the past and present regarding the strategy and tactics of information warfare.

THE CONFLICT ENVIRONMENT

With the recent explosion of information technologies, the growing reliance of advanced societies on them, and the burgeoning of capabilities to manipulate information and disrupt its flow, the role of information warfare has become central to nearly every discussion of adversarial relations, military and commercial. Conventional wisdom says that we have entered an age where information is not only an adjunct to conventional military and business operations, but has become a key arena of conflict and competition.

In important ways, information warfare continues trends that were already underway in the evolution of combat. Like strategic bombing and counter-value nuclear targeting, efforts to deter or defeat an adversary by bypassing destruction of his armed forces and directly attacking his society predate the information technology age. Techniques of information warfare simply provide attackers with a broader array of tools and an ability to target more precisely and by non-lethal means the lifelines upon which advanced societies rely: power grids, phone systems, transportation networks, and aeroplane guidance systems. IT can also make conventional combat more accurate, thereby improving the efficiency of high explosive attacks. Here again, IT continues trends in warfare that have improved the lethality of military force over time.

In other ways, information technology has altered the environment of conflict. It has changed the way we think about vulnerability. Control of information and knowledge is a central engine driving human activity, evident in the incredible growth of computing power, the increasing reliance on information technology for business transactions (credit cards, electronic banking), the rise of consumer electronics, and most of all, the increasing reliance on the internet. The distribution of a computer virus that can be activated on command, the electronic theft of funds from a credit card company, the spread of disinformation via the internet or the media, or tampering with e-mail present contemporary society with new points of vulnerability.

Paradoxically, IT has made the most advanced and powerful societies, by traditional indices, the most vulnerable to these types of attack. A distinguishing hallmark of the information age is the 'network', which exploits the accessibility and availability of information, and computational and communicative speed, to organize and disseminate knowledge cheaply and efficiently.[5] The strength of the network lies in the degree of connectivity. Connectivity can increase prosperity and military effectiveness, but it also creates vulnerabilities. Information-intensive military organizations are more vulnerable to information warfare simply because they are more information-dependent, while an adversary need not be information-dependent to disrupt the information lifeline of high-tech forces. Information-dependent societies are also more vulnerable to the infiltration of computer networks, databases and the media, and to attacks on the very linkages upon which modern societies rely to function: communication, financial transaction, transportation and energy resource networks. From a competitive perspective, it would be foolish for a well-financed and motivated group not to attack the technical infrastructure of an adversary.

IT has also changed the way we think about threats. The information revolution has empowered traditionally weaker actors by diffusing and redistributing power. Information warfare is not confined to interstate interactions. Individuals and non-state actors, be they corporations, interest groups, criminal organizations, or terrorist groups, can acquire the means to wage some level of information warfare. The US GAO estimates that 120 groups or countries have or are developing offensive information warfare capabilities. It is not necessary to be a high-tech networked society to have access to information warfare capabilities because of their relative cheapness, accessibility and commercial origins. Relatively low entry costs mean that the diffusion of information technologies is likely to accelerate far more quickly than did nuclear or aerospace weapons.

For all these reasons, information has become one of the most valuable commodities and strategic assets. A nation's (or corporation's) ability to produce and utilize information and to protect its information assets has become synonymous with protecting its national (or corporate) security and ensuring its citizens' (or shareholders') prosperity. Information systems will be a key arena of operations and a primary means for conducting offensive operations, and information warfare a key element in any 'strategy' of conflict or competition.

HOW TO THINK ABOUT INFORMATION WARFARE

Information warfare conjures up all sorts of definitions, taxonomies and images. We find it useful to think in terms of the conceptual categories laid out in Figure 1. The four domains of attack capture many of the prevailing taxonomies of information warfare.

We start from the assumption that the means of attack and the targets of attack can be classified as predominantly physical or cyber. We do not find it useful to focus on the target of attack as do many other taxonomies. Schwartau distinguishes personal IW which targets

FIGURE 1

DOMAINS OF ATTACK

Means of attack	Target of attack	
	Physical	*Cyber*
Physical (hurling mass and/or energy)	*I – Traditional War and Cyber-enhanced Physical Attack* Bombing military or civilian facilities; conventional warfare or terrorism	*II – Blast-based Information War* Physical strikes on information infrastructure (e.g., 9-11 impacted cell phone switching area); EMP from directed-energy weapons that destroy or disrupt digital services
Cyber (hurling information)	*III – Cyber-enabled Physical Attack* Attacks on aircraft navigation system; spoofing air traffic control system; attacks on specialized digital devices that control electrical power and dam floodgates	*IV – Non-lethal Information War* Denial-of-service attacks, worms, logic bombs inserted into information systems

individuals, corporate IW targets which targets business, commercial and economic interests, and global IW which targets assets associated with the national interest.[6] A more common way of distinguishing targets is to separate the domains of 'strategic' and 'battlefield' IW. The former comprises targets in the societal realm, the latter in the military realm. Information war is frequently associated with new military targets (e.g., enemy air defences; radar facilities) for conventional and cyber forces.[7] It is also frequently used to refer to new civilian targets for cyber forces, such as denial of service attacks on the nation's critical national infrastructure.[8] These distinctions, however, obscure the fact that what is really new is the widening ability, due to both the changing nature of the capabilities of state and non-state actors and the increasing vulnerabilities of advanced society, to disrupt the information and networks that support crucial day-to-day workings of civilian, commercial and military systems alike. The civilian–military distinction is even less useful in a world where military systems increasingly use and rely on civilian information infrastructures, and where there are important commonalities in the vulnerabilities of military and civilian information systems.[9]

Despite the characterization of this era as the information age, attacks will surely continue to combine physical and cyber capabilities, as, for example, when IT is used in combined-arms operations to improve the efficiency of high explosive attacks. The means of attack in this case remains predominantly physical. Information simply improves the efficiency and accuracy of physical attack. In the near future, national militaries in particular are unlikely to adopt purely non-physical strategies of conflict.[10] Physical destruction will remain a compelling proximate goal and cyber-attacks are likely to be used in support of lethal operations on the battlefield and against the adversary's homeland. Cell I of Figure 1 captures these characteristics of traditional warfare and cyber-enhanced physical attack. Information technologies augment conventional attack, as enablers of existing technologies by boosting the ability to find targets, direct fire to targets, as well as facilitating planning and communication among one's own forces. In several post-Cold War military engagements including the Persian Gulf War, Kosovo and Afghanistan, information technologies have been used quite effectively in battle to support and enhance traditional destructive warfare.

Cell II captures the idea that the information systems that undergird the operations of modern day societies and military organizations can be directly targeted through physical attack. Blast-based information war targets information systems with firepower, be it mass or energy. Physical attacks with conventional munitions on command and control targets, as well as on civilian critical infrastructure, such as electrical power generation and transmission systems, have been hallmarks of recent Western military campaigns. These attacks can have consequences far beyond the physical assets directly destroyed as the impact of losing services ripples throughout society. In recent years, attention has turned toward a new category of firepower – directed-energy weapons – which use high-power microwaves to disable electronic targets, in contrast to traditional jamming equipment that blocks communications devices from functioning but does not physically damage them. The new generation of directed-energy weapons 'is meant to emulate the sort of damage that nuclear EMP [electro-magnetic pulse] can inflict upon electronics but at far less range, with more control of the damage and without all the ancillary physical destruction and radioactivity'.[11]

Our analysis focuses in detail on cyber attacks directed against physical and cyber targets. Cell III, cyber-enabled physical attack, captures the destruction of physical targets by means of attacks on underlying technical systems. These attacks may be lethal, destroying lives and property, although only indirectly so. Recent attention has been directed toward the potential for terrorists to use the internet to target specialized digital devices, namely the distributed control systems (DCS) and supervisory control and data acquisition systems (SCADA) that throw railway switches and adjust valves in pipes that carry water, oil and gas. Increasingly, these digital control devices are connected to the internet and lack rudimentary security. Moreover, utilities worldwide allow technicians to remotely manipulate digital controls, and information on how to do this is widely available.[12]

Information warfare has been used to refer to combat waged solely within the domain of information and information systems. Cell IV captures this pure form of information warfare, or what we call non-lethal warfare. The tools are 'digital' and the targets include enemy population beliefs, enemy leadership beliefs, and the economic and political information systems upon which society relies to function.

Arguably the most distinctive quality of conflict in the information age is the capacity to coerce and deter adversaries, and influence and shape the strategic environment in non-lethal ways. Information technologies used in a non-destructive mode can serve a variety of preventive conflict goals. They could enhance transparency, build confidence and possibly prevent conflict if used in support of arms control verification regimes or peace operations. The increased abilities of sensors to detect military build-ups and disseminate that intelligence could reduce strategic surprise and deter conflict. Information technologies could be used to combat terrorism and international crime through the creation of global databases that track the movements and activities of these transnational actors. Information technologies could possibly prevent genocide and ethnic clashes *before* they start by ensuring accurate information supplants inflammatory nationalist rhetoric.[13]

Information technology, we argue, will also be used increasingly in a non-lethal mode during conflict, as a substitute for high explosive attacks via cyber operations that target an adversary's coordination capacity (military or societal) rather than their physical assets, that disrupt rather than directly destroy. The ultimate end goals of competition will remain the same: they may be political, material or symbolic. Those goals may be pursued by states, organizations, or personal actors. The weapons, however, will be cyber rather than physical, hurling information rather than mass or energy. The targets, whether military or civilian, will be the digital systems or coordinating capacity that undergirds physical capabilities rather than the physical capabilities themselves. The proximate or technical means of attack may in fact be destruction of information and information systems but more often than not given limited resources and system vulnerabilities, it will be the disruption of those systems.

The reasons for this are two-fold. First, the IT revolution has begun to alter expectations about conflict. In democratic nations today, there is a decline in the legitimacy accorded to lethality as well as a redefinition of innocents to include non-military members of an enemy's society.[14] Together, these make anything other than extremely accurate killing increasingly unacceptable in Western societies. The speed and accuracy of information warfare capabilities, coupled with the intolerance of democratic publics for casualties, indiscriminate destruction, and attacks on innocents has raised the attractiveness of this type of information warfare.

Second, because the United States dominates the global battlefield in conventional weapons, foreign governments and non-state actors are likely to resort to asymmetric strategies, of which information warfare is one. Attacking computer network systems is one way to balance the odds against a conventionally superior opponent. For weaker actors that cannot marshal the physical capability necessary to harm or influence more powerful adversaries, cyber attacks on information assets may become the strategy of choice. Particularly given an adversary with a highly informatized society and military, it makes logical sense to target the information systems of the adversary that provide intelligence about the opponents' tactics and strategy, that exercise command and control over, and direction of, capabilities and assets, and that undergird the functioning of the adversary's society and economy.

Information warfare of this disruptive variant is particularly challenging for our understanding of conflict because it blurs the peace–war boundary. Given the technological potential for intrusion, the temptation to pre-emptively disrupt in order to 'prepare the battlefield' before conventional hostilities or a crisis begins, or to incapacitate an adversary's war-making system by causing a complete or partial loss of function, is strong. A pre-battle information suppression operation might shatter an enemy's will to fight but does this first strike constitute a use of force?[15] The peace–war boundary may become virtually meaningless. Moreover, it is no longer self-evident what the battlefield is in an IW context, whether warfare is really occurring if there is no loss of life, and whether an actor would expend other types of personnel and equipment if attacked solely by electronic means.

The ultimate objective of information warfare – the use of information assets in the service of strategy – is to make the war or competition more costly for the adversary such that the adversary submits to one's will or never engages in the conflict or enters the competition/market at all. The proximate objective toward this end is always to compromise the adversary's information security. Information security rests on three pillars: confidentiality, integrity and availability (see Figure 2).[16] Confidentiality involves keeping secrets a secret. Integrity involves evaluating and maintaining the trustworthiness of data. Availability involves ensuring data and systems are available for use. Every IW attack compromises one or more of these three pillars.

Generically, all IW attacks are an assault on the security of information–the information itself and/or the systems that collect, process and disseminate the information. The targets are the enemy's beliefs, knowledge and information gathering, processing and disseminating capabilities. In the military realm, information attacks aim to send enough messages to convince the enemy to stop fighting or to

FIGURE 2

ASSAULTS ON INFORMATION SECURITY

Information Security Pillar	Goal of Attack	Technical Objective
Confidentiality	Exploit adversary's information systems	Theft or unauthorized use of valuable data
Integrity	Distribute misinformation or disinformation	Corrupt or modify adversary's information or information systems
Availability	Deny, destroy, or cripple adversary's information systems	Destroy key information; paralyze adversary's information systems

refrain from fighting, or to disrupt or destroy the communication channels to affect the adversary's implementation of strategy and ability to fight or resist. Messages may be direct – aimed at civilian and military leaders and their armed forces – or indirect – aimed at the public whose support may be necessary to wage a war. In the commercial realm, the goal is to influence the behaviour of actors in the marketplace – competitors, customers, suppliers, the public – to achieve business objectives.

Beyond this generic description, however, there is a vast array of modes of attack. Most discussions of IW focus on the dichotomy between destruction and disruption. But there are important differences between disrupting, disabling, crippling, corrupting and delaying such that the techniques short of destruction provide attackers with the ability to finely calibrate their assault. Moreover, destruction may be physical or logical. Finally, advances in IT have dramatically expanded the modes of diversion, distraction, distortion, monitoring and controlling.

The rest of this paper discusses the underlying logic and technical prerequisites of various types of information attacks focusing chiefly on Cell IV of Figure 1, non-lethal warfare. It is useful to think in terms of technical or cyber goals, and higher order political, material or symbolic goals. We first discuss the technical goals of attack, such as the use of cyber resources to cripple systems. Our discussion of these cyber goals applies equally to strategic information warfare – or attacks on the homeland directly – and to battlefield information warfare. Cyber goals however do not speak directly to the larger impact on society; rather, they characterize the effects upon the systems and infrastructure involved. The distinction between cyber goals and higher order goals is important. Cyber goals are primitives, in the sense that they cannot be broken down further. Higher order goals result from an attacker achieving cyber goals in such a way that the effect of achieving those goals also achieves a more general political, material or symbolic goal. Any particular campaign is likely to be comprised of several different cyber goals (See Figure 3).

In what follows, we discuss each goal individually. However, different cyber goals, and hence different types of attack, can and probably will be combined to achieve the attacker's end purpose. Obtaining a desired result may require intermediate results. For example, suppose an attacker wishes to monitor or control an adversary. In order to do this effectively, the attacker may need to distract the enemy so the attacker can tamper with the system to be monitored. Hence two sets of attacks are launched. The first involves much activity that is likely to be detected but will require some set of defences to be created. This diverts the enemy from noticing the second, subtler set of attacks that tamper with the system (for example, by adding a kernel loadable module) to insert keystroke recorders in appropriate places, thus achieving the desired goal. The reader is encouraged to construct multi-level attacks in which the ancillary efforts aid in achieving the desired goal.

CYBER GOALS

Destruction requires disabling a system in such a way that it cannot be recovered. It must be rebuilt or recreated. Destruction may occur in either the virtual realm or the physical one, but the key point is that something in the virtual realm triggers the destruction.

Clausewitz championed the principle of destruction as the most expedient way to achieve one's political objectives, as the shortest and surest way to defeat the enemy and impose one's will. Destruction has typically required the maximum concentration of physical force at the decisive point to irreparably damage the adversary's armed forces, or 'centre of gravity'. Destruction is the most decisive method for achieving one's political objectives, the most costly if it succeeds and the most damaging if it fails. Though Clausewitz's 'principle of destruction' is usually equated with physical destruction, Handel notes that 'by destruction, Clausewitz does not necessarily mean physical eradication or devastation of the enemy; he is also referring to destruction of the enemy's will to go on fighting'.[17] Destruction, in other words, encompasses both the physical and moral destruction of the enemy's forces.

FIGURE 3
GOALS AND TACTICS OF INFORMATION ATTACKS

Goal of Attack	Information Security Pillar Compromised	Tactics	Type of Goal
Destroy	Availability	Insert information that causes destruction of system; messing with refresh rate on some early monitors	Cyber
Disable, cripple, disrupt	Availability	Targets conduit; denial-of-service; swamp system (distributed denial of service attack); ping of death (sending a special packet that causes system to freeze, effectively disabling it); some worms and viruses	Cyber
Delay	Availability Integrity (e.g., trustworthiness of information degrades over time)	Prevent timely delivery of messages (e.g., that authorize payment on contract or delivery of critical supplies to different military theater); increase traffic on some segments of network to increase time to delivery; increase load on routers or servers	Cyber
Divert and distract	Availability	Divert target's attention and resources; hide other attacks or delay their discovery; script kiddie attacks while others are working much more subtly	Cyber
Distort	Confidentiality Integrity	Targets content vs conduit; perception management; psychological operations	Cyber
Monitor and control	Confidentiality Integrity	Code breaking; feeding misinformation (mimicking known signal so well that receiver cannot distinguish phony signal from real signal); mirror image sites; use of various techniques to mask identity of penetrating party into network or system	Cyber
Swagger	Confidentiality Integrity Availability	Demonstrations of one's abilities by attacking high value targets, highly protected systems, or by launching simultaneous attacks	Symbolic
Punish	Availability	Attacks on electrical, water, and medical infrastructure to maximize societal pain and suffering	Political
Deter	Availability	Impressive simulations and exercises; prebattlefield information attacks against command and control networks or leadership to shatter will to fight	Political
Coerce	Integrity Availability	Limited attacks that demonstrate power to hurt and inflict calibrated pain and damage to induce compliance	Political
Undermine confidence and legitimacy	Integrity	Infiltrate bank's computer system; alter critical files on system to allow unauthorized users entry to alter/delete user files unexpectedly; Trojan horses	Symbolic
Market manipulation	Confidentiality Integrity	Industrial espionage; information denial; break in and copy files; plant backdoors to allow reentry; plant sniffing programs to obtain user keystrokes and other actions	Material
Personal gain	Confidentiality Integrity Availability	Infiltrate bank's computer system to transfer money into or out of account; infiltrate registrar's computer to change semester grades; extortion; blocking access to a competitor's service	Material

Destruction has always required knowledge of how the system interacts with external entities, and this is true in the virtual world as well as the physical world. Physical destruction in particular requires knowledge of the environment of the system, such as characteristics of its hardware or its location. Two examples are changing the refresh rate of some older monitors (which causes them to burn out), and modifying the programming of avionics systems that control aeroplanes (which could cause the aeroplane to crash). The refresh rate is a function of the monitor's hardware. The avionics computer is in a precarious location, and its well-being depends upon its programming (and inputs) being correct. In both cases, the attack is designed to override any constraints intended to ensure the system functions within acceptable parameters, causing destruction.

Logical destruction, in which the hardware of the system is left alone but the logic or data of the system is rendered unintelligible and unrecoverable, typically requires physical destruction of backup information. If no backup information is present, deleting the software or data suffices for the attack to succeed. This requires either inserting code to delete the information (using a buffer overflow attack, for example), triggering resident code (such as resides in some servers), or acquiring privileges (for example, by compromising a privileged server). In order to determine which of these approaches is feasible, the attackers will probe the system to determine first, what servers are active and second, whether any of the active servers have these capabilities. The probes may request identifying information or characteristics of the server or simply send command sequences to the servers to determine how they react.[18]

The attacker needs information about the system to identify the most effective way to destroy it. Thus, an attack with the goal of destruction will begin with some type of analysis of the target's relationship to its environment. This phase again may be logical, in which case the attacker will probe the target, or physical, in which case the attacker will acquire instruction manuals and descriptions of the target system and its uses. In this case, probing the target will establish the characteristics that enable an attacker to discover the needed information to launch the attack, but the information will be obtained from manuals. Hence the level of probing may be much less.

Thus, the precursors to an attack intended to destroy the target system will require identifying the ways in which the system interacts with its environment. This in turn requires identifying the target system type, and its function. Probing network servers and the network protocol stack will help establish this information. Further, the attacks will target specific functions and features of the target.

Disabling renders equipment inoperable but repairable (e.g., by reboot). With *crippling*, equipment continues to operate but some key functions, those that are central to the goal or purpose of the system, fail. For example, a mail server may no longer be able to process mail but will respond to other requests. With *disruption*, equipment continues to function with intermittent failures, or a message changes unexpectedly as it moves from one point to another. A key tactic to achieve these results is denial of service. In principle, denial of service is nothing new in warfare, given that bombing a target takes it out of service. However, cyber attacks allow one to disable, cripple and disrupt non-lethally, and to pre-emptively disrupt in order to prepare the battlefield before conventional hostilities begin. In the military domain, the object of a denial of service attack would be to make the enemy blind and deaf, to cut off his ability to see and deny him access to information necessary to fight the war and command his troops. Though computer software operators disrupting other computers are not likely to be seen as dangerous, let alone as acts of war, disruption can be as great a security threat as destruction.

Disabling, crippling and disrupting are all goals that require that the system be overwhelmed in some fashion. In this context, 'overwhelmed' means that all resources of a particular type are serving an attacker, and none can be deallocated to be reassigned to a legitimate user. An example is the distributed denial of service attack. This attack simply swamps the target system (or its gateway), preventing network connections from users who wish to use the system. The requests for network connections from the attackers absorb all available space in the connection queue, and whenever a connection is terminated (by a time-out, for example), the deallocated resource is immediately reallocated to the attacker. If network connections unrelated to the distributed denial of service attack occur, they are highly unlikely to succeed.

A variant is to block the use of resources, as in the ping of death. An attacker sends a ping packet of maximum size, with the offset also set to maximum size. This causes the receiver to freeze, or lock its resources so they are unavailable to other senders. This achieves the same effect as overwhelming the system, except that the attacker need not send requests continuously. One request is enough.

In this case, the attack will either exploit known characteristics of the target or simply overwhelm resources. This suggests two characteristics. Either the attack uses specific inputs to block the resources, or the attack uses resources repeatedly. The first of these is difficult to characterize a priori, because the inputs that will cause the system to freeze are not known. However, an attacker will likely try inputs that are known to block some systems in the hope that one will succeed with the target. The second is characterized by an anomalous increase in the amount of traffic, the goal being to prevent the target from having resources free to assign to the non-attacking users.

An interesting insight into the nature of this attack is that the system recovers when the attack ends, or when the system managers reallocate resources to avoid the attacker being given any. This distinguishes it from destruction, in which the system managers must take specific steps to make it recover. Once a destructive attack is launched, the attacker cannot restore the system.

With *delay*, equipment continues to function as before but more slowly; or a message takes an unexpectedly long time to go from one point to another. The goal of delay is to disrupt the timely delivery of messages. The attack may either disrupt the network components of the sender or receiver, or of the path that the message will take. Two approaches are possible. Either the sending or receiving machine will be attacked, or a network component will be attacked. In both cases, the attack is similar to that of disabling, crippling and corrupting, except that the attack aims at overwhelming the target system intermittently rather than until the next reboot.

The boundary between delay and disruption lies in the fate of the messages. Disruption requires their destruction. Delay simply prevents them from arriving in a timely fashion. Hence a delaying attack will not disrupt all components of the communication path, but merely some. This type of attack is more localized than disruptive attacks. It is comparable to a 'surgical strike' that disables critical resources that can be replaced, but the time required to replace the resource causes delay. Thus, delaying attacks are characterized in the same way as those for disabling, crippling and corrupting, but are localized to particular elements of the path rather than attacking the entire path (by flooding) or discarding messages at the end points.

Diversion and *distortion* are forms of deception. The logic behind deception is to 'fabricate a pattern, albeit a bogus one, which will result in your adversary building up a false picture of reality. You hope that, as a result of his conclusion, he will either act incorrectly or fail to take advantage of a situation which, although he may not realize it, is favourable to him.'[19] *Diversion or distraction* is the simplest and most common form of deception. The mechanism employed is the disposition of one's own forces, physical or cyber, to dilute the adversary's ability to concentrate resources and efforts at the decisive point to achieve swift victory.[20] According to Sun Tzu, victory depends on superiority at the decisive point of engagement but this goal is best achieved not by focusing only on concentrating one's own forces while ignoring the enemy. It requires a method to force the enemy to disperse his forces, resources, capabilities and attention. Deception through diversion becomes central.[21]

Distortion is a form of deception that targets the content of the population's information space. It is frequently referred to as 'perception management'.[22] In this respect, it differs from many other types of information warfare that target the conduit of information whether through destruction, disabling, crippling, disruption or delay. However, distortion requires that one exploit the conduit of the information, or the communications medium, whether it is face-to-face contact,[23] print, telecommunications, broadcast or computer networks.[24] The mechanism employed in distortion is the manipulation of the accuracy of information (through fabrication of information or falsification of existing information) in order to shape the adversary's perceptions, and by extension influence his reasoning, decision making and actions.[25]

While Clausewitz viewed destruction as the core principle of warfare, Sun Tzu accorded deception to that paramount position because successful deception may allow one to achieve surprise. If the deceiver can conceal his true objectives, the enemy may concentrate his forces in the wrong places, thereby weakening himself at the decisive point of engagement.[26]

Deception is intimately related to security. Dewar summarizes the purposes of security as preventing the enemy from deducing your location, capabilities, plan of attack, timing of attack, means of attack, and sources of intelligence.[27] Conversely, the purposes of deception are to persuade the enemy that you are elsewhere, your capabilities are different from what they are, your plan is to do something else, somewhere else, at a different time and in a different manner. The successful deception is difficult to achieve. It requires centralized control and coordination; thorough preparation; consistency with the pattern of events the enemy has come to expect; redundancy (e.g., false indicators presented to the enemy through as many intelligence or surveillance sources as possible); careful timing to allow the enemy enough time to react to false information but insufficient time for analysis to uncover the deception; and maintenance of normal security precautions so as not to arouse the enemy's suspicions.[28] Dewar emphasizes that 'All deception has a limited and relatively short life span before it is exposed. The degree of sophistication required to make a ploy successful is directly related to the length of time over which it has to be sustained.'[29] Moreover, individuals, groups and populations will vary in their susceptibility to deception. In the information age, those who have come to rely heavily on electronic and digital sources of information and intelligence are likely to be the most susceptible to the manipulation and distortion of those sources of information.

Dewar contends that the battlefield has not always presented the same opportunities for deception. In the eighteenth century, the battlefield was completely visible; hence Clausewitz's scepticism about the chances for successful deception and surprise. In the nineteenth century, the battlefield became much larger and visibility declined. The Second World War was the apex of the 'Empty Battlefield' while reconnaissance and surveillance technologies in the post-1945 era have returned a much larger battlefield to near complete visibility. Yet today's digital technologies allow one to easily create and manipulate documents and digital images. While the physical battlefield may be more transparent, the digital battlefield provides unprecedented opportunities for deception.

The essence of diversion is to attract the enemy's attention. While the enemy is otherwise occupied, the attacker can launch the 'real' attack. This makes diversion and distraction uniquely suited to be a precursor to, or component of, other attacks. This suggests a simple characterization of such an attack: obviousness. If the attack cannot be detected, the enemy cannot respond. Hence the attack must be of a nature that the enemy can detect. Ideally, the enemy will be forced to divert resources to handle the attack as well. Thus, the attacker may use well-known attacks that require the enemy to take procedural steps to protect the enemy. The enemy must then focus on the attack, and may not notice the more subtle attack from which her attention is being diverted.

Diversionary attacks can be defensive, as in the classic diversionary response launched when some East German attackers broke into a computer at Lawrence Berkeley Laboratory in the mid-1980s. Cliff Stoll, a system administrator, was determined to trace the attackers, whom he realized were coming over a telephone line from somewhere in

Germany. But tracing an international call required time, and the attacker was never connected for long enough. So Stoll created a false document that contained information the attacker would desire. It would also take several hours to download over a telephone line. When the attacker found the document, he downloaded it – and that diverted the attacker's attention from the telephone trace, which located him.[30]

Distortion manages the enemy's perception of what is happening. The goal of distortion is to make the enemy believe something that the attacker wants the enemy to believe. For example, one can configure an electronic mail server to greet a client with a declaration that it is *sendmail* version 8.9, when in reality it is a *postfix* mailer. As different mail servers have different vulnerabilities, this leads to an attacker wasting resources on attacks that work on *sendmail* version 8.9 mail servers but not on *postfix* servers. In a parallel fashion US surveillance and reconnaissance aircraft not only can collect and jam enemy radar and radio emissions but also plant false targets in enemy radars and spoof enemy air defence systems.[31]

A characteristic of distortion attacks is control of resources. The attacker must control the enemy's access to information involved in the distortion. If the enemy can obtain information indicating inconsistencies, then the enemy may realize that the attack is under way. Thus, the attacker must identify all paths along which the enemy can obtain the information to be distorted. This requires a complete understanding of the enemy's relationship to the information involved in the distortion. This would require probing not only the enemy, but also intermediaries along the paths of information flow to determine if they can detect the distortion (and feed information back to the enemy).

While distortion and deception usually involve replacing information with a phoney signal, *monitoring* and *controlling* involve infiltration of the enemy's information space and hiding the signal in order to gather information. Infiltration for the purposes of monitoring creates opportunities for deception since the enemy presumably is unaware that his information resources have been compromised and will continue to trust them. Monitoring is a crucial foundation for deception. Good intelligence and penetration of the enemy's camp are the means to understand the enemy's thoughts, expectations, and plans.[32]

The distinction that is important is your ability to predict the resulting actions of the enemy. With distortion/deception, we are simply misleading the enemy, either in his information space or our space, by feeding the enemy false or distorted information. With monitoring/ controlling, we are attempting to see what the enemy is doing, and force her to specific actions or situations. For example, we may place false documents in our information space to mislead the enemy, but not know what the results will be. This is distortion/deception. Or we may concoct the documents to produce specific results or actions. This is controlling, of which deception is a part. Or, we may instrument the system to record who grabs the documents. This is monitoring.

The difference between monitoring and controlling is that monitoring is passive, whereas controlling is active. Monitoring may require action to initiate the monitoring, but once the mechanisms for monitoring are in place, the attacker need take no further action. An example of monitoring is to record keystrokes. The attacker must insert appropriate code into the kernel (usually done via a kernel-loadable module), but after the insertion the mechanism simply records all keystrokes entered at the system. In some cases, the attacker need only persuade the enemy to take some action, such as downloading a file or executing a program. The Trojan horse is an example of this technique.[33]

Controlling is similar to distortion, except that the goal of control is to force the enemy to take specific actions or to enter specific states of operation. Distortion may be a component of control, as it was in Cheswick's manipulation of Berferd.[34] By distorting the environment that Berferd perceived, Cheswick made Berferd take specific actions which (he hoped) would identify Berferd. Contrast this to the use of honeypots,[35] in which the distortion fools the enemy into thinking they are on a system with sensitive information or desired resources. They then try to compromise the system. The attackers can monitor every action, and by changing the configuration of the system, trick the enemy into revealing their capabilities.

Controlling may be more direct. The NetBus[36] attack tool allowed the attacker to perform system administrative tasks, such as monitoring the other users of the system, inserting keystrokes, reading screens, and shutting the system down. This tool was placed into a computer game that was made publicly available. A number of sites downloaded and installed the game, giving the attackers complete control of their system.

Monitoring requires the ability to read traffic. This means that the attacker must have, or obtain, read access to some part of the communications channel. Similarly, controlling requires the ability to write or modify traffic, meaning that the attacker must have, or obtain, write access to some part of the communications channel. Thus, a characteristic of these attacks is an analysis of the communications paths that the enemy uses, in order to obtain the needed access. A secondary characteristic is that the attacker must penetrate some component of the channel, such as the kernel (or sending or receiving process) of an endpoint, or an intermediate system such as a router. The attacker may compromise the component directly, through a penetration attack, or indirectly, through a Trojan horse that contains the compromise when it is executed.

HIGHER ORDER GOALS

Swaggering traditionally has involved the peaceful use of military force to display one's might. Typically, nations display their military prowess at military exercises, national demonstrations, or through the purchase or manufacture of prestigious weapons.[37] According to Art, 'the swagger use of force is the most egoistic: It aims to enhance the national pride of a people or to satisfy the personal ambitions of a ruler. A state or statesman swaggers in order to look and feel more powerful and important, or to be taken seriously by others in the councils of international decision making, to enhance the nation's image in the eyes of others.'[38] In the short run, swaggering serves no specific instrumental purpose. In the long run, it may enhance the state's offensive, defensive, and deterrent capabilities. Der Derian argued that impressive cyber demonstrations and exercises could serve the same purpose as nuclear testing. Through technological exhibitionism, swaggering one's cyber capabilities could render visible and plausible one's power, thereby acting as a cyber-deterrent.[39]

As swaggering is primarily a public activity, the attacker must create an effect that others can see. The attack, or its effects, must be obvious to all. The attacker who penetrated Stanford's network is a good example of swaggering, because he discussed with the Stanford administrators what he was doing as he did it.[40] The (possibly apocryphal) compromise of a sensitive Air Force system, in which a group of Air Force computer security experts were assured the system was impenetrable and promptly demonstrated the falsity of the claim by having the computer print a parody of the press release, is another example.

The characteristic of an attack with swaggering as its goal is visibility. The result need not be visible to all; it may only be visible to a select few (as in the above examples). But it must be visible to someone. Hence these attacks tend to be obvious either in their execution or their results. This suggests the use of well-known techniques of attack for which adequate responses are not available, so the enemy can detect the attack, or publicly visible results, such as the recent spate of defacements of web pages. In this sense, swaggering attacks are similar to attacks used to divert and distract.

Punishing involves the use of force to inflict pain and suffering. Schelling distinguishes brute force, which seeks to overcome another's strength, from the threat of pain, which seeks to structure another's motives.[41] Punishment is a form of coercion designed to induce compliance. Successful use of the strategy of punishment requires knowing what an adversary treasures and fears. According to Schelling, the difference between brute force and coercion is less in the instrument than in the intent. Brute force seeks to eliminate a military obstacle while the coercive use of force seeks to convince an adversary to behave or to surrender by inflicting unacceptable anguish and pain. Punitive attacks on people can also be used in a broader military campaign to subdue short of a direct military engagement.

Historically, victory has resulted from defeat of an enemy's military forces rather than simply hurting people to make the conflict terrible beyond endurance. Terrorism, blockade and strategic bombing – all examples of violence against civilians intended primarily to coerce rather than weaken the enemy militarily – have rarely been effective in and of themselves to achieve victory. The major exception was probably the atomic bombs released on Japan, weapons of terror and shock whose value lay in inflicting pure pain as much as direct military destruction. Nuclear weapons have also made it possible to inflict unacceptable pain without first achieving military victory. Typically, such violence was reserved for the victors over the vanquished. Not only have nuclear weapons changed the amount of destruction that can be inflicted but also the role that destruction plays in the decision process.

Punishment is a strategy that not only blurs the distinction between combatants and non-combatants but also specifically targets non-combatants, either during or preceding war, in order to intimidate, coerce or deter governments.[42] Information attacks on critical infrastructure may not produce the same destructive impact as conventional bombing but they serve a similar purpose although the result may be to confuse more than to hurt.

Punishing through technical means requires targeting infrastructure systems that disrupt the use of the internet. As the internet is not yet a necessary component of people's lives, the degree of disruption must affect the use of the internet to distribute products or services that are necessary for society to function. Hence attacks designed to punish would target the suppliers of services or the network infrastructure. The technical types of attacks involved could be drawn from any of the above set of technical goals. The specific technical goal that would create the greatest havoc would dictate the nature of the attack.

Deterrence seeks to make an attack unattractive so that an opponent does not initiate action. This goal may be achieved either through threats of retaliation and punishment as discussed above, or through denial of the attacker's likelihood of success. The problem with deterrence through retaliation is well-addressed by Harknett, who warns that deterrence is likely to fail if launched by a non-state actor that can retain its anonymity and that has no physical assets or population against which to retaliate. Deterrence through denial could involve improving one's own defences against attack, through robust computer security, or incapacitating the enemy's offensive capabilities through a pre-battle information suppression operation designed to dissuade the enemy from attacking. This would involve attacks that destroy, disable, corrupt or disrupt.

While deterrence is aimed at dissuading an adversary from undertaking a damaging action, *coercion* is used to persuade an adversary to stop or reverse an action. Coercion can use threats of punishment if the adversary does not comply. Or, exemplary or symbolic uses of limited military force – mass, energy or information – could be employed to persuade the opponent to back down.[43] Exemplary actions must use just enough force to demonstrate resolve and lend credibility to further uses of force if deemed necessary. But as George notes, coercion does not require the use of force; it may be executed entirely through diplomacy and persuasion. If force is employed, it is used flexibly, as a 'refined psychological instrument' in contrast to a blunt instrument of destruction. A strategy of coercion with or without force necessarily includes appropriate communications to the opponent to signal intent and negotiate an acceptable compromise. IW attacks could be very useful in a coercive strategy because they can be finely calibrated to limit damage yet also demonstrate resolve. Like swaggering, coercive uses of information warfare must be visible and distortion must be minimized.

Undermining confidence and legitimacy involves attacks that reveal an enemy's weaknesses, or that distort others' perceptions of the enemy.

Revealing weaknesses may require attacks that destroy, disable, corrupt or disrupt. If availability and timeliness are services that the enemy provides, delay may also be a goal that will undermine confidence and legitimacy. Diversion and distraction undermine confidence in the enemy's ability to cope with attacks. Monitoring and controlling may reveal actions that the enemy wishes to keep secret, and publicizing them may achieve the social goal. Similarly, controlling an enemy allows the attacker to force them to take action inimical to their best interests, undermining confidence.

Distortion as a goal towards undermining confidence and legitimacy has two effects. The first is as a form of control, in which the enemy is presented with a distorted view of reality and takes discreditable action as a result. The second is to distort observers' perceptions of the enemy's actions, causing them to discredit the enemy. If the enemy is viewed as a 'black box', the first view arises from the attacker controlling the inputs upon which the enemy bases her decisions and actions. The second arises from the attacker controlling the conduits from the enemy to the observers, and distorting the outputs from the enemy. The difference dictates the response of the enemy: whether to gather inputs from other sources that the attacker cannot (or does not) control, or whether to find alternate channels of communications with the observer.

Market manipulation is a social goal that arises from the 'cyber' goals of monitoring and controlling. To acquire data, the attacker monitors the enemy. To manipulate the market, the attacker uses the data to determine what actions to take to achieve the desired result. *Personal gain* may require any of the 'cyber' goals to help the attacker achieve the desired result. Hence the characteristics and precursors of that 'cyber' goal will arise for this social goal.

CONCLUSION

Our approach to understanding the dynamics of information warfare is grounded in a belief that an 'attack-based' analysis has merits over an 'effects-based' analysis. It is important to understand the effects of attacks in order to recover. But defence against information warfare requires foremost an understanding of the likelihood of different types of attack, and all attacks are not equally likely, nor equally executable by all types of attackers. Nor are systems equally vulnerable to all types of attack. The choice of attack will vary in some systematic way based on the type of attacker (e.g., state, non-state actor, or individual) because different types of actors are likely to have different motives, capabilities, adaptability and time horizons.

Accordingly, attack-based analysis has diagnostic potential. The type of attack launched should tell us about the motivations and capabilities of the attacker, and indicate the attacker's understanding of the vulnerabilities of the target. There should be similarities in the dynamics of warfare across the military and commercial domains that did not exist in the past because entrepreneurs and warriors have similar requirements for information systems – that those systems be resilient and can function correctly under uncertainty whether due to human error, system failure, or malicious attack. However, attackers working for a government are likely to launch different types of attacks than attackers working for a company because their goals and training may differ significantly.

From an attack-based perspective, we see that despite the levelling affect of information technology, states and state-sponsored groups will retain certain advantages in waging information warfare. A common belief holds that IT is levelling the field of attackers, making it possible for a lone individual to create the same havoc that was once the purview of states and organizations with large amounts of resources. Certainly, the attacks used may be the same; the repertoire of attacks may be available on the internet for both individual and state use. Certainly, the lone attacker may cause great damage. But equating a lone attacker with states and similar organizations overlooks three factors: organization, intelligence about the target, and sustainability.

First, the state-sponsored attack allows the attackers to be better organized. If the defenders resist the attack by, for example, adding more powerful routers to handle an increase in traffic (from a distributed denial of service attack), the state-sponsored attackers can quickly increase their delivery of packets to overwhelm the new router. An individual attacker, or a group of loosely organized attackers, would need to co-ordinate the response without having planned for that contingency. They would be unable to respond to the defence quickly or effectively. The state-sponsored attackers have the advantage of resources, more robust communication abilities, and support for planning that would allow them to anticipate defences and plan counters.

Second, while the attack tools provide the capabilities to launch attacks, they do not provide the knowledge to use the attacks effectively.

A lone attacker may be able to use some number of attack tools effectively, but an organized group that could draw upon team members with a wide variety of experience and knowledge would be able to determine which attack tools to use effectively, and how to use them to reach their goal swiftly. If the attackers had resources beyond the team members, so much the better; especially if they were able to learn about their target's organization and response capabilities. Further, in the technical realm, the attackers could practice against a duplicate of the enemy's systems, networks and organizational procedures, just as professional militaries have practised the art of war in training situations, so they could more quickly proceed to their goal. An individual attacker could not do this.

Third, the effectiveness of an attack is a function of the resources needed to sustain the attack. When an individual launches an attack, her resources are limited to those she has available. When a state supports the attack, the attackers have more resources (and more money) at their command. For example, a state-sponsored group could sustain the attack in the face of detection and interference, because they can simply move the origin of the attack to a new location. A lone attacker, once caught, could not do this.

The observations above hold true not just for state sponsored attacks, but for attacks that spring from a non-state entity with resources and the ability to organize. Attacking can be an individual activity or a group activity. But the basic requirements for sustaining a campaign in warfare that have existed in the past have not changed fundamentally. They have simply moved to a new arena.

NOTES

1. Geoffrey L. Herrera, 'Inventing the Railroad and Rifle Revolution: Information, Military Innovation and the Rise of Germany', paper prepared for The Center for Strategic and Budgetary Assessments workshop on 'Military Revolutions: The Role of Information Capabilities' (Washington DC, 4–5 March, 2002).
2. Robert Citino, 'Beyond Fire and Movement: Command, Control, and Information in the German *Blitzkrieg*', paper prepared for The Center for Strategic and Budgetary Assessments workshop on 'Military Revolutions: The Role of Information Capabilities' (Washington DC, 4–5 March, 2002).
3. David Zimmerman, 'Information and the Air Defense Revolution, 1917–1940', paper prepared for The Center for Strategic and Budgetary Assessments workshop on 'Military Revolutions: The Role of Information Capabilities' (Washington DC, 4–5 March, 2002).
4. Information as 'content' refers to a signal that contains meaningful content and can be transmitted, either in the form of intelligence or as messages between commanders and troops. Information as 'conduit' focuses on flow, or on the *communication* of signals rather than signal content. A view of information as conduit focuses one's analysis on information technologies

138   National Security in the Information Age

that permit one to transmit and receive messages.
5. See Richard J. Harknett, 'Integrated Security: A Strategic Response to Anonymity and the Problem of the Few', in this volume.
6. Winn Schwartau, *Information Warfare: Chaos on the Electronic Superhighway* (New York: Thunder's Mouth Press, 1994).
7. Roger W. Barnett, 'Information Operations, Deterrence, and the Use of Force', *Naval War College Review*, Vol. 51, No.2, pp.7–19; T.L. Thomas, 'Deterring Information Warfare: A New Strategic Challenge', *Parameters* (Winter 1996–97), pp.81–91.
8. See Harknett in this volume; L. Sullivan, Jr., *Meeting the Challenges of Regional Security* (Carlisle, PA: US Army War College Strategic Studies Institute, 1994); G.F. Wheatley and R.E. Hayes, *Information Warfare and Deterrence* (Washington DC: National Defense University Press, 1996).
9. Berkowitz reports that approximately 95 per cent of all military communications are routed through commercial lines and that the US government buys most of the microchips used in military systems from commercial vendors. Bruce D. Berkowitz, 'Warfare in the Information Age', *Issues in Science and Technology* (Fall 1995), pp.59–66.
10. See Chris C. Demchak, 'War of Disruption: International Competition and Information Technology-Driven Military Organizations', in this volume for a discussion of why lethality will remain a defining characteristic of how states, particularly the United States, wages warfare in the information age.
11. Seth Schiesel, 'Taking Aim at an Enemy's Chips', *New York Times*, 20 Feb. 2003, pp.E1, E5.
12. Barton Gellman, 'The Cyber-Terror Threat', *Washington Post National Weekly Edition*, 1–4 July 2002, pp.6–7.
13. Joseph S. Nye, Jr. and William A. Owens, 'America's Information Edge', *Foreign Affairs*, Vol. 75, No.2 (March/April 1996), pp.20–36.
14. Chris C. Demchak, 'Watersheds in Perception and Knowledge: Twenty Years of Military Technology', draft manuscript (June 1999).
15. Thomas G. Mahnken, 'War in the Information Age', *Joint Force Quarterly* (Winter 1995–96), pp.39–43.
16. Schwartau, *Information Warfare*, p.265.
17. Michael I. Handel, *Masters of War* (third edn), (London: Frank Cass, 2001), p.150.
18. Fyodor, 'The Art of Port Scanning', <http://www.insecure.org/nmap/namp_doc.html>; D. Lee, J. Rowe, C. Ko and K. Levitt, 'Detecting and Defending Against Web-Server Fingerprinting', *18th Annual Computer Security Applications Conference*.
19. Michael Dewar, *The Art of Deception in Warfare* (Devon, England: David and Charles Publishers, 1989), p.19.
20. The classic example of deception through diversion was Operation FORTITUDE, the codename for the deception plan associated with Operation OVERLORD, the Allied invasion of Europe in 1944. The diversion focused German attention on the Pas de Calais and other parts of Europe. When the Allied invasion took place in Normandy, the Germans were not sure for nearly two months whether it was the main invasion or merely a feint to draw attention away from a subsequent invasion of the Pas de Calais. Ibid., p.11.
21. Handel, *Masters of War*, p.159.
22. Dorothy E. Denning, *Information Warfare and Security* (Boston: Addison-Wesley, 1999), pp.101–29 examines five areas of perception management: lies and distortions, denouncement, harassment, advertising and censorship.
23. Sun Tzu discussed the use of expendable agents who unknowingly would be given false information and sent into enemy territory, in the hopes that they would be captured and forced to reveal the false information.
24. Denning, *Information Warfare and Security*, p.101.
25. Ibid.
26. Handel, *Masters of War*, p.217.
27. Dewar, *The Art of Deception in Warfare*, pp.18–19.
28. Ibid., pp.14–15.
29. Ibid., p.10. Dewar provides a list of techniques of deception. The first is encouraging the enemy to believe that the most likely way of achieving the objective will in fact be adopted thereby diverting his attention from an alternative plan. The lure presents the enemy with what

appears to be sudden or ideal opportunity, which he would be wise to exploit whereas in fact he is being lured into a trap. The repetitive process lures the opponent into a false sense of security. The double bluff involves openly revealing the truth to the enemy – who has come to expect deception – in the conviction that he will not believe it. The unintentional mistake leads the enemy to believe that valuable information has come into his hands through a break of security or by negligence or inefficiency on the part of the enemy. The piece of bad luck encourages the enemy to think he has acquired information of vital importance by accident because of a train of circumstances over which his adversary has no control. Substitution encourages the enemy to recognize something as false and to continue in the belief that it is false even after it has been covertly replaced by the real – and vice versa. One can disguise one's own forces in enemy uniforms. Finally, Dewar notes that deception techniques can be categorized in terms of the senses. Camouflage and concealment involve visual deception. Sound can also be used to deceive.

30. C. Stoll, 'Stalking the Wily Hacker', *Communications of the ACM*, Vol. 31, No.5 (May 1988) pp.484–97.
31. Thom Shanker and Eric Schmitt, 'Firing Leaflets and Electrons, U.S. Wages Information War', *New York Times* (24 Feb. 24 2003), pp.A1, A7.
32. Handel, *Masters of War*, pp.217–8.
33. J. Anderson, 'Computer Security Technology Planning Study', Technical Report ESD-TR-73-51, Electronic Systems Division, Hanscom Air Force Base, Hanscom, MA (1974).
34. W. Cheswick, 'An Evening with Befrerd, in Which a Cracker is Lured, Endured, and Studied', *Proceedings of the 1992 Winter USENIX Conference* (Jan. 1992) pp.163–73.
35. L. Spitzner, *Honeypots: Tracking Hackers* (Boston, MA: Addison Wesley Professional, 2002).
36. Symantec, 'Information on Back Orifice and NetBus', <http://www.symantec.com/avcenter/warn/backorifice.html>.
37. Robert J. Art, 'The Four Functions of Force', reprinted in Robert J. Art and Robert Jervis, *International Politics* (fourth edn) (New York: Harper Collins, 1996), pp.159–60.
38. Ibid.
39. James Der Derian, 'Cyber-deterrent', *Wired*, Vol. 2, No.9, pp.116–22.
40. B. Reid, 'Reflections on some Widespread Computer Break-Ins', *Communications of the ACM*, Vol. 30, No.2 (Feb. 1987), pp.103–5.
41. Thomas C. Schelling, 'The Diplomacy of Violence', reprinted in Art and Jervis, *International Politics*, pp.169.
42. Ibid., p.178.
43. Alexander L. George, 'Coercive Diplomacy: Definition and Characteristics', in Alexander L. George and William E. Simons, ed., *The Limits of Coercive Diplomacy* (Boulder: Westview Press, 1994), p.10.

Information Warfare and Democratic Accountability

MIROSLAV NINCIC

American history, it has been observed, progresses as the intertwined march of democracy and technology: the joint product, on the one hand, of political institutions and a political culture favouring individual freedom and collective effort and, on the other hand, of applied science as a multiplier of human attributes and an engine of change.[1] It is also recognized that democracy and technology are not mutually independent forces: that science, both pure and applied, thrives best in certain political climates, and that socio-political structures are, in certain ways, a reflection of the technologies a society has mastered. Still, our appreciation of the first part of this mutual relationship has progressed further than our grasp of the second, and the purpose here is to explore one manner in which US democracy may be shaped, for better or worse, by a form of technology – specifically information technology – and by the policy objectives to which it is tethered. Moreover, the lessons learned in the US case may have a broader potential application to democracies seeking security in the information age.

The expansion of information technology may affect two defining features of democracy: how power and accountability are structured at the apex of the political system, and how government and governed interact. Both are shaped not only by norms that establish what is appropriate in this regard but, often incrementally and inadvertently, by the actual policies governments pursue and the tools by which they are pursued. The information age, in turn, has determined the contours of many policy objectives and the means used on their behalf.

Because of its importance and its scope, national security policy has, arguably, had a greater impact on political life than any other facet of national policy. At the same time, the nature of its missions and the resources at its disposal have made the military enterprise a major beneficiary of information technology, while this technology's role as a force multiplier for other nations has made adversary information systems one of its major targets.[2] Accordingly, this paper concerns itself with the implications of information warfare for US democracy – in particular, for congressional checks on executive branch autonomy, for the ability of citizens to monitor and evaluate the activities of government, and for governmental respect for the civil liberties protected by the Fourth Amendment to the Constitution. Specific implications depend on the purpose of the military activity.

Offensive information warfare, the business of targeting the enemy's information and its functions while seeking to protect those on which one's own military effort depends, is acquiring a significant role in US military doctrine and planning.[3] It may carry consequences for democracy at two levels at least. In the first place, by rendering ambiguous the very definition of warfare, it makes it harder to ensure democratic controls over its conduct. Attempts to corrupt and degrade information systems may involve minimal physical destruction, whereas the destruction of life and property has traditionally been warfare's defining characteristic. Democracy assumes accountability and control of the executive branch, but the constitutional and other norms that regulate decisions on the use of armed force abroad may have no clear applicability in this context, impairing the proper operation of checks and balances. At another level, tools of offensive information warfare may seek to influence an adversary's will and capacity to fight by dint of what is referred to as 'perception management'. As this often means manipulating the adversary's perceptions with a view to distorting his view of reality, it may convey the distortions to a domestic audience, undermining the public's ability to form an autonomous judgement of government actions and to hold it accountable for these actions.

If the purpose is not to impair the adversary's information systems but to protect those upon which US society is crucially dependent – i.e., if the purpose is *defensive* information warfare – a different threat must be considered. Here, it is not so much a matter of accountability but of civil liberties – as government's efforts to ferret out threats to critical information infrastructures may involve a level of monitoring and surveillance whose scope, in some eyes, may threaten Fourth Amendment protections and other norms limiting governmental intrusiveness into the lives of its citizens. Consequently, the broad concerns crystallize into the following three problems: (1) the implications of information warfare for decisions to initiate war, (2) its potential to distort judgements that are at the roots of public control of its leaders, and, (3) the possibility that the requisites of defensive information warfare may lead to excessive government intrusiveness into the lives of its citizens.

WHO DECIDES?

Given the potential costs and the extensive implications of war, few democracies allow complete executive discretion in the use of military force, and the general rule is that war involvement requires positive parliamentary action, in many cases with a qualified majority. Nevertheless, changing historical circumstances, including the growing scope of what technology makes possible, often affect the meaning of very fundamental norms of a nation's political order, including those governing the initiation and conduct of war.

There is little doubt that America's Founding Fathers wished to ensure that decisions to go to war would not be left up to the executive. As James Madison explained, the Framers' purpose 'supposes, what the History of all Govts demonstrates, that the Ex. Is the branch of power most interested in war, & most prone to it. It has accordingly with studied care, vested the question of war in the Legisl.'[4] Accordingly Article I, Section 8, of the Constitution places the power to declare war, as well as the power to 'raise and support armies' and to 'provide and maintain a Navy', solely in congressional hands. At the same time, the Constitution designates the President as 'Commander and Chief of the armed forces', a designation bestowing much autonomy in decisions to repel sudden attacks and to oversee the conduct of military operations.

While US presidents have interpreted the Commander in Chief clause as allowing them considerable latitude to initiate military action abroad, this almost certainly was not the Framers' intention. As Louis Fisher, perhaps the foremost scholar of congressional–executive relations in foreign affairs, observes, 'The framers were quite deliberate about placing with Congress the fundamental power to deploy armed forces.'[5] Hamilton certainly would agree: writing in *Federalist 69*, he observed that the Commander in Chief authority 'would amount to nothing more than the supreme command and direction of the military and naval forces as first General and admiral of the Confederacy.'[6] The Supreme Court seemed to hold the same view. Commenting on the power conferred upon the president by the declaration of war in *Fleming*

v. *Page*, it observed that the commander in chief clause implied that 'his duty and power are purely military.'[7]

Even if congressional supremacy in decisions to go to war is accepted, the boundary between war-*declaring* and war-*making* powers are blurred. Doubts may remain over the appropriate congressional role once the nation is committed to fighting, and about how much autonomy the Commander in Chief clause really implies with regard to war-initiation. Although the actual course of military entanglements typically is guided by an appreciation that war requires national unity, and that parliamentary bodies have neither the expertise to manage military action nor the organizational aptitude to react nimbly and decisively to fluid circumstances, there are few democracies in which legislative bodies cannot, if they so choose, terminate hostilities via the powers at their disposal. There is, in any case, no reason to assume that Congress cannot, or should not, use its legislative power and power of the purse to decide when a military entanglement should be terminated. Even here, however, arguments about constitutionally unjustified congressional forays into the executive realm, as defined by the commander-in-chief-clause, must be expected.

The important point, for our purposes, is that the norms behind any political order are a product of the historical awareness accumulated at the time, and the enduring principles they reflect may not forever be adequately captured by the same specific norms. Because of this, in a dynamic world, constitutional requirements must sometimes be interpreted in light of the evolving conditions linking them to the more basic principles they express. Constitutional purpose can be trumped by the evolution of circumstances that could not have been foreseen at the time a political order was designed. Altered circumstances may mean that original provisions are, appropriately or not, ignored or reinterpreted in light of altered needs, at least by some parts of government. Thus, the nation's extensive international interests and responsibilities could not have been anticipated at the time of the Philadelphia Convention, nor could the frequency with which armed force would be relied upon in defence of these interests and in pursuit of these responsibilities. Had this been predicted, it may be that war powers would have been dealt with differently by the Founding Fathers.

Similarly, the range of military operations the United States might undertake could not have been foreseen, for this stems from the forms and levels of military power at the disposal of a technologically sophisticated and economically powerful nation. At the lower ends of this range, some military operations, while constituting warfare in the general meaning, might be thought to fall short of War, in the sense of a significant and active commitment of military power over an extended period of time. Had this been foreseen, the Founding Fathers might have devised a different system of constitutional controls for actions amounting, say, to a show of force, punitive expedition, police action, and so forth. Conceivably, the President might have been granted greater autonomy in such cases.

Aside from the *range* of military activities, constitutional intent regarding war powers can be, and has been, superseded by science and technology, yielding possibilities that could not have been considered when the nation's political system was initially devised. Types of military force which could not have been imagined by those who designed the initial contours of America's political system, have emerged, bearing little relation to notions of warfare originally conceived, and raising dilemmas about how they should be regulated democratically. The most widely commented upon example has involved long-range nuclear weapons, which, at least within the logic of Cold War doctrines of deterrence, allowed for no congressional or popular input into the specific circumstances of their use, despite the unparalleled levels of destruction and unfathomable political consequences implied.

Of direct bearing on our current concerns, information warfare, particularly in its offensive form, raises questions about the democratic control of new forms of military activity whose answers cannot be found in constitutional provisions: in current debates on their proper interpretation, or even in general tenets of democratic theory. No particularly novel issues may arise where information warfare is an adjunct to conventional forms of warfare: i.e., where physical destruction of lives and property goes hand in hand with impairments of the adversary's information infrastructure. Physical destruction is the defining feature of warfare in this case, and the issues surrounding permissible presidential autonomy to deploy armed force abroad present themselves in their usual form. That many of these issues remain unresolved does not alter the fact that they probably would be cast in habitual terms, involving premises and arguments similar to those deployed in the past.

But information warfare may be the principal, even the sole, form of operations undertaken. Computers may battle computers, information systems may be disrupted in various ways, the communications infrastructure on which the adversary depends may be thoroughly impaired, while all along very little ordnance is fired. It has been suggested that 'Information warfare is a very remote form of confrontation and if executed correctly may very well permit the United States to avoid the conventional deployment of troops and munitions.'[8] Similarly, it has been observed that 'IW changes the rules. With the appropriate information, it may now be possible to accomplish objectives without the use of force.'[9]

Where information warfare becomes an offensive objective *in and of itself*, the essence of the activity assumed by constitutional provision, and around which debate has developed, is altered. Here, we must address not only the relation between warfare and democracy (e.g., which branch of government should have the final say in these matters) but, more fundamentally, the relation of this form of military activity to the notion of warfare on which thinking in this area had previously focused. Is there so much discontinuity between information warfare, pursued as an end in itself, and conventional forms of warfare that thinking about how it should democratically be controlled must rest on entirely new premises? The crucial difference is that information warfare, thus conceived, can be deemed an application of force (thus warfare), in the sense of an attempt to induce the adversary to act contrary to his will, but it need involve no US casualties, not even adversary casualties, nor meaningful physical damage. Firepower simply is not involved, whereas reliance on firepower, and the corollary prospect of human death and material destruction, are core assumptions of the conception of warfare on which arguments for democratic control have largely been based. The question, then, is whether the relation between information warfare, on one hand, and the postulates of US democracy, on the other hand, should be thought of in entirely different terms? Most obviously, should a freer hand be given the executive branch in this case, given the lesser lethality?

The answer is not necessarily affirmative. The executive branch's ability to use force should be constrained, not only because of the prospect of human and material harm, but also because warfare's *political* consequences may be vast, profoundly affecting the national interest, whereas decisions with very significant implications for the country should, it could be argued, be governed by the principle of checks and balances. It is this *dual* implication of warfare (tangible costs and political consequences), not just the prospect of casualties and destruction, that seems to prompt the architects of democracy to place special limitations on decisions to use military power. Since the international political implications of a resort to information warfare may be as great as those of conventional fighting, it could be argued that democratic controls over war-declaring and war-making should apply either equally to both, or that some arrangement recognizing the special character of information warfare should be devised. In any case, it cannot be asserted that information warfare should be exempted from controls without a full democratic debate on the matter. This debate, in turn, would involve difficult conceptual and practical issues.

If democratic controls should attend war's initiation, then one must recognize that it is hard to define the point at which information warfare has been launched, and, consequently, the point when congressional war-declaring powers, its authority as defined in the War Powers Resolution, or whatever authority it might be granted for the specific case of information warfare, are activated. Clearly, the initiation of such operations is harder to pinpoint than for conventional warfare. With the latter, initiation is usually thought to occur when elements of the nation's armed forces are sent into combat abroad, or deployed in such a fashion that they are very likely to become embroiled in conflict. Thus, the War Powers Resolution states that its provisions apply to 'introduction of United States Armed Forces into hostilities, or into situations where imminent involvement in hostilities is clearly indicated by the circumstances and to the continued use of such forces or in such situation.'

By most reasonable conceptions, and assuming that war is conducted beyond US borders, the congressional role is activated by the physical displacement of armed force with a high probability of combat. But there is no similarly defined threshold at which information warfare can be said to be triggered: largely because of the long and finely grained continuum of activities involved in affecting the informational capabilities of other nations, some of which do not cross the threshold of information warfare. Thus, one might ask whether the introduction of a single, mildly damaging computer virus would amount to information warfare, or at which point psychological operations breach the boundaries of public diplomacy[10] to become such warfare. These thresholds could be defined in a variety of ways, but the criteria would be significantly less straightforward than those associated with conventional warfare. Moreover, the implications of these conundra reach beyond the democratic control of war-initiation to the democratic control of war-making: if there is no agreement on whether the operations amount to warfare, then the unresolved problems extend to both.

Even if agreement could be reached on the general criteria pinpointing the initiation of information warfare, democratic oversight might be thwarted by secrecy surrounding these operations. While it is difficult to conduct conventional military operations with no publicity, it is easier clandestinely to damage an adversary's information processing ability. Thus, two problems coexist: a definitional problem (does some activity amount to information warfare?) and an informational problem (has that activity occurred?). Taken together, these are significant, but not necessarily insurmountable, obstacles to the democratic control of information warfare.

At this point, one might argue that information warfare simply does not amount to military activity, requiring corresponding control and oversight. In the absence of direct physical destruction, and given the disguised forms in which it might occur, it may make more sense to place information warfare under the heading of *covert operations*. Both the fact that the specific activities involved in information warfare as an end in itself would not, as a rule, be publicly acknowledged and identified (although the operations would be recognized by the adversary), and the fact that it would seek to affect the adversary's political will without express physical destruction might qualify such operations as covert subversive or paramilitary operations, rather than warfare. Ambiguity remains, for much of this would be conducted by the Department of Defense (although the intelligence community would play a role), implying that one would have to focus on the nature of the activity, rather than its authorship.

For obvious reasons, democratic control is even more difficult in the case of covert operations than of outright warfare, the former offering US presidents a way to avoid public debate on controversial external activities. While ample national security justifications for covert operations may be provided, in the absence of democratic oversight they are incompatible with open and accountable government. Shielded from the public eye, popular accountability can never be assumed; congressional supervision encounters many obstacles, and even executive control may be impaired.

Congress has never offered comprehensive legislation on covert operations and intelligence activities, but there is a statutory foundation for some forms of oversight. Since the main purpose of the National Security Act of 1947 was to establish the Department of Defense, and only secondarily to establish the Central Intelligence Agency, responsibility for intelligence oversight initially was vested in the armed services committees. During the coldest years of the Cold War, neither committee showed much interest in monitoring or second-guessing the intelligence community. It was only after the U-2 embarrassment and again after the Bay of Pigs fiasco, that Congress, via the Senate Foreign Relations Committee, held meaningful hearings on covert operations. Extensive concern about unfettered covert activities, and the foreign policies with which they could be associated, surfaced in the early 1970s with revelations about the CIA's role in Chilean politics. One product of these revelations was passage of the Hughes-Ryan amendment, requiring that covert operations be reported 'to the appropriate committees of the Congress.'[11] Following the recommendations of the Church and Pike committees, the Select Committee on Intelligence was established in the Senate in 1976 and the following year the Permanent Select Committee on Intelligence was created in the House. Reporting is a foundation of oversight, and Congress explicitly required that the executive branch keep these committees 'fully and currently informed' of covert operations.

Accordingly, a framework for congressional intelligence oversight does exist. While Congress and the executive branch do not always identically interpret the rules, and though the system was devised with conventional forms of covert activity in mind, it provides a foundation on which democratic supervision of information warfare might build. The purpose is to avoid excessive executive autonomy on issues probing the heart of the national interest: an autonomy resulting, in part, from the fact that technology has provided methods of conducting foreign policy for which sufficient accountability is not ensured by the current framework of US democracy. The goal would be to adapt and improve the present institutional and normative structure, recognizing the new circumstances. One challenge is to craft an understanding on the types of activities, under the general rubric of information warfare, for which accountability to Congress must be assured. Another is to devise an appropriate division of responsibility between the armed services committees and the intelligence committees. Yet a third is for Congress to decide, in specific instances, whether there are activities to which it would choose to put a stop – by legislative methods or via the power of the purse.

It must be appreciated that democratic accountability is not the sole objective of adequate oversight; for this is a condition for a stable foreign policy as well. External operations, especially those to which a meaningful cost is attached, cannot be maintained very long without national support. As the House Intelligence Committee observed, the president 'cannot expect sustained support for foreign initiatives, including covert action operations, that are generally unpopular or where a covert action mechanism can be viewed as having been chosen to avoid public debate or a congressional vote on the matter'.[12] Accountability is, therefore, also a way of rooting policy in the wisdom of multiple perspectives and of ensuring that chosen policies are those that stand to be supported and with which the nation can persevere.

THE ISSUE OF PERCEPTION MANAGEMENT

An aspect of information warfare with potentially worrisome implications is that designated by the euphemism 'perception management', which 'refers to operations that exploit an information medium available to a target population ... in order to affect their beliefs and ultimately behavior'.[13] Perception management is similar in intent, but broader in scope, than psychological operations (psy-ops). While the latter is directed at an opponent's willingness to pursue its military objectives, the former may involve the manipulation of the most general national values, perceptions and objectives. Perception management is related to public diplomacy, but it is not the same thing. Public diplomacy amounts to public relations with a foreign policy purpose: it involves bringing the facets of an issue considered beneficial to one's own aims to the other nation's attention, convincing the other of the merits of one's position. It does not, as a rule, involve falsehood and deception, whereas these are important ingredients of perception management: the purpose is to get the other side to believe what one wishes it to believe, *whatever* the truth might be.

Before the information revolution, perception management focused mainly on 'psy-ops' – the methods involved, such as distributing leaflets from aeroplanes or beaming radio broadcasts to the other side, did not allow a more ambitious purpose. While possibilities are limited by the extent to which the adversary has entered the information age, available techniques are now potentially much more effective. If television ownership is at all extensive, many avenues for affecting a society's perceptions, or at least those of its elites, through the manipulation of visual images become available. The extensive use of fax machines provides additional, though more limited, possibilities. A society penetrated by the internet furnishes exceptional opportunities for perception management via the creation of widely accessible websites purveying the desired disinformation; this also implies access to, and the ability to tamper with, the websites of others.[14] At the limit, digital technology opens the possibility of creating wholly concocted images that appear entirely authentic, including images of people engaged in fabricated activities, or speech. As one theorist of information warfare asked:

> Can anyone who saw Tom Hanks conversing with John F. Kennedy in the movie *Forrest Gump* have any doubts that it is technologically possible to produce computer-enhanced or 'morphed' videotape that clearly and conclusively shows adversary leadership violating sacred religious or cultural precepts, in order to destabilize a regime …What will happen to the old saw 'seeing is believing' when the eyes can be so easily fooled?[15]

Perception management raises two concerns. The first is that the tools of perception management might be turned inward, to ensure support for national policy. The assumed context is a dire threat to national security, a threat before which the executive reckons that normal democratic principles, including speaking truth to its people, must yield before the policy objective. The second, more probable, danger is that information distortion targeted abroad becomes, unintentionally but predictably, the information on which Americans form their own opinions: there is no way to mislead foreigners without misleading one's own citizens.

The technology of conveying misinformation and manipulating perceptions that may be applied against an adversary can as easily be used domestically, since 'many of the weapons of information warfare are equally well suited for employment against domestic constituencies'.[16] Despite the overwhelming ethical argument against doing so, a twofold danger looms. The first is that a President, or some segment of the executive, might feel that nothing whatever should be allowed to stand in the way of some national security objectives: if the nation must be misled in certain ways, then so be it. Deceiving the public in pursuit of foreign policy objectives is hardly unknown. For example, it was apparent in the Johnson administration's early reports on the Vietnam War's progress, and in President Nixon's reports on the peace he was crafting.[17] What makes past abuses appear modest compared to future threats is the immense scope of deception made possible by the technology of information warfare. Existing statutory prohibitions against this sort of activity may not provide a sufficient barrier. On the one hand, some of the more egregious abuses of the Nixon presidency[18] suggest that, in exceptional conditions, the chief executive's state of mind may induce utter disdain both for ethical and legal principle. Beyond this eventuality, segments of the governmental bureaucracy may, and have at times, adopted a code of conduct of their own, much at variance with statutory and moral norms. Thus, it was revealed in 1974 that the Central Intelligence Agency, with no presidential authorization and in defiance of prohibitions against this sort of activity by the National Security Act of 1947, had, in the hope of discovering foreign links to anti-war movements, kept intelligence files on some 10,000 Americans.[19] More recently, the Iran-Contra affair gave evidence of willing involvement in illegal activities by a component of the national security apparatus, and of lying to hierarchical superiors by the President's National Security Adviser, Vice Admiral John Poindexter, and by NSC staff member Oliver North. Their activities were counter to the instructions of the secretaries of state and defence; in fact, according to the Tower Commission, 'on one or more occasions Secretary Schultz may have been actively misled by VADM Poindexter'.[20] Claiming the primacy of his policy objective, Poindexter admitted that 'Our objective here all along was to withhold information.'[21] The point is that, when portions of the federal apparatus feel that the claims of policy justify scorning basic tenets of democratic practice, they may do so. Also, it is unlikely but possible that those with ultimate control over the tools of perception management, rather than their wayward subordinates, might direct these instruments against those who fail to support a policy to which they are profoundly committed.

A second danger remains more plausible: deception and misinformation targeted toward enemies also shape the understanding of people at home, leading to indirect manipulation of the thinking and perceptions of one's own citizens (as well as of one's friends and allies). As a practical matter, the issue is unavoidable since it is almost impossible to build firewalls separating the information systems used by friends and enemies. Deception funnelled through websites affects all who may access it, morphed images mould the perceptions of all who see them or to which, directly or indirectly, they may be reported; factual disinformation furnished foreign governments may be picked up by one's own media, and so forth. When perception managements was largely a matter of dropping propaganda leaflets into enemy territory, the threat did not arise, but information technology has made it difficult to deceive enemies without deceiving one's citizens.

These are not remote contingencies. In February 2002, leading newspapers reported, with some concern, that the Department of Defense was considering establishing an Office of Strategic Influence intended to shape foreign public opinion about US military operations. This mission was, *inter alia*, 'to manipulate information and even knowingly dispense false information'.[22] For example, a task might be to plant 'news' items with foreign media organizations in a manner not traceable to the Pentagon. Worries included the danger of blurring the distinction between intelligence operations and public relations, and of impairing the effectiveness of the latter, since organized misinformation might undermine the credibility of government officials.

It was also observed that 'The problem with disinformation is that it has the potential to corrupt the channels of public discourse. Today, as never before, there is a global media network and it is no longer possible to plant a story in a particular foreign outlet and have any assurance at all that it will not feed into the global information stream.'[23] It was recalled that, in the mid-1970s, some CIA programs to plant disinformation abroad had resulted in articles published by the American media.[24]

In the face of much controversy, it was decided not to proceed with the Office. Still, the project suggested that manipulation of foreign opinion, even at the cost of collateral domestic misinformation, was not considered beyond the pale – a problem with a scope proportionate to the effectiveness of available tools of perception management. But a decision to forego an office devoted to that purpose does not imply abandonment of the function itself, and less than a year after the Office of Strategic Influence had been scrapped, it was reported that a new and secret Pentagon directive was being considered, with the aim of manipulating public opinion in friendly and allied countries.[25]

DEFENSIVE INFORMATION WARFARE AND CIVIL LIBERTIES

If the business of conducting offensive information warfare involves questions of democratic principle, the same applies with some variations to its defensive counterpart. Here, the challenge is to protect one's own information systems and infrastructure from hostile attack,[26] raising in turn questions of government power and oversight, of civil liberties and freedom of information. Although tension between national security and democratic imperatives is as old as the Republic, current concerns stem from the pervasiveness and importance of information networks in US society – creating on the one hand, vulnerabilities and on the other hand, broad spheres of life in which government intrusiveness is unwelcome.

The capabilities involved in the Revolution in Military Affairs depend considerably on digital technology and other systems of advanced electronic communication. In addition, the functioning of as large and complex an organization as the Department of Defense, the individual military services, and the intelligence community relies, in manifold ways, on advanced computer systems. Beyond that, the society in which these institutions are imbedded – its industry, financial institutions, transportation, energy distribution, and so forth – depend on the smooth functioning of its information networks. But threats of major magnitude to the nation's information networks are relatively recent, and responses that are both effective and compatible with basic national values, have not yet been devised.

The danger of attack and disruption highlight asymmetries in vulnerability between the United States and most of its potential adversaries. On the one hand, the US ability to disrupt the information networks of other countries, is greater than that which any other country can boast. On the other hand, given its exceptional dependence on information systems and networks, the United States is more vulnerable to information warfare than just about any other nation, and far more so than some of the countries it has come to view as its leading enemies. At the same time, the barriers to entry to information warfare are not very high. If the goal is to implant viruses, worms and logic bombs in another country's systems, a personal computer and modem may suffice, and the ability to create websites and to intervene in the flow of Internet traffic is a basis for perception management. Thus, and far more than with regard to any other form of warfare, profound asymmetries may characterize cyber-war. The threat must be addressed but the implications for democratic principle are profound: the free flow of information is a cornerstone of democracy, as is the right to privacy, but both may collide with attempts to limit vulnerabilities to information warfare.

The vulnerability of information networks was first seriously addressed at the federal level during the Clinton presidency, with the report by President's Commission on Critical Infrastructure Protection (PCCIP). In May 1998, a critical infrastructure protection policy was established, as well as an institutional framework for its implementation. The key institution, here, was to be the National Infrastructure Protection Center (NICP) placed within the Federal Bureau of Investigation, and a Critical Infrastructure Assurance Office (CIAO) to support a National Coordinator for Security Infrastructure Protection and Counterterrorism, located within the National Security Council. On 7 January 2000, the government issued an expanded and updated National Plan for Information Systems Protection. Its main thrust was a call for a partnership between government and the private sector wherein the latter would provide timely information to the government on attacks on private systems, while the latter would provide vulnerability assessments and try to develop systems for attack warnings.

The Homeland Security Act, signed by President Bush on 25 November 2002 and consolidating numerous agencies with domestic security responsibilities into a single Department of Homeland Security, has provided for NICP's and CIAO's absorption into the new body.

While plans to defend against information warfare are a work in progress, issues bearing on the policy's impact on civil liberties have been raised. One involves the compatibility of some of the policy's elements with Fourth Amendment protections of the 'right of the people to be secure in their persons, houses, papers and effects, against unreasonable searches and seizures', the requirement of 'probable cause' and the issuance of a 'warrant' being conditions that must be satisfied before search and seizure can occur. The framers had physical objects in mind when seeking to protect against government search and seizures[27] but here again, technology has forced an expansion of conceptual understanding. With the ability to tap telephone wires and to eavesdrop on conversations with electronic devices, the notion developed that persons and their communications, not just physical areas, should be protected from intrusion by government. Thus, in its 1967 *Katz* v. *United States*[28] decision, the Supreme Court held that the Fourth

Amendment also applies to a person's telephone conversations. Further technological developments, the internet in particular, have expanded the ways in which persons communicate and the ways in which their communications can be monitored by the state. Within the spirit of this broader definition of privacy, the worry is that defensive information warfare will create a disturbing governmental capacity to monitor the electronic communications of its citizens. The Department of Homeland Security provides for the position of Privacy Officer, but privacy guidelines had not been fully developed by the end of 2002.

Other issues concern encryption policy. Encryption is the principal means of protecting the confidentiality of commercial and other electronic communications: by scrambling electronic communication and information, it ensures the privacy of internet traffic. An ability to translate the encrypted text into plain text requires a 'key', i.e., the algorithms behind the code. In order to deny criminals or foreign enemies the ability to shield their internet communications through encryption, President Clinton's PCCIP proposed that government be allowed to ban encryption programs that do not contain the possibility of 'back door' government access in the form of encryption 'keys' deposited with government-approved third parties. An article published in the *Depaul Business Law Journal* worried that this 'could be seen as a cynical effort by the Administration to advance its position on a surveillance issue that has little or nothing to do with infrastructure protection and everything to do with the attempt to preserve wiretapping and computer evidence seizures used in law enforcement investigations unrelated to critical infrastructures'.[29] Ultimately, the government did not press the issue, and legislation sponsored by Rep. Bob Goodlatte (R–Va) and Zoe Lofgren (D–Ca) would prohibit domestic key recovery.

A matter of particular Fourth Amendment concern involves direct surveillance of electronic communication. The PCCIP recommended developing an early warning and response capability, including an ability to monitor the telecommunications infrastructure in real–time to search for anomalies suggestive of attacks and to locate and isolate the electronic signals implicated in the attack. In the summer of 1999, this capability was established in the form of the Federal Intrusion Detection Network (FIDNET), based on intrusion detection software designed to identify suspicious contacts with government computers ('anomalies'), the evidence of which would be directed to the NIPC. Eventually, the system would come to encompass private sector systems, expanding the reach of intrusion-detection to private communications.

By most standards, this would amount to a capacity, housed in the FBI, to monitor private communication, with implications for constitutional protections of privacy. In one view, the plan 'goes further than ever before toward the automated collection of private information without any due process: robotic rights violation'.[30] The government has argued that FIDNET would be consistent with privacy laws such as, for instance, outlined in the Electronic Communications Privacy Act of 1986. The complaint, even if that were the case, is that current law is so out of step with technological developments as to fall short of Fourth Amendment standards.[31] At the moment, and in the face of significant criticism, the FIDNET initiative appears to have been suspended.

Similarly, the FBI has developed a wiretapping system, the Carnivore system, focused on e-mail traffic and whose purpose is to track a criminal suspect's e-mails among the flood of other communications passing through an Internet service provider. But there is concern that this may involve trawling through e-mails of ordinary citizens to identify those that are targets of an investigation. The FBI has responded that it selects messages to be tracked on the basis of narrow guidelines specified in a court order (e.g., messages between particular parties), not broad criteria. In November 2000, the Department of Justice undertook a review of the Carnivore system, concluding that it did not pose a Fourth Amendment threat.[32] However, the independence of the review panel has been questioned, as have the boundaries of its charge. In any case, critics observe that the system *could* intercept virtually every e-mail communication.

The terrorist attacks of 11 September 2001 have predictably further stoked fears of cyber-attacks against the United States, as the barriers to entry for information warfare may be lower from a terrorists perspective than for some of the more conventional forms of warfare.[33] An early response by the Bush Administration was to encourage adoption by Congress of a new anti-terrorism law, referred to as the USA Patriot Act (USAPA), signed into law by the President on 26 October 2001. A number of its sections concern electronic communications, amending the ECPA.

Previously, under the ECPA and with a warrant showing probable cause, the government could seize from a service provider e-mail no older than 180 days. If older than 180 days, seizure could be on the basis of a subpoena (not requiring judicial review) bearing on an administrative or criminal matter. One USAPA provision allows internet service providers (ISPs) and other system operators to disclose private communications of their users if the system operator feels that s/he has encountered a situation involving imminent danger of death or serious injury. Further, the Act (Section 210) expands the scope of the subscriber and user records the government can seize via subpoena (thus without judicial review). One controversial section expands pen/trap surveillance to the area of electronic communication. A 'pen register' provides the number dialled from a subject's telephone, a 'trap and trace' furnishes incoming numbers to that phone. This information may be used in criminal investigations when there are insufficient grounds for a full wiretap, and pen/trap orders are issued when law enforcement shows that they are *relevant* to an ongoing investigation – a standard for lower than probable cause, or even than the standard of 'reasonable grounds'. USAPA's Section 216 extends the provision of pen/trap orders to cover internet communications – a very significant expansion of this surveillance authority given the considerable and growing scope of e-mail, peer-to-peer communication, and net-surfing.[34]

Legislation designed to expand the Patriot Act may further affect civil liberties. A new cyber-security bill taken up by the House in 2002 (HR 3482) relaxes the provisions of the Patriot Act, allowing ISP providers to reveal private communications when there is, in their opinion, *some* danger of death or serious injury: a much looser requirement than the previously specified requirement of *imminent* danger. It also allows the release of such information, not only to law enforcement authorities, but to any governmental entity, further extending the scope for government surveillance conducted with no judicial oversight.[35]

A particularly ambitious post-11 September project with regard to electronic data-mining is the Total Information Awareness (TIA) effort – a project of the Defense Advanced Research Projects Agency (DARPA) and with a reach beyond that of the Carnivore program. TIA's purpose is to detect terrorists by massively scanning information in internet mail and in the commercial databases of health, financial and travel companies. The US Senate, troubled by what one Republican Senator described as 'the most far-reaching government surveillance proposal we have ever heard about', voted in January 2003 to bar deployment of the project pending Congressional legislation specifically permitting its use.[36]

Protection of privacy from excessive government intrusion is a cornerstone of any democratic order. Although there is little evidence that there have been serious invasions of privacy connected to defensive information warfare, the requisite capacity has been developed.

CONCLUSIONS

The specific norms around which a democratic order is established must occasionally be revisited if its foundational principles are to be maintained under changing circumstances. Among these circumstances is the development of technologies on which the functioning of a society depends, that enhance a government's ability to pursue civilian and military goals and that, at the same time, make a country vulnerable to previously unknown forms of external assault. New pressures on democracy emerge in the process, some of which are illustrated by the implications of the capabilities and policies connected to information technology as it applies to information warfare.

Grounds for concern appear firmest regarding: (a) the operation of checks and balances in decisions to engage in information warfare; (b) the ability of the public (and of those who inform democratic opinion) to obtain an accurate enough view of information warfare operations and their consequences to hold their government properly accountable; and, (c) the implications of the intrusiveness associated with defensive information warfare for certain civil liberties.

If there is cause for worry, this is not because democracy has actually been undermined but because it is possible to conceive of ways in which it could be. The purpose of this essay was to identify such possibilities, an awareness that makes it easier to anticipate problems and devise solutions.

The forms information warfare can assume raise the question of whether the activity is sufficiently similar to conventional warfare to be covered by the democratic controls specified in the US Constitution. If the scope of IW's political implications lead to an affirmative answer, then it is necessary to think of effective ways of applying these controls. If the answer is negative, then standards of control compatible with this new variant of warfare must be considered.

The implications of perception management are troubling. That this could be directed at a domestic audience appears implausible, but given the record of certain presidential administrations, not entirely farfetched. Even if the deception is targeted at a foreign audience, it remains very difficult to mislead foreigners without also misleading one's own citizens. At a minimum, it is necessary to create democratically acceptable rules governing the circumstances, if any, under which this could be done, as well as a system of effective oversight ensuring that the rules are not violated by those who would place policy goals too far above norms of democratic governance.

How much of a threat to privacy springs from defensive information warfare is hard to gauge – but the potential for damage does exist, especially since the fervour over security following the September 11 events has led, in the opinion of some, to a somewhat cavalier governmental stance toward civil liberties.[37] Friction between individual rights and national security is not unknown, in this and other democracies, and the excesses which bellicose emotion can produce are frequently viewed with remorse in hindsight. Nevertheless, as suggested by the implications for defensive information warfare drawn in the Patriot Act, the terrorist attacks may have increased the vulnerability of some core tenets of civil liberty to the claims of security. In any case, an objective awareness of the dangers and a democratic dialogue on the acceptable terms of the security-civil liberties trade-off is necessary.

NOTES

1. This is the theme of Edward Wenk, Jr's intriguing book *The Double Helix: Technology and Democracy in the American Future* (Stamford Ct.: Ablex, 1999).
2. Many of these issues are discussed in John Arquilla and David Ronfeldt (eds), *In Athena's Camp: Preparing for Conflict in the Information Age* (Santa Monica, CA: RAND, 1997).
3. See, for example, 'Bush Orders Guidelines for Cyber-Warfare', *Washington Post*, 7 February 2003.
4. Gaillard Hunt (ed.), *The Writings of James Madison: Including his Public Papers and Private Correspondence* (New York: Putnam's, 1900), pp.312.
5. Louis Fisher, 'Historical Survey of the War Powers and the Use of Force', in Gary M. Stern and Morton H. Halperin (eds), *The US Constitution and the Power to Go to War* (Westport Ct.: Greenwood Press, 1994), p.11.
6. In Jacob E. Cook (ed.), *The Federalist* (Middletown Ct: Wesleyan University Press, 1961), p.166.
7. *Fleming v. Page*, 9 Howard 601 (1850).
8. Bernard C. Lewis, *Information Warfare*. <http://www.fas.org/irp/eprint/snyder/inforwar>.
9. Keith D. Anthony, 'Information Warfare: Good News and Bad News', *Military Intelligence Professional Bulletin*. <http://www.fas.org/irp/agency/army/tradoc/usaic/mipb/1997>.
10. Public diplomacy implies an attempt to affect public opinion within the target nation. There is no necessary assumption that it is conducted in the public eye.
11. These were initially the Appropriations, Armed Services and, when they were established, the two intelligence committees.
12. House Permanent Select Committee on Intelligence, *Intelligence Authorization Act, Fiscal 1987*, H.Rept. 99–690, part 1, 99th Congress, 2d Session, 1986, 7.

13. Dorothy E. Denning, *Information Warfare and Security* (Boston: Addison-Wesley, 1999), p.34.
14. See Denning, *Information Warfare and Security*, pp.101–12.
15. Dan Kuehl, 'The Ethics of Information Warfare and Statecraft', www.infowar.com/mil_c4/mil_c4ij.html-SSI
16. Richard Szafranski, 'A Theory of Information Warfare: Preparing for 2020', *Airpower Journal* (Spring 1995).
17. See, for example, Larry Berman, *No Peace, No Honor: Nixon, Kissinger, and Betrayal in Vietnam* (New York: The Free Press, 2001).
18. Much of this is detailed in Anthony Summers, *The Arrogance of Power: The Secret World of Richard Nixon* (New York: Viking, 2000).
19. Seymour M. Hersh, 'Huge CIA Operations Reported in US Against Antiwar Forces, Other Dissidents, in Nixon Years', *New York Times*, 22 Dec. 1974.
20. S. Res. 21, 94th Congress. 1st session, 1975.
21. House Select Committee, *Iran-Contra Affair*, Report, p.123.
22. 'Defense Department Divided Over Propaganda Plan', *New York Times*, 20 Feb. 2002.
23. 'New Defense Office Won't Mislead, Officials Say', *New York Times*, 21 Feb. 2002.
24. 'Pentagon Readies Effort to Swing Sentiment Abroad', *New York Times*, 19 Feb. 2002.
25. 'Pentagon Debates Propaganda Push in Allied Nations', *New York Times*, 16 Dec. 2002.
26. A good overview is provided in David. S. Alberts, *Defensive Information Warfare* (Washington DC: National Defense University Press, 1996).
27. J.W. Peltason, *Understanding the Constitution* (seventh edn) (Hinsdale, Ill.: 1976), p.145–50.
28. *Katz v. United States*, 389 US 347 (1969).
29. Michael J. O'Neil and James X. Dempsey, 'Critical Infrastructure Protection: Threats to Privacy and Other Civil Liberties and Concerns With Government Mandates on Industry', *Depaul Business Law Journal*, Vol. 12 (1999/2000), p.103.
30. Don Lobo Tiggre, 'FIDNET: Another Step Closer to Orwell's Nightmare' *Laissez Faire City Times*, 23 Aug. 1999.
31. O'Neil and Dempsey, 'Critical Infrastructure Protection', p.105.
32. *Wall Street Journal* Online, 'DOJ Review Clears Carnivore', 20 Nov. 2000.
33. See, for example, Yael Shaharm 'Information Warfare: the Perfect Terrorist Weapon' <http://www.ict.org.il/artcles/infowar>.
34. For critical discussions of the Fourth Amendment implications of USAPA, see Electronic Frontier Foundation, 'EFF Analysis of the Provisions of the USA Patriot Act That Relate to Online Activities', Center for Democracy and Technology, 'Summary Analysis of Key Sections of the USA Patriot Act of 2001', and Center for Constitutional Rights, 'The USA Patriot Act'.
35. See Center for Democracy and Technology, *Policy Post*, Vol. 8, No. 3 (25 Feb. 2002).
36. 'Senate Rejects Pentagon Plan to Mine Citizens' Personal Data for Clues to Terrorism', *New York Times*, 24 Jan. 2003.
37. See, for example, the report by The Center for Constitutional Rights entitled *The State of Civil Liberties One Year Later*. <http://www.ccr-ny.org>, Sept. 2002.

Information Warfare and Domestic Threats to American Security

PATRICK M. MORGAN

INTRODUCTION

This essay looks at the other side of war in the information age, the domestic security threats arising from both the advance of surveillance technology and its application against terrorism. The argument is that, like many other kinds of disasters, a marked deterioration in the freedom of citizens and organizations can come not from a particular disturbing development so much as from an unanticipated blend of several such developments, and that many of the elements for a serious erosion of domestic security in this way are in place or on the horizon. What might occur is explored through the use of analogies, as are potential remedies.

THE SITUATION

Warfare is now influenced by the information age in numerous ways. Cyberwar is about dealing with old threats in new ways and new (cyberwar-related) threats in new ways. To begin with, improvements in information technology are now used to fight more effectively with existing military instruments. Thus soldiers now use information from satellites or surveillance aircraft to attack enemy units in the usual ways. Then there is the use of new weapons born of the information age, or new generations of old weapons enhanced through information-age improvements: everything from viruses that attack the other side's information and communications systems to Boeing kits that turn dumb bombs into precision guided munitions. Finally, there are capabilities devised to help fend off enemy efforts to disrupt or destroy one's own information-age systems, military and non-military – a threat posed with either traditional or information-age weapons – someone may disrupt your satellite communications by bombing the down links or target the crucial computer systems with a virus.

All this has to do with an external enemy – national security as threatened by *outsiders*. American concern about these traditional security implications of the information revolution has rapidly expanded recently. Many implications of the new technology are very positive militarily. The information revolution has enhanced American military power in many ways that have received intense study within the framework of the 'Revolution in Military Affairs' (RMA).[1] However, other implications are quite disturbing. For instance, there are the threats when others who are hostile acquire some or all of the same military enhancements. Also, the information revolution makes a society and its government vulnerable to attack in new ways. We now see analyses of the vulnerability to terrorism of the nation's money supply which consists mostly of computer symbols; of how transportation and energy systems could be disrupted by attacks on their computers and communications; or how a nation increasingly dependent on space-based systems could suffer a 'space' or 'electronic' Pearl Harbor.[2] Strictly speaking, none of this is new. Americans have lived for decades with technological enhancements that vastly expand our military capabilities but provide actual or potential improvements in others' military capabilities, and have long had to adapt to how technologically induced changes in how we live and work make the US newly vulnerable. After all, that is what the nuclear revolution and ballistic missiles was all about, or how all modern societies now worry about disruptions in the world flow of oil.

A secondary concern now is that the same harm enemies abroad might inflict because of the new vulnerabilities can also be inflicted by domestic enemies – hackers, thieves and other criminals, domestic terrorists. Another relevant concern, getting much attention but not in connection with cyberwar, is not about being attacked. It is about being observed and, on that basis, potentially controlled, manipulated or repressed. The information age has already produced a major escalation in actual and potential monitoring of Americans by the national government, state and local governments, criminals, and economic or other entities that market and/or deliver goods and services. This is only occasionally considered a national security matter and not regularly listed under cyberwar or war in the information age.

It should be. We need a suitable appreciation of the links between these threats. To correct this requires reviving and updating an old tradition in American history of regarding balefully all advances in the power of the state, no matter how benign the intent. Traditional fears of an intrusive state, and parallel private power, still flourish but they have been only slowly adapting to better fit the information age. Such fears also invite the application of a traditional practice in discussions of security affairs. For years I have wanted to try my hand at a worst-case analysis, the pernicious stock in trade of many a security specialist but sometimes quite appropriate. This paper offers a worst-case analysis of the domestic security implications of a series of recent developments – technological, political and economic.

SOME GENERAL CONNECTIONS

To start with it has long been held acceptable that the government go further in encroaching on civil liberties in national security, terrorism and related matters, including the rights of foreigners, than in dealing with domestic crime, and the government has rarely held back on its own. Congress has found it difficult to decide whether this should be changed and the courts have not challenged it.

By extension, the oldest and best appreciated link between war and domestic threats to civil and human rights is that, beginning with the Civil War, national security crises, particularly wartime emergencies, always erode domestic constraints on the state. Its power *vis-à-vis* society and individuals increases. In national emergencies this is usually granted legislative approval when sought, though often the executive does not want outright approval and proceeds on its own, partly to avoid having to compromise or face delays but particularly to reassert the primacy of national security and the state's special power and authority on security matters. The increase in state power is typically upheld by the courts, particularly when there is legislative approval. Security trumps rights. This is almost always popular as well. In general, people approve of shrinking the rights of Americans or foreigners who deliberately endanger national and citizen safety.

The expansion of state power comes in removing constraints on pre-existing capabilities and through creation of new powers and capabilities. An excellent example of both has been in the Bush Administration's reaction at home to the 11 September attacks and the war on terrorism. There is always a strong response from civil liberties advocates. The usual compromise between expanded state power in a national security crisis and objections to its civil liberties encroachments has normally been to handle the conflict sequentially – first the expansion to get the crisis handled, then trimming back that expansion once the crisis has passed.

Less attention has been paid recently to an older, certainly more traditional, American view linking external threats and citizen liberties. Prior to independence, Americans were already suggesting that serious involvement in international politics would promote the state's power *vis-à-vis* the society and the citizens, a concern that did much to shape the nation's early development. One justification for American 'non-involvement' in the issues and fissures of international politics was that this would contain the power of the government. In that way the US could avoid a large standing army, intelligence activities, many national controls over economic activity, and other standard tools for dealing with foreign threats which enhanced the power of government. From this perspective it was better to defend the nation with a militia, letting citizens 'keep and bear arms' to make that feasible.

We should revisit this perspective with respect to information warfare and related capabilities. It is not a matter of slashing American involvement in international security management and its associated burdens, but of developing a constant sensitivity to how such an involvement inevitably expands government capabilities in ways that are bound to be uncomfortable. Designers of national security policies should consider more carefully how those policies and the necessary capabilities will adversely affect domestic liberties, and make an effort to contain those effects – if necessary, by redesigning the policies.

There are ways in which the problem is potentially much greater than before. Adopting new ways to cope with external threats needs to be done with much more care about the domestic after-effects because some distinctive conditions now can make the problem more serious. It is not any one development that has done this, it is the synergy among a series of developments.

TECHNOLOGICAL CONSIDERATIONS

I need not say much about the relevant shifts in technology – the information age hardly arrived silently. In standard national security affairs its impact has been primarily evident in the RMA. Three clusters of change dominate the RMA and the domestic implications of the information age. The first is shifts in *surveillance*. Our ability to find people or things, then track them if they move is growing prodigiously and this will continue. Of greatest value here is the ability to directly observe the other side in doing this, but it extends to indirectly observing and tracking as well.

The second is changes in *information processing and communication*. We have become much better at processing vast amounts of information, in particular for getting information from surveillance to those who need it. Processing is no good unless the information can be communicated effectively for taking action, so an associated explosion in communications and information processing – including more effective presentation methods – is an important development.

The third is the emergence of ever better ways to 'hit' the target – to do something to it if and when you want to. In military operations that 'something' could be to destroy or neutralize it. In counterterrorist operations it might be to arrest the target. For intelligence operations the goal could be to disrupt or manipulate it. Or the goal might be just to better prepare for what is coming by knowing what the target is up to, much like how surveillance, information processing, and communications help when it comes to dangerous storms we can't do anything to stop.

This is quite clear with regard to many aspects of cyberwar and other elements of the RMA. But these technological changes apply equally well to the domestic scene. The rising ability to find and track people and things is equally apparent; often it uses the same, or even more advanced, sorts of technology. It is steadily expanding, considered worth doing because of our growing ability to turn information into something useful. Finally, everyone – from the police to telephone salespeople to advertisers – is getting better in reaching whoever and whatever can be tracked – to arrest, rescue, sell, convert, scam. There is good reason for concern.

Spelling out the exact nature of the concern is important. The tendency is to see the problem as stemming from our ability to gather and utilize ever more information, that this can only lead to greater control over each of us. But that is only partly true. The constant improvement in surveillance capabilities is *unavoidable*. And in many ways it contributes greater security, more freedom of action. This is why we often readily trade information about ourselves for a variety of important services – financial, communications, health, educational, employment, welfare, etc. Expanded detection and tracking can be endlessly beneficial – from finding lost or stolen children to reaching emergency personnel quickly about a disaster. The problem is not technological change *per se*.

What is worrisome is the potential for *misuse* or *abuse*. But to describe the problem this way doesn't get us far either; after all, what else is new? The threat of abuse or misuse is normal. We expect information to be improperly used sometimes for all sorts of reasons and purposes and we live with that. Unusual concern, or even alarm, is called for only if the abuse or misuse is rising, or the capacity for it is rising steeply now and will continue to do so in the future, or if the consequences will be much greater, or our ability to control or correct that has declined or will decline greatly.

This is how to understand the problem. In our era surging technological improvements can readily be used to diminish and compromise the liberty of citizens and groups. The overall capabilities of the state, at all levels, to gather information about and exercise greater control over citizens are growing; the same is true for various private-sector actors. This heightens a broad and growing threat to privacy that is inherent in the technologies and enlarges the possible scope of harassment and control. An analogy to what is taking place is the set of state capabilities installed and exploited in the Soviet Union, and widely imitated elsewhere, to produce a *surveillance-dominated society*. People acted as sensors, employed to track who came and went from apartment buildings and apartments, who checked into or visited hotels and hotel rooms, who visited public buildings, who talked with foreigners or others not in the good graces of the authorities. All citizens carried an internal passport which was required to move about the country or change one's residence and was used to prevent much of the population from moving anywhere. Informers filled police files on the political and behavioural reliability of nearly everyone. Profiling was widespread: people with 'unreliable' backgrounds, behaviour or associations were especially suspect – files detailed their relatives, class background, past occupations, former political and other activities. All printing items, even typewriters were licensed and their distribution noted, along with the distribution of paper and other media materials. There were efforts to record what people listened to on the radio. Mail was opened, hotel rooms bugged, phones often tapped. All this took place without today's technological resources.

Capabilities for carrying on all of these ways of monitoring people are steadily building in the US and other advanced societies. The accumulation of information about people from myriads of sources, the build-up of resources for locating and tracking them at almost any time in almost any place, the monitoring of what people read or watch is all quite impressive. One difference is that the work is now being done for the most part by advanced technology. The other is the way in which these capabilities are being used.

However, as noted above, we must be concerned only if the threat of abuse or misuse is rising or soon will be or our ability to control it is about to or will sharply decline. What would make these things true? While it is hard to be certain, here are several developments of special concern. The *first* is the desire to develop advanced forms of war in the information age now driving the American armed forces, an approach that emphasizes disrupting a society and its forces by paralysing its information systems. This leads to heightened concern about what others will be able to do along the same lines, and a desire to control or restrict that threat by monitoring and interdicting elements of it inside the country. Together they foster huge capacities that could readily be turned to monitoring Americans on an unprecedented scale. This development is partly secret given its roots in threats to national security, and that is almost an invitation for abuse. It is reinforced by private sector demands for the same technologies and private sector responses to them, which also invite abuse and misuse.

A plausible analogy is our experience with development of a regular peacetime intelligence capability, which began with the National Security Act in 1947. There was apprehension that this would pose civil liberties threats but Pearl Harbor and the new responsibilities the nation was embracing abroad led to brushing those concerns aside. The CIA was followed by numerous other agencies and the growth of intelligence responsibilities and activities in traditional agencies like the FBI and the State Department. This new government capability was eventually abused and misused.[3] Intelligence resources allowed several presidents to conduct foreign policy activities that violated the law or disregarded known or probable preferences of Congress or the public. This included covert actions of later ill repute which the intelligence community had no obligation to report, much less secure approval for, from the Congress or any regulatory agency.

In domestic affairs several presidents used the CIA to spy on groups and secure information about political figures, ignoring the ban on this in the National Security Act. The CIA's CHAOS program compiled files on some 7,200 citizens and a computerized index of more than 300,000 people and organizations. Other programs developed files on 57,000 more citizens and indexes covering another 115,000. The CIA also wiretapped or conducted other surveillance on reporters between 1959 and 1972 in trying to trace leaks. The FBI illegally broke into offices of organizations over 230 times in 1942–1968. It illegally wiretapped citizens. Its COINTELPRO program tried to disrupt or denigrate many organizations and individuals, often drawing on file materials gathered by surveillance – legal and illegal – of thousands of Americans.

The army anticipated having to enforce martial law during the Vietnam War and therefore developed files on 'radicals' and others who might pose trouble, presumably to be watched or incarcerated if necessary. Since trouble might have developed anywhere the files covered people everywhere – reportedly over 200,000 individuals. Elements of the files were gathered from and in turn shared with state and local law enforcement organizations.

The National Security Agency illegally tapped international phone calls and cables (something started well before the Second World War) for information on narcotics activities, terrorism, and anti-Vietnam War protests. It maintained watch lists on about 1,650 Americans on request from other government agencies. The CIA and FBI illegally opened mail for years. The CIA opened as many as 13,000 a year between 1952 and 1973 (some 215,000 in all), including the mail of prominent officials, national leaders, and distinguished people in various walks of life. Ex–CIA personnel were used to break into offices by the White House, and the CIA infiltrated domestic groups in Washington in the late 1960s to detect plans to damage the agency or other government facilities. The agency also illegally obtained tax returns. Both the CIA and FBI provided secret information about citizens to presidents solely for political purposes – information on reporters, critics, opponents of particular policies, members of Congress.

There are parallels in this to recent developments of particular interest. The government capability involved was developed to help deal with foreign threats and then turned to domestic use. In several instances the illegal domestic activities were a response to a belief that the domestic targets had links to foreign governments. And at least part of the illegal activity was undertaken as an extension of US involvement in a war, when concern about national security is naturally at a very high level and the constraints on the state are eroded or circumvented.

The *second* matter of special concern these days is the proliferation of types of threats that tend to erase the foreign–domestic division. What causes this is fear of the equivalent of a fifth column; a threat arises abroad but seems to have a very substantial domestic component so one part cannot be met without getting into the other, which is what drove a good deal of the intelligence community activity recounted above. The threat posed by drug imports into the US by organized gangs/cartels is a good example. So are contemporary kinds of fraud and money laundering, and some illegal immigration. These types of threats are an extension of globalization – they will continue to proliferate and should grow in scale.

Why is this foreign–domestic entanglement significant? For one thing, US political and legal systems treat foreign security threats differently in terms of what it is permissible to do to defeat them. Foreigners, including resident foreigners, do not enjoy the same protections as citizens. The government can carry surveillance further, in more intrusive ways, to deal with potential crimes. It faces a much lower burden of proof that surveillance is necessary and can conduct the surveillance longer without displaying evidence of success. When the foreign and domestic are entangled there is an obvious temptation to treat those involved in the domestic component in the same fashion as the foreigners – either by securing legal authority for this or engaging in illegal activity to trace the foreign threat's domestic resources and impact. And foreign involvement makes it possible to sharply increase the search for domestic evidence, which can sweep many more citizens into surveillance. The foreign threat and the domestic activity have a reciprocal reinforcement effect on surveillance.

Officials may also either believe or cynically suggest that their opponents have foreign backing and a foreign connection. This is very common in other political systems and has put in appearances in the US. Finding foreign links to domestic opponents of the president that could be politically exploited was probably the chief rationale for orders to spy on them during the Vietnam War.

Meanwhile the proliferation of threats that erase the foreign–domestic distinction has been a staple in studies of the threats posed by international crime. It has been obvious in the drug trade and its associated money laundering but extends to many other areas: flows of goods and people into the US illegally, illegal international arms transfers, etc. The War on Terrorism simply drives this even harder.

Terrorism is now a foreign-based threat and that can have a significant domestic presence. This is exactly the sort of threat that, if sustained for a long period, promotes a steady expansion of domestic monitoring of citizens and non-citizens alike. Profiling is likely to play a major role in this sort of monitoring.

Which brings us to the *third* element that now should provoke special concern. The War on Terrorism is almost certain to be a long-standing national emergency[4] of the sort which typically brings a sharp increase in state (and sometimes private) encroachments on citizen liberties. This has already begun to happen. Intelligence and surveillance are standard tools of warfare; expanding both domestically is a logical extension of the war on terrorism. Suppose that the US suffers another major terrorist attack, on the scale of 11 September or greater, or a string of significant terrorist attacks linked to al-Qaeda. To anticipate some of the results we can reflect on reactions of the federal government to the 11 September disaster.

Prior to the disaster the government had been concerned for a decade about possible terrorist attacks and steadily boosting its authority for greater surveillance to deal with the threat. Quite separately, new laws and regulation were steadily expanding the information collected on segments of society for purposes of improving health care, monitoring immigrants, tracking treatment of workers, etc. Under the Federal Wiretap Act of 1968 and the Foreign Intelligence Surveillance Act of 1978, wiretapping was widely practised on the basis of warrants from judges, while outside the country intelligence agencies were entitled (under US law) to engage in types of surveillance that would have been illegal in the US. (In 2000 the government secured 1,190 wiretaps – a figure that had risen sharply since 1996; under the FISA there were over 1,000 other wiretaps approved.)[5] The Clinton Administration moved to expand that authority and tried to keep new technology wiretap-friendly, to exempt cybersecurity activities from the Freedom of Information Act, and to develop a Federal Intrusion Detection Network for expanded internet monitoring.[6]

The Cyber Security Enhancement Act of 2001, introduced before 11 September, proposed that electronic communication providers be enabled to disclose information about their clients and customers to *any government entity* with no prerequisite required in terms of an impending threat. There was provision for emergency wiretapping of electronic communications without a court order as well.[7]

In June 2002 the Attorney General announced new guidelines for the FBI in domestic operations that allow much greater internet scanning for all investigations, not just those on terrorism, reversing rules put in place after the earlier scandals in the intelligence community. This includes the use of preliminary investigations even without an indication of criminal activity. The FBI can also tap commercial profiling and data mining companies for services in profiling people even though there is no related investigation. It can do far more to monitor groups, including checking on mosques and other religious institutions.[8]

The new guidelines were an extension and implementation of provisions of the USA Patriot Act. Those provisions are now being cited by police departments to allow them much greater leeway in conducting surveillance as well. In the 1970s and early 1980s evidence of illegal or questionable surveillance by police let to numerous laws, regulations, consent decrees, and the like in New York, Chicago, Seattle, Los Angeles, San Francisco and other cities imposing restrictions on local police surveillance without evidence of a crime or criminal activity. The police are now going to court or pursuing other avenues to remove these restraints, citing the need, for instance, to be able to infiltrate mosques.[9]

After 11 September the government broadened its powers to tap phones and plant listening devices – making it easier to justify use of these methods, relaxing the reporting requirements, lengthening the time allowed for any particular effort, broadening the range of activities permitted under any warrant for this surveillance, and weakening limitations on hearing and retaining information gathered by such activities that has no connection with the matter for which judicial permission was granted. The government has expanded its ability to do surveillance via the internet in investigations of peoples' past internet communications and secret monitoring of their current ones. It has enlarged its ability to secure financial records, student records, and records on visitors and immigrants. It has expanded its right to seize records on personal computers.

For instance the Justice Department, with regard to the Foreign Intelligence Surveillance Act, moved under the post-11 September USA Patriotism Act and other legislative changes to:

- reduce restrictions on who could be subject to surveillance, so that it could cover persons not previously known to be affiliated with any (possibly) terrorist group or foreign power;

- remove requirements that agencies which monitor communications must specify the locations of the systems to be tapped – to deal with cell phones and to permit roving wiretaps with neither the location nor the persons to be wiretapped specified;
- remove requirements that probable cause to believe that a person is engaged in illegal activity be shown for permissions for surveillance;
- gain access to large data bases about foreigners that also contain information about myriads of Americans;
- secure approval for the FBI to compel disclosure of almost any information if it is described as part of an intelligence or terrorism investigation – medical records, educational records, library records, etc.;
- extend the lower standards in foreign intelligence wiretaps and secret searches to domestic investigations – overriding federal and state privacy statutes to gain access to wireless phone location information as a way to track the movement of individuals;
- expand the use of pen registers (that detect phone numbers dialled) and trap and trace capabilities (which detect phone numbers of incoming calls) in wiretaps;
- extend the time an initial surveillance can be conducted before it must be approved by a court;
- extend the time surveillance can be continued until renewed by a court;
- permit lists of groups supposedly engaged in terrorism to be the basis for seizures of assets, deportations, denial of admission to the country;
- treat support of groups supposedly engaged in terrorism as illegal even if it occurred before the groups were identified as terrorist-linked;
- arrest and hold people indefinitely for investigations of threats to national security.[10]

Since then a number of other steps have been taken. Shortly after the 11 September attack the FBI moved to make its material from secret wiretaps under the Foreign Intelligence Surveillance Act much more widely available to agents throughout the bureau so they can better pursue leads on domestic terrorists.[11] Previously such information had been carefully segregated since it cannot normally be used in prosecutions and its wide distribution could compromise intelligence operations. By November 1991 the FBI moved to enlarge its surveillance authorization under the FISA.[12] Since then the FBI has also undertaken to make its surveillance information and secret grand jury testimony available to the CIA in the interests of better interagency coordination on terrorism threats.[13]

Also to deal with the War on Terrorism the FBI Carnivore system, which had been under attack, has been revived. This system can be imposed on an internet provider to gain access to all e-mails the provider handles, using pre-programmed indicators to select e-mails to read. Key logging programs (a sniffer keystroke logger) – the so called 'Magic Lantern'– record every keystroke allowing detection of passwords to encrypted materials. This can be combined with tapping phone calls made over the internet.[14]

In addition the government arrested over 2,000 people for investigations into their possible terrorist connections with nearly all normal safeguards for prisoners suspended, including private conversations with counsel. These people often had no access to counsel and their relatives had no right to see them. There was no application of normal time limits on when they must be charged or released. The government was not required to admit who it is holding or to specify its charges or suspicions.

Federal, state and local authorities have been vigorously investigating new surveillance technologies, often secretly, such as comparing faces filmed or on live cameras with criminals or illegal immigrants or suspects via mass screenings (in airports, for example, and government buildings). This is part of a surge in the use of biometrics technologies to identify people by retinal scans, fingerprints, facial scans, hand geometry, voice verification, and even signature analysis.[15] Facial screening is now being tried in some airports and by police in various cities, as well as in casinos and in the preparation of drivers' licences. There is a huge flurry of interest in this technology in the private sector as well. It all stems from the effort to develop such a technology that started in DOD in 1993 – the Face Recognition Technology Program[16] and some of the firms involved now have large contracts with DOD and the intelligence community. The technology is widely criticized as ineffectual but it is in a very early stage of development. Most importantly, it requires building a large database of photos for comparison with the images.

We can anticipate marked extensions of video surveillance. There are now more than 2 million surveillance cameras in the US, most producing crude images and recording on film, and use of the cameras is exploding. Coming are cameras that produce far better images linked to police or other agencies to allow real-time monitoring (and intervention/reaction). Very sophisticated video equipment is already being used for research on shoppers – cameras detect every minor reaction to displays, packaging, etc.[17]

However, in addition to providing local surveillance or being part of a broader surveillance net, many of the video systems in stores, 'nanny-cams' in homes, and similar items produce signals that can readily be picked up and amplified by people cruising the area. This can produce a new version of the peeping Tom, and offers ways for outsiders to case stores or homes for possible break-ins. Many wireless computer networks can be tapped by people driving by with suitable aerials and electronic sniffers – one popular antenna is a Pringles potato chip can! – allowing access to sensitive data from, for example, hospitals.[18]

In a related move, government agencies are vigorously exploring ways to merge separate collections about Americans and foreigners into much larger databases and then make the information available to numerous parties. This makes much of what is known about any individual or group public property. The private sector began doing this some time ago when data bases on people began to be bought, sold, and merged into larger collections for commercial purposes. Drivers' licence information is already widely sold, as are public records on property deeds, court records, unlisted phone numbers, etc. 'College students, who often have free access to the Lexis-Nexis database, are using it to see if their dates' claims of age and marital status check out. Sales agents look for bankruptcies and tax liens in their customers' pasts.'[19]

The Defense Department's Total Information Awareness project is attempting to link many of these sorts of surveillance – airport surveillance cameras, phone records, credit card transactions, airline reservation data, etc. – to permit computer sifting of the data to look for suspicious patterns of activity. It would make use of new programs to facilitate software collaboration and the new Extended Markup Language which translates numerous isolated data bases into a universal form so the information they contain can be widely shared. The civil liberties implications are disturbing enough that even the director of the project has suggested that it should be operated by and independent non-government organization.[20]

The Patriot Act has requires that the Treasury Department make security firms, banks, etc. go much further than they already were in efforts to detect and report suspicious financial transactions or transaction patterns. The firms do this through powerful computerized search systems that process millions of transactions daily.[21]

Another effect of 11 September is that a national identity card is now on the agenda as a supposedly important weapon against foreign terrorists.[22] Companies and officials are campaigning vigorously for a national identity card and for Congressional action to ensure that the cards, when issued by state and local authorities, or other common means of identification such as drivers' licences, conform to national standards on how the holders are initially identified or on the kinds of information to be included in the card holograms. The card would include the holder's fingerprint and perhaps carry a great deal of personal information such as health data, the person's criminal record, if any, social security number and biodata, even financial information or the data necessary to operate as a library card, licences of various sorts, confirmation of voter registration status, etc. and be used to pay for parking or tolls, for public transit, and even for taxes.

The American Association of Motor Vehicle Administrators has proposed standardizing all state drivers' licences so they become the national identity card, making the administrators the verifiers of Americans' identities. If licence data continue to be sold, licences as national ID cards would provide larger benefits for those who want the information for commercial purposes. And when the licences are screened for verifying identifications, the record of those screenings would track when and where the person had gone, into what places that required identification – bars, hotels, airports, stores. To operate the licences as ID cards those issuing them would need access to social security records, vital statistics bureaux, INS records, etc. Already the police are increasingly issued powerful computers to access many data bases on individuals, such as the ones that would be backing drivers' licences.[23]

There are proposals to go further and use chip implants to broadcast a brief signal that indicates, when combined with GPS satellite data, the location of the card holder. The chip could also monitor the person's physical condition and signal whenever his physical condition deteriorated. Others note that cell phones can be designed for the same purpose, tracking people and containing all the above information. In fact, cell phones in operation can already be used to track their owners and are very easy to wiretap. There are also proposals to make black boxes used in airliners more ubiquitous – in cars or rental vehicles to supply data on the vehicles, passengers and the surrounding conditions (for instance, detecting when drivers are high or drunk).[24]

The War on Terrorism has incited strong efforts to consolidate data bases to improve surveillance, consolidations of:

• holdings of federal agencies such as the FBI Criminal Justice Information Services Division and the National Crime Information Center, the Integrated Automated Fingerprint Identification System, and the National Instant Criminal Background Check System;
• state holdings with those at the federal level;
• state and local government holdings.

This could be very powerful because of the vast and growing range of data about individuals that federal, state and local agencies are now required to collect. Developments in the past decade include requirements that:

• Social Security numbers (SSNs) be used to identify all federal employees and on all tax returns, DOD personnel records, in Medicare and Medicaid;
• all children claimed as dependants on tax forms have SSNs, issued at birth;
• various federal data bases (nearly 50) be linked via SSNs;
• huge amounts of data on employees be sent to the federal government – on new hires, wages, unemployment benefits, etc.;
• electronic profiles of students be kept with the data made available to federal education agencies especially the National Center for Education Statistics; information on personal accounts, including copies of all cheques, be kept by banks for use by the government when needed.[25]

There is a *fourth* cause for concern already alluded to above. As noted, many of the new technologies that escalate the potential threats to citizens are not being developed and applied by the government for national security concerns. Instead, they are emerging from domestic commercial and research outfits to meet domestic civilian needs. Hence, this sort of resource is *already suitable for domestic surveillance* and is being made widely available. The associated threats are expanding – we are swimming in a widening sea of surveillance.

The build-up of firms in this area is bound to increase the difficulty of responding to inappropriate surveillance – their lobbying against suitable responses will be terrific. But concern is unavoidable since the government's data accumulations, and many private ones, are not necessarily tamper-proof. Exploiting improper access will very likely turn out to be a widespread criminal activity.

Companies are now actively promoting biotech sensor inserts or attachments that can be used, via the GPS system, to determine a person's exact location and to monitor his or her general condition. This is a simple extension of having such sensors in vehicles, on parolees, on livestock and pets, in buried nuclear wastes, etc. Many companies are promoting card systems to give priority access to airports, building, etc. for holders who exchange a great deal of personal information to gain the privilege.[26] Illustrating the public–private sector connections is the fact that one of the chief officials of Oracle, the most vivid proponent of consolidating government data bases for widespread use was formerly the third highest official of the CIA.

A particularly widespread development of surveillance has occurred with respect to traffic, with cameras at intersections to detect speeding, running red lights and other violations and on freeways to track congestion. This is expanding. In the San Francisco area, for example, electronic passes that thousands of motorists use to pay tolls on the Bay Bridge will soon be monitored by transponders on hundreds of miles of freeways to track the speed and location of cars. To meet civil liberties concerns each pass is to have a generic identification, separate from the billing one, encrypted – with the key changed daily, and the data purged from the records daily, but civil liberties groups fear those features could readily be changed to deal with 'emergencies'.[27]

As a summary, four broad developments, especially in combination, are cause for concern:

(1) the acquisition by the state of huge new capabilities for surveillance and the effective coordination, analysis and application of the resulting information, capabilities that will readily be abused or misused.

(2) the proliferation of threats that erase the foreign–domestic distinction;

(3) the conditions linked to the War on Terrorism, and the prospect that they may deepen and remain for years.

(4) the fact that most of the new technologies involved are readily available in the civilian economy and are being rapidly expanded for commercial purposes, broadening greatly the possible sources of abuse and the political pressure for their further development and application.

How do we know there will be misuse? One reason is that the new capabilities have already outstripped existing regulatory arrangements, and under the War on Terrorism this is developing even further. The technology is spreading widely and continues to improve. It is displayed and shown everywhere. The typical private detective or security agency has a huge assortment of surveillance items to choose from, and the computer technology to get the most out of it. Next, all modern enhancements of the state's power have been abused – it is in our nature. In the past some of the abuse was deeply institutionalized, as in Hoover's FBI. Finally, these developments will collectively *erode the concept of abuse*. When many good purposes can be and are served it will become steadily more difficult to sort out, *in principle*, what is harmful. (We will see similar processes at work in genetics research and its application.)

The prospects of serious abuse are probably enhanced by another discouraging development. The administration culminated its adaptations to terrorism by moving to consolidate about 100 separate agencies into the new Department of Homeland Security (DHS). This will come much closer to creating a national police force. One reason for concern is how this was done. The plans were prepared with the utmost secrecy in the White House for fear of widespread opposition. Only a handful of people prepared the bill; heads of relevant cabinet agencies and even high White House aides were not consulted. This reinforces the assertion that a national emergency exists and that extraordinary measures are required that dispense with much normal decision making. Once again, imagine how this new department is likely to develop if there are further terrorist attacks in the near future.

In the end it was considered unwise to assign the DHS broad powers for domestic spying or enforcement. But the same concentration of power could readily arise from the terrific pressure that now exists to consolidate the work of the FBI, CIA and others on terrorism and other matters. For instance there are now many proposals to set up a new agency, apart from the FBI, to do domestic intelligence work and investigations on terrorism or even to serve as an enforcement agency, and on the other hand to centralize analysis on domestic threats from all foreign and domestic sources (and thus from the FBI, CIA, State Department, DHS, etc.) in a single place. Along the same lines are proposals to far more closely coordinate intelligence work and information sharing between the federal government and state and local police, using the new technology to integrate the various efforts into a vast network.[28] After another major terrorist attack major steps along these lines would probably become inevitable.

Much about the topic of this paper is discussed under the heading of threats to privacy; after all, Article 12 of the Universal Declaration of Human Rights refers to privacy as a fundamental human right. We are said to be debating the proper tradeoffs to make between security and privacy. This does not quite do justice to the problem. *Privacy is a form of security*. Hence the trade-off is between two sorts of security, a serious matter. Individuals, groups, and institutions often treat privacy as a form of security. People who are robbed, particularly in home burglaries, say that one of the most disturbing emotional reactions come from how their privacy is violated. Privacy is a central element of autonomy, of self-control. Growing up is normally a steady expansion of privacy – children face serious restrictions on their privacy and one of the most stressful elements of being a teenager is that a rising need for privacy outruns what parents, institutions, and the law are willing to grant.

Governments seek privacy in decision making to get candid advice. They also claim to have many things to do that must be kept secret for the proper function of decision making and implementation. Government bureaucracies resist transparency – they treat whistle-blowers as the dregs of the earth, try to evade open meeting laws, etc. Private sector organizations do the same. Faculty members resist transparency in writing recommendations.

Constant surveillance is, after all, potentially a version of police hounding and surveillance of minority men on the streets, a form of profiling, or the rousting of ex-convicts on general principles – the biggest difference is that most of us behave ourselves so it does not turn into harassment. If it was announced that every organization holding meetings would have someone in attendance who will secretly report to outsiders what went on, who said what, who favoured what this would arouse an immense level of insecurity. Even for innocuous groups this would feel excessive, intrusive, very uncomfortable.

Increased and increasingly intrusive surveillance is usually sold as strongly benefiting security. It is easy to see how this can be so – detecting criminals, tracking children or the elderly or those with serious health problems, finding people who are lost, providing evidence of criminal wrongdoing so justice can be done. And it enjoys a good deal of support in public opinion polls. After all much of the public does not believe that criminals are entitled to civil rights, particularly the right to be absent from public view and free of restraint and surveillance until a crime has been committed.

Proponents of the new transparency point out that privacy has already been lost and yet we have survived, that important advances can be made by the greater accumulation of information about all of us, that we regularly give up more privacy in exchange for this. It is also the case, however, that while we give up information for a specific purpose the loss of privacy is typically carried to much greater lengths than we expected through use of the information for many other purposes. Too often, to supply information is to lose custody over what is done with it.

Another reason to fear that harm will result is because the definition of a crime shifts over time. Giving money to Muslim charities, seemingly innocent enough, has now become suspect. Information can be reconfigured, or merged with data of other sorts, to yield an impact not originally anticipated, such as when you become a target of certain marketers on the basis of visiting internet sites or your selection of particular cable TV programs and channels. Supplying information can readily have quite unexpected consequences.

Part of the problem is that the thrust of technology is mostly in one direction – in favour of a rising tide of observation and penetration. Technological change is mostly whetting the appetites of those people eager to gather data on virtually every narrow element of people's lives for governmental, criminal, or commercial purposes. We could use the equivalent of stealth technology for individuals.

REMEDIES

What can be done? Remedies come in legal and regulatory, bureaucratic, technical, economic and political forms. The first category covers policies and rules, laws and regulations for controlling highly intrusive surveillance and the misuse of information gathering. This category has been taking a beating in the wake of 11 September. It is always vulnerable to the impact of emergencies – normally there are important exceptions allowed then – and to public and political pressures to 'do something'. It is also difficult for laws and regulations to keep up with a rapidly changing technology. The second category has to do with setting up agencies charged with guarding against abuse – external agencies or sections of the government (like the Inspector Generals in intelligence agencies). The third category consists of efforts that turn technological change into an ally against excessive surveillance and control, examples of which are discussed below. The fourth arises from the expectation that firms will arise to sell a highly valuable thing like privacy, producing market pressures to develop items that limit surveillance. The fifth refers to the proliferation and strengthening of countervailing political pressures, i.e. complaints about surveillance and abuses keep up resistance. For example, beyond the American Civil Liberty Union privacy advocacy is carried on by such lobbying organizations as the Electronic Privacy Information Center; Americans for Computer Privacy; the Center for Democracy and Technology; Cyber-Rights and Cyber Liberties; the Electronic Frontier Foundation; the Global Internet Liberty Campaign; and the Internet Privacy Coalition.

Here are some actual and suggested remedies and a consideration of their strengths and weaknesses. One traditional step is the insertion of sunset provisions on authorizations for highly intrusive surveillance, some of which were included in the USA Patriotism Act (taking effect in 2007[AU?]). This ensures some debate, and possibly some accounting, at a later point – time when abuses can be uncovered and highlighted. It encourages all parties to keep records and develop evidence for the coming struggles. But this approach has important defects. The problem may not be constant abuse but the good possibility of serious abuse *someday*, and that day may not fall within the sunset provision time frame. The provisions may be continued for lack of disastrous abuse yet. And when expanded surveillance yields important benefits, the costs of abuse may be underestimated in any reassessment of legislation and regulations.

Some people put their faith in technological solutions. For instance, it is possible to very tightly define what is to be sought by computerized searches of millions of e-mail messages or other communications. Advocates of facial recognition technology argue that it is less intrusive because it only looks for certain faces and discards the rest; other forms of scrutiny would be more extensive. Such arguments rest on the notion that the technology really looks only at a small sample of the faces or messages canvassed, that sampling is inherently less intrusive. Cameras can be made that automatically destroy their exposed film after a certain time has passed, or film can be made that readily deteriorates unless specifically set aside for special treatment. More and more communications now go by buried fibre optic cables that are much harder to tap, and by digital rather than analogue signals which are also harder to tap. It is now possible to make unbreakable codes thanks to computers, and the government has been very concerned when they are used by criminals or terrorists. At one point the NSA sought to discourage publication of mathematical research with direct relevance for the development of unbreakable codes. (It failed.) There were proposals for a key escrow system – vendors would hand over keys to their cryptographic systems to a third party, and the government would be able to gain access, via a warrant and special court approval, when it could demonstrate a strong public policy need to break into the relevant communications. The government at one point proposed to distribute an unbreakable code system itself if the recipients would agree that the government would hold keys, once again to be used only when there was a demonstrated need, and periodically bills introduced in Congress proposed banning systems without a key available to authorities.[29] These proposals aroused strong objections. There might be more confidence in key escrow arrangements if the warrant system had a better history of controlling abuse.

Various people have argued that an effective market in privacy will soon produce solutions. Numerous companies are eager to enhance privacy for customers.[30] (Lester) This includes companies that develop and market codes, create ever better firewalls for protecting against hackers, install equipment to frustrate unwanted surveillance or at least detect its presence, and private intelligence firms hired to prevent industrial espionage, protect against kidnapping of executives or terrorism, etc. There is now software that reacts to unwanted advertising and other spam by reaching out to the source and eliminating your name from its mailing list. Unfortunately, there are obvious problems. Not all of these solutions can be readily made available to everyone for reasons of cost, complexity and feasibility. Those seeking greater protection from monitoring often do so, in part, by elaborate monitoring of their employees, buildings, grounds and communications. They deal with a part of the problem but not all of it (such as visual surveillance). The companies involved may well also be in the business of developing new technologies for surveillance, playing both sides of the street. Finally, is there a good example of a widespread, profitable, abuse that has been suitably contained by the market for halting it? Insurance fraud? Piracy of trade names, video disks, etc.? Illegal drugs, immigration, business scams, embezzling, hacking, poaching? I can't think of one. The market for abuse typically pays better than the market for preventing it, and the result can be the erosion of standards that came to afflict the accounting profession and was uncovered in the recent Wall Street scandals. Often the effective use of market incentives goes only as far as rewards to whistle-blowers.

It seems that the most viable long-term solution will have to be in *enlarging the monitoring* of those in a position to abuse surveillance. Thus another remedy would be to expand arrangements for requiring prior approval on highly intrusive searches for information and the related technology. The list of requirements that must be met to get judicial approval could be expanded, along with narrowing the descriptions of what can be collected and for what purposes, to prevent fishing expeditions. Bringing back the criminal standard for authorizations is a good example – no intrusive surveillance by public agencies unless there is good reason to suspect a crime is being or has been or is about to be committed. There are numerous proposals to require that surveillance be disclosed to the target individual or group at some point during or after the operation.

Several defects come to mind. The arrangements of this sort that already existed have been shredded in the aftermath of 11 September – new ones will be vulnerable to the same political pressures. In addition, they are most suitable for curbing official agencies and do less to limit abuses in the private sector. And they may fall flat with official agencies too – the existing system of prior approval requirements for wiretaps prior to 11 September was seemingly very strong but in fact the FBI made thousands of wiretap requests for years and was denied perhaps once. Applications go to judges known to be easier, standards are eroded by familiarity among the participants, and the applicants chip away at the rules through building precedents – all weaknesses that are heightened when there is little time for making a decision.

Separate agencies could be set up to oversee compliance – being charged with protecting rights and paying close attention to privacy concerns by conducting inspections, setting standards, etc. The justification would be that the logical agency for this, the Justice Department (and corresponding units at the state level), is responsible for many of the current activities that raise serious concerns. For instance, proposed new laws, regulations, and practices are typically defended by the relevant officials against fears that they go too far or are liable to be abused. This could be carried much farther if both public and private steps that raise such fears had to be accompanied by a civil liberties impact statement, analogous to the required environmental impact statements for public and private construction projects, with prior approval of the statements before any action could be undertaken assigned to a new government agency.

This is the sort of system academic researchers face in doing human or animal subjects research. It doesn't work perfectly in academic and would not work perfectly in controlling surveillance. Part of the problem is the constant complaints from those under scrutiny that the standards prevent them from doing their work, that compliance takes up more time than the work it is supposed to authorize, that the regulators just don't understand the point of view of those they are overseeing – the usual complaints about regulation that, over time, can erode its effectiveness. The Environmental Protection Agency has not been immune to political pressure from unfavourable administrations, Congress, and various interests. But such a step would heighten the barriers to be surmounted in designing new responses to security and criminal threats where important civil liberties will be affected.

Among those expected to curb abuses of rights and privacy, a major resource in fighting excesses in the War on Terrorism has been the US federal courts. The Fourth Circuit Court of Appeals has attacked the indefinite incarceration of Americans without charges or access to legal counsel because they were labelled 'enemy combatants'. A Federal District Court judge has ruled that the government cannot conceal the identities of those arrested after the 11 September disaster in its anti-terrorism campaign. This is resistance to the administration's claim that the campaign required no judicial review, no public disclosure and public hearings, no right of counsel for those arrested, and no access to them even by family members.[31] Obviously, the courts can be important. However, this is unlikely to hold true if, in a true worst case analysis, further significant terrorist attacks deepen the national emergency on terrorism. Then the courts will defer to the executive branch, Congress, and the public on more intrusive measures, and if the emergency lasts for years those measures will become that much more entrenched.

More work should be done on how to enlarge the costs of gathering information improperly, gathering more than necessary, or abusing the responsibility of having it. Too often the major cost for the state is inability to use improperly gathered information to prosecute, and even prosecutors may be satisfied to gather information they shouldn't, and which they can't use, if it helps gather information they can use. And all this is of little concern to those without a prosecutorial objective. It would also be nice to see stronger punishments for abuse. There is often little punishment for overzealousness, poor judgement, lying about probable cause, and the like – nothing comparable to being roasted for failing to do enough if an 11 September occurs – so it is easy to choose the side on which to err once a disaster has occurred. There is often no punishment, sometimes even a reward, for employees who advance interpretations or cut corners to suit the interests of their agency, as long as their actions were on the 'right' side. So serious punishments are often possible only after a major disaster or huge shift in the political climate. The intelligence community eventually paid a huge price for the abuses catalogued earlier but only in the unusual political situation after the Vietnam War. We might seem to have done better with the serious prison time given to a few notorious hackers, but since the pentagon alone experiences over 250,000 instances of hacking every year and almost no one gets caught it is clear that the penalties are not a serious recourse.

A possible way to enlarge the costs is a hair-of-the-dog approach I have yet to see proposed anywhere. What if monitors to prevent abuse were authorized and equipped to carry out their monitoring of an agency or firm by using, among other things, the techniques that the agency or firm had been caught using in the past to carry surveillance too far. In other words, let those who intrude be just as subject to intrusion in the same arbitrary ways and for the same reason: suspicion as to their honesty, competence, or goals and to gain an extra advantage for carrying out the monitors' responsibilities. If very intrusive surveillance is necessary because people can't be trusted then the people doing the surveillance can't be trusted. But how would they like it if their computers were bugged, their phones tapped, their e-mail messages ransacked by the equivalent of the hated 'internal affairs' people in police departments? In intelligence agencies this sort of thing is well known – in pursuit of moles almost no holds are barred – but it is not used to deal with unwarranted invasions of privacy by other organizations.

Of course, there would be furious resistance from the targets, citing everything from morale considerations to violations of civil rights! It took the Robert Hanson case to finally get the FBI to agree to put intelligence-related personnel through polygraph testing periodically. These people much prefer approval to be flexible in gathering information and strenuously resist transparency which would limit that flexibility – the extent to which they seek the maximum amount of secrecy for what they do and how, such as exemptions from Freedom of Information Act pressures, is very disturbing. But such a solution might make people developing technology and the implementation procedures for greater surveillance give serious thought to building in more barriers against abuse and misuse right from the start. As it stands those pressing for, or designing, ways to carry out more intrusive surveillance do not treat the potential for abuse as a serious cost that must be considered in policy making. We seem to count instead mainly on countervailing pressures to do this – someone will take steps to critique the proposed legislation or regulations, will mobilize to get changes, will campaign for the necessary public support. But we are on the verge of developing a new 'surveillance industrial complex' which will make the political struggle even more uphill for those defending civil liberties and privacy.

CONCLUSION

All these remedies share an underlying defect. An old problem can now reach a frightening new dimension because of the confluence of unusually favourable conditions for the expansion of misuse and abuse that are highly likely to overwhelm standard remedies. The remedies would deal more with the symptoms and not the powerful underlying cause. New solutions are needed. In any worst case analysis it is easy to look too alarmist but the threats to national security associated with the information age are real and this applies just as well to the domestic as the foreign ones. People helping generate the threats should give more attention to this. So should the rest of us.

ACKNOWLEDGEMENTS

I had invaluable help in preparing the essay from the research work of Melissa Rodriguez and Andrea Reyna.

NOTES

1. On the RMA see John Arquilla and David F. Ronfeldt, *The Advent of Netwar* (Santa Monica, CA: RAND, 1996); John Arquilla and David F. Ronfeldt, *In Athena's Camp: Preparing for Conflict in the Information Age* (Santa Monica, CA: RAND, 1997); Stuart E. Johnson and Martin C. Libicki, *Dominant Battlespace Knowledge* (Washington DC: National Defense University Press, 1996); Patrick M. Morgan, 'The Impact of the Revolution in Military Affairs', *The Journal of Strategic Studies*, Vol. 23, No. 1 (2000), pp.132–62; Williamson Murray, 'Thinking About Revolutions in Military Affairs', *Joint Force Quarterly* (Summer 1997), pp.69–76.
2. Examples of the burgeoning literature on such threats: Harvey W. Kushner, *Cyberterrorism in the 21st Century* (a special issue of *American Behavioral Scientist*) (Thousand Oaks, CA: SAGE, 2002); Yonah Alexander and Stephen Prior (eds), *Cyber Terrorism and Information Warfare: Threats and Responses* (Ardsley, NY: Transnational Publishers, 2001); Director of Central Intelligence, 'Proceedings From the Carnegie Mellon Workshop on Network Security', (DCI Scientific and Technical Intelligence Committee, Aug. 1997); John Arquilla, 'Preparing for Cyberterrorism Badly' *The New Republic*, 1 May 2000, pp.16–18; Bob Drogin, 'US Scurries to Erect Cyber-Defenses', *Los Angeles Times*, 31 Oct. 1999; Kenneth A. Minihan, 'Defending the Nation Against Cyber Attack: Information Assurance in the Global Environment', USIA, *US Foreign Policy Agenda*, Nov. 1998. <http://usinfo.state.gov/journals/itps/1198/ijpe/pj48min.htm>.
3. *Congressional Quarterly*, 2002, *Probes of Intelligence Agencies and the FBI – Part I*, available at: <http://www.infowar.com/class_2/02/class2_02190a_shtml>.
4. The state of emergency proclaimed by the Truman Administration for the Korean War, which expanded the government's powers, was not officially cancelled until the attacks on the government in the 1970s over the Vietnam War.
5. See 'The Nature and Scope of Government Electronic Surveillance Activity', Center for Democracy and Technology, 2001. <http://www.cdt.org/wiretap/wiretap_overview.html>.
6. 'Statement of David L. Sobel' to House Committee on Government Reform, (Subcommittee on Government Management, Information and Technology, 22 June 2000). From the Electronic Privacy Information Center at <http://www.epic.org/security/cip/hr4246_testimony.html>.
7. 'Testimony of Alan Davidson, Associate Director Center for Democracy and Technology before the Subcommittee on Crime of the Committee on Judiciary, U.S. House of Representatives' (12 Feb. 2002) Available at: <http://www.cdt.org/testimony/020212 Davidson.shtml>; 'EPIC letter on HR 3482' 26 Feb. 2002. Letter on Cyber Security Enhancement Act. Available at: <http://www.epic.org/security/infowar/csea.html>.
8. The FBI Guidelines; Impact on Civil Liberties and Security – the Need for Congressional Oversight' (6 June 2002), Center for Democracy and Technology.
9. <http://www.cdt.org/wiretap/020606guidelines.shtml>, 'The Nature and Scope of Government'; Adam Lystak, 'Changing the Standard', *New York Times*, 31 May 2002.
10. Michael Moss and Ford Fessenden, 'Across U.S. Police Seek More Power to Spy', *International Herald Tribune*, 11 Dec. 2002.
11. See 'Analysis of Provisions of the Proposed Anti-Terrorism Act of 2001 Affecting the Privacy of Communications and Personal Information' 24 Sep. 2001. Analysis by the Electronic Privacy Information Center available at: <http://www.epic.org/privacy/terrorism/ata_analysis. html>; 'Legislation Gutting Privacy Standards Passes Congress; Several Provisions survive Sunset', 25 Oct. 2001, Center for Democracy and Technology report; 'EFF Analysis of the Provisions of the USA PATRIOT Act that Relate to Online Activities', 31 Oct. 2001, Electronic Frontier Foundation, Available at: <http://www.eff.org/Privacy/Surveillance/ Terrorism_militias/20011031_eff_usa_patriot_analysis.html>; 'USA Patriot Act Boosts Government Powers While Cutting Back on Traditional Checks and Balances', 1 Nov. 2001, ACLU Legislative Analysis.

12. Eric Lichtblau, 'FBI Criticized on Data Access' *Los Angeles Times*, 10 May 2002.
13. 'DOJ Proposed Further Surveillance Expansion Changes to Intelligence Authorization Would Again Increase FISA Eavesdropping', 30 Nov. 2001 Center for Democracy and Technology. Available at: <http://www.cdt.org/security/011130cdt.shtml>.
14. James Risen and David Johnston, 'Not Much Has Changed in a System That Failed' *New York Times*, 8 Sep. 2002.
15. John Schwartz, 'Nanny-Cam May Leave a Home Exposed', *New York Times*, 14 April 2002; 'Fourth Amendment Issues Raised by the FBI's "Carnivore" Program', Hearing, Subcommittee on the Constitution, Committee on the Judiciary, House of Representatives, 24 July 2000, Washington, DC: US Government Printing Office; Neil Brindis, Jr. and Ted Brindis, 'FBI System Covertly Searches E-mail', *The Wall Street Journal Online*, 10 July 2000; Ariana Eunjung Cha and Jonathan Krim, 'Privacy Trade-Offs Re-assessed After Attack' *Washington Post*, 13 Sept. 2001.
16. Electronic Frontier Foundation, 'Biometrics' 2002, Available at: <http://www.eff.org/privacy/surveillance/biometrics.html>; 'Face Recognition' Electronic Privacy Information Center, EPIC Face Recognition Information Page, <Http://www.epic.org/privacy/facerecognition/default.html>; Veronica Henry, 'Biometrics: Face Recognition Technology', Sans Institute: Information Security Reading Room, 12 March 2001, <http://rr.sans.org/authentic/face_rec.php>; Robert O'Harrow, Jr, 'Face ID Technology Gets Federal Funding', *Washington Post*, 1 Aug. 2001; <http://www.epic.org/privacy/facerecognition/default.html>; John D. Woodward, Jr., 'High-Tech Human Identification Can fight Terrorism', RAND: Op-eds by RAND Staff, 2002, <http://www.rand.org/hot/op-eds/092401ppg.html>.
17. See 'FERET: DOD CDTDPO's Facial Recognition Project', 2002. Available at: <http://www.dodcounterdrug.com/facialrecognition/FERET/feret.htm>.
18. Stephanie Simon, 'Shopping With Big Brother', *Los Angeles Times*, 1 May 2002; 'What's Wrong With Public Video Surveillance?' 2002, American Civil Liberties Union Available at: <http://www.aclu.org/issues/privacy/CCTV_Feature.html>.
19. Charles Piller, 'These Nets Have Security Holes', *Los Angeles Times*, 18 April 2002; Schwartz 'Nanny-Cam May Leave a Home Exposed'.
20. Rajiv Chandrasekaran, 'When the Personal Becomes Public', *Washington Post National Weekly Edition*, 30 March 1998.
21. John Markoff and John Schwartz, 'Many of Big Brother's Prying Tools are Up and Running', *International Herald Tribune*, 24–25 Dec. 2002.
22. Robert O'Harrow, Jr. 'Security Versus Privacy', *Washington Post National Weekly Edition*, 10–16 June 2002.
23. See Shane Ham and Robert D. Atkinson, 'Using Technology to Detect and Prevent Terrorism', Progressive Policy Institute Policy Brief, Jan. 2002; Robert O'Harrow, Jr. and Jonathan Krim, 'Is Big Brother Watching?' *Washington Post Weekly Edition*, 24 Dec. 2001; William Glaberson, 'Technology's Role to Grow in a New World of Security', *New York Times*, 18 Sept. 2001; Jeffrey Rosen, 'Spy Game' *New York Times Magazine*, 14 April 2002; Electronic Frontier Foundation, 'National Identification Systems', June 2002, available at: <http://www.eff.org/Privacy/Surveillance/nationalidsystem.html>.
24. 'Your Papers Please: From the State Drivers License to a National Identification System', Electronic Privacy Information Center, Policy Report, Feb. 2002; Shane Ham and Robert D. Atkinson, 'Modernizing the State Identification System: An Action Agenda', Progressive Policy Institute Policy Report, Feb. 2002.
25. Cullen Murphy, 'Innocent Bystander', *The Atlantic Monthly*, 20–22 Dec. 2001.
26. Charlotte Twight, 'Watching You: Systemic Federal Surveillance of Ordinary Americans', *CATO Institute Briefing Paper*, excerpted from Twight, *Dependent on DC: The Rise of Federal Control Over the Lives of Ordinary Americans* (New York: Palgrave/St. Martins, 2002).
27. Simon Romero, 'Location Devices Use Rises, Prompting Privacy Concerns', *New York Times*, 4 March 2001; David Streitfeld, 'First Humans to Receive ID Chips', *Los Angeles Times*, 9 May 2002; Alex Canizares, 'Human Implant Tracking Device Excites MDs, Worries Privacy Groups', 15 Aug. 2000. <http://www.space.com/businesstechnology/technology/human_tracker_000814.html>.

28. Adam Clymer, 'Tracking Bay Area Traffic Creates Concern For Privacy', *New York Times*, 26 Aug. 2002.
29. 'Getting the Intelligence Services a Vulnerable Nation Needs', *New York Times*, 8 Sept. 2002; Risen and Johnston, 'Not Much Has Changed in a System That Failed'. 30. Brendan I. Koerner, 'Technology and Its Discontents', *The Village Voice*, 26 June 2002; 'Big Brother in the Wires: Wiretapping in the Digital Age, March 1998 ACLU Special Report, available at: <http://www.aclu.org/issues/cyber/wiretap_brother.html>.
30. Toby Lester, 'The Reinvention of Privacy', *Atlantic Monthly*, 27–39 March 2001, at <http://www.theatlantic.com/issues/2001/03/lester-p1.htm>.
31. Linda Greenhouse, 'The Imperial Presidency vs. The Imperial Judiciary', *New York Times*, 8 Sept. 2002.

Rewarding IT Security in the Marketplace

WALTER S. BAER

INTRODUCTION

Keeping information systems and the information technology (IT) infrastructure secure has important public good aspects. As a recent National Research Council report points out, 'The overall security of a system is only as strong as its weakest link.'[1] The security of my IT system depends not just on the firewalls and authentication measures I have installed, but on how well other computers and networks linked to me are protected. This represents a classic example of a network externality, in which an individual's or firm's action has uncompensated economic consequences for others connected to the network.[2] IT security thus must deal with the market failures that often result from such externalities; that is, private stakeholders alone are highly unlikely to invest sufficiently in IT network security to provide an optimal (or even adequate) level of societal protection.

This essay focuses on ways to better align private incentives with the overall public interest in IT security. While it is written from a United States perspective and refers primarily to US institutions and processes, the issues and approaches discussed should be generally applicable internationally. In fact, they must be considered in an international context; since attacks on IT systems often cross national borders, and effective defences involve a wide range of national and transnational entities.

Nearly everyone agrees that improving IT security demands greater efforts from both the public and private sectors, as well as better coordination and cooperation between them. Within the US federal government, most of the offices, centres, boards and councils created to oversee and coordinate federal activities have been brought into the new Department of Homeland Security (DHS). These include the Critical Infrastructure Assurance Office (CAIO) and the National Infrastructure Protection Center (NIPC), which were established in 1998 with responsibilities to develop a national strategy for, and promote government/industry collaboration on IT security.[3]

As prominent examples of such collaboration, a series of industry-specific Information Sharing and Analysis Centers (ISACs) have been created since 1998 to develop 'secure database[s], analytic tools, and information gathering and distribution facilities designed to allow authorized participants to submit either anonymous or attributed reports about information security threats, vulnerabilities, incidents and solutions'.[4] The ISACs collect and analyse such reports, compare them with baseline data, and provide early notification to their members about security threats and possible responses. Membership is voluntary, and membership criteria differ: the financial services ISAC accepts only industry members, while the ISACs for telecommunications and information technology include both industry and government participants.

It seems too early to judge the ISACs' effectiveness in improving IT security, although the financial services ISAC has been credited with helping its members avoid the widespread denial of service attacks launched in February 2000.[5] US industry sectors as diverse as surface transportation, food and water supply have established ISACs in the past two years, and the concept has spread to Canada, Japan and other OECD countries. However, many US firms worry about the potential downsides from joining ISACs, including increased antitrust scrutiny from sharing security data with competitors, legal liabilities arising from leaks about information security breaches or vulnerabilities, or the public release under the Freedom of Information Act of sensitive information shared with the federal government. Such concerns may well limit the ISACs' growth and effectiveness, at least in the short-run.[6]

Beyond encouraging public/private collaboration, another key pillar of the US national effort is to strengthen the incentives for private sector (and other non-government) organizations to improve their own IT security. Bruce Schneier, a leading expert on IT security, states the point clearly: 'good security [should be] rewarded in the marketplace'.[7] The remainder of this paper discusses how such incentives can be put in place so that markets will reward investments in IT security. The next section considers how well known principles of risk management and private insurance can be applied to IT security problems. The third section, Current Status of and Trends in Cyber Insurance, describes how the insurance industry is responding to the market opportunities presented by IT security, while the forth section focuses on problems that currently limit the scope and effectiveness of private insurance covering these risks. I then explore potential rationales and roles for government involvement to help private insurance markets function better to provide incentives for IT security. Findings and prospective conclusions are outlined in the final section.

APPLYING RISK MANAGEMENT PRINCIPLES AND PRACTICES TO IT SECURITY

In a perceptive speech to the Digital Commerce Society of Boston in November 1998, Daniel Geer called for a change in IT security thinking from trust management to risk management.[8] Traditionally, IT security designers have thought in terms of building trusted systems for trusted users.[9] IT security thus has emphasized trust management technologies – e.g., smart cards with encrypted passwords, public key infrastructure, and increasingly sophisticated biometric devices – for identifying and authenticating trusted users, as well as firewalls, intrusion detectors and other technologies for protecting systems against malicious code and malign users. But since no systems are or will be 100 per cent secure, the problem with trust management approaches is that when they fail, the losses may be open-ended, or at least unestimated.

In contrast, risk management focuses on identifying and quantifying potential losses and the uncertainties surrounding them.[10] Quantitatively estimating IT security risks permits enterprise managers to decide how much to invest in measures, like the technologies mentioned above, to mitigate them and/or whether to package them in forms that others will assume (for a price). The latter depends, of course, on well-functioning markets for insurance covering the risks that the enterprise wants to lay off. Such insurance is available to cover most normal business risks from property loss or damage, business interruption, and liability for harm or damage caused to others. Applying risk management principles to IT could bring IT security within the more familiar and workable paradigms of insurance, risk sharing and risk securitization – realms in which US financial service firms excel and actively seek new business opportunities. That is why Daniel Geer titled his 1998 talk on IT security: 'Risk Management is Where the Money Is'.

As a risk management tool, insurance can encourage greater protective measures and help achieve other social goals. Fire insurance is often cited as a case in point. A building owner must have fire insurance to obtain a mortgage or a commercial business license. Obtaining insurance requires that the building meet local fire codes and underwriting standards, which may involve visits from local government and insurance company inspectors. Inspectors also follow up on serious incidents and claims, both to learn what went wrong and to guard against possible moral hazards of insurance such as arson or fraud. Insurance companies often sponsor research, offer training classes and publish materials on fire prevention and mitigation. Most important, insurers reduce premiums to building owners who keep their facilities clean, install sprinklers, test their control systems regularly and take other protective measures. Fire insurance markets thus involve not only underwriters, agents and clients, but also code-writers, inspectors, and vendors of products and services for fire prevention and protection. While government remains involved, well-functioning markets for fire insurance keep the responsibility for and cost of preventive and protective measures largely within the private sector.

The fire insurance analogy seems to have considerable applicability and appeal to IT security problems. Workable markets for insurance covering IT risks could, in principle, have a number of desirable incentives and outcomes, including:

- Processes to set IT security standards for underwriting;
- Security consulting firms that audit and monitor clients' IT security practices as an integral component of insurance underwriting;
- Institutions that test and certify IT security products and services;
- Incentives and means to promulgate industry best practices;
- Incentives for firms to increase IT security to reduce insurance premiums;
- Incentives to keep responsibility for and cost of protection within the private sector.

Bruce Schneier, the founder and CTO of Counterpane Internet Security, agrees: 'Sooner or later, the insurance industry will sell everyone antihacking policies. It will be unthinkable not to have one. And then we'll start seeing good security rewarded in the marketplace.'[11]

However, as discussed in the next two sections, we are still a long way from obtaining such positive results from private markets for insurance covering IT security risks, commonly known as 'cyber insurance'.

CURRENT STATUS OF AND TRENDS IN CYBER INSURANCE

As recently as five years ago, there was very little commercial demand for insurance covering damage, loss or liability from hackers or other IT network failures. However, growing national concerns about US vulnerability to information attacks, coupled with well publicized distributed denial of service (DDOS) attacks that brought down many commercial websites in early 2000, has led many firms to request insurance against such perils. The insurance industry is responding – albeit slowly.

Insurance underwriters and brokers – including industry giants such as AIG, Chubb, Lloyds of London, Marsh & McLennan, St. Paul and Zurich Financial Services, as well as more specialized firms such as Wurzler Underwriting Managers and INSUREtrust – now offer policies that explicitly cover some IT security risks. For an additional premium, for example, 'commercial crime bonds' will cover loss of funds from cyber crimes as well as ordinary fraud, embezzlement or extortion (but not losses from business interruptions due to cyber crimes). State banking regulators generally require banks and other financial institutions under their jurisdiction to carry such coverage.

For businesses that sell goods and services online, insurers offer several kinds of e-business coverage of liabilities due to technology errors or omissions, intellectual property violations, privacy infringement, theft of customer credit cards or viruses transmitted to and from the insured's websites. Other 'breach of security' losses from hacker attacks may also be covered. Premiums typically are one to five per cent per year of the policy limit, depending on the specific coverage. According to the Insurance Information Institute, the market for e-business liability insurance will grow from about $75 million in 2001 to $2.5 billion by 2005.[12] Still, even the $2.5 billion figure in 2005 would represent less than two per cent of total property/casualty premiums.

Business losses due to direct physical loss or damage to computers and other IT hardware are generally covered under standard business property insurance. An Arizona federal district court decision recently broadened that coverage to include computer loss of use and functionality under 'direct physical loss or damage'.[13] In this case, an electrical power outage shut down computer systems at an Ingram Micro, Inc. data center in Tucson, Arizona. Although the systems were not physically damaged, the company could not conduct business for some eight hours while the computers were manually reprogrammed. The insurer's denial of Ingram's claim of loss was rejected by the Arizona district court, stating:

> At a time when computer technology dominates our professional as well as personal lives, the Court must side with Ingram's broader definition of 'physical damage.' The Court finds that 'physical damage' is not restricted to the physical destruction or harm of computer circuitry, but includes loss of access, loss of use and loss of functionality.[14]

Although the US Ninth Circuit Court of Appeals affirmed the *Ingram* decision in August 2000, it remains highly controversial within the insurance industry. Some believe it could be used to claim any loss from hacker attacks and other breaches of computer security under standard property coverage. As a consequence, *Ingram* may accelerate insurers' efforts to write separate coverage for IT security breaches and explicitly exclude them from standard policies.[15]

To qualify for specific insurance covering losses from breach of security, businesses may have to pass an IT security audit and risk assessment. Insurers typically have arrangements with third party IT security firms to conduct such assessments,[16] although INSUREtrust and a few others operate their own risk management services groups. AIG has been particularly aggressive in offering free security assessments to prospective clients.[17] And while initial audits clearly are essential to maintain underwriting standards, security experts emphasize the importance of routine, continuing monitoring of clients' IT systems and security processes. Such arrangements for regular security assessments as part of insurance renewals do not yet appear to be in place.

Overall, despite growing recognition of IT security vulnerabilities, and increased business interest in insuring against IT security risks, actual insurance coverage remains spotty and limited. The latest 'Benchmark Survey' published by the US Risk and Insurance Management Society reports that while nearly 70 per cent of business respondents are engaged in electronic commerce, 'only 2 percent indicated that their organization carries a separate e–business insurance policy'.[18] Present–day policies have relatively low coverage limits, high premiums and numerous exclusions that make them problematic to many potential customers and thus reduce their effectiveness as incentives for better IT security practices. The next section outlines the reasons why this remains the situation today.

Since the concept of insurance against IT security risks is quite new, it is perhaps not surprising that current markets for such coverage are still undeveloped and limited. Cyber insurance faces a number of relatively serious, interrelated problems.

Lack of Agreement on Basic Policy Definitions and Language

Rapid and constant changes in information technology can bring ambiguity or misunderstanding about precisely what is insured, what perils and risks are covered, and how losses are to be assessed. The *Ingram* case points to such problems in interpreting what is meant by 'physical damage' to computer systems. As another example, insurance law generally holds that coverage applies to risks that are 'fortuitous'; that is, unforeseeable and subject to chance, like an accidental fire or an electrical outage. However, an insured must take active protective steps against foreseeable, 'non-fortuitous' risks in order for coverage to apply. Are hacker attacks fortuitous or non-fortuitous? Neither policy language nor case law makes this clear. Similar ambiguities surround whether coverage applies everywhere in cyberspace (on hosted servers, mirrored sites, etc.), and how information stored on IT systems should be valued for insurance purposes.

Because case law involving IT security is uncertain and changing, insurers seek to limit their exposure by narrowly defining coverage on new cyber policies and excluding coverage on other contracts. As of now, no standard policy language has been agreed on that would encourage more rapid market expansion.

Lack of Underwriting Standards or Experience

Insurers have little experience with IT security claims on which to base premiums, both because the field is so new, and because firms have resisted revealing losses from security breaches. Similar to the policy definition problem, setting standards for policy underwriting is difficult in a rapidly changing environment. And clients' fears of damaging publicity or liability if their IT vulnerabilities are revealed make them loath to file claims. According to a *Fortune* article in July

2000, 'Not one of the ... big insurers said it has ever actually paid a claim on e-policy.'[19]

Client reluctance to file claims works to the insurers' advantage, of course, at least in the short run. On the other hand, limited actuarial experience makes underwriters wary of substantial exposure, especially post-11 September. A recent article in Information Security Magazine on '2002 Industry Trends: Cyberinsurance', states:

> In the past, companies seeking a $25 million policy could find someone to cover them. Now it's much more difficult. Underwriters who didn't blink at $5 million or $10 million policies would rather insure $1 million policies, say cyberinsurance underwriters.[20]

Lack of Adequate Reinsurance

Insurers' concerns about their inability to judge the level of future exposure is compounded by the lack of a strong reinsurance market to lay off IT security risks. In other fields of property/casualty insurance, underwriters commonly purchase reinsurance to protect themselves against unusual, extreme losses. But the paucity of claims experience for IT security worries the reinsurance industry as well the initial underwriters. Prospective reinsurers are particularly concerned about the possibility of coordinated, 'structured' information attacks by organized criminals, terrorists or state-supported hackers, which could result in far greater losses than have occurred to date.

Catastrophe bonds ('cat bonds') are a recent innovation in reinsurance that could be applicable to IT security risks. Beginning in the mid 1990s, reinsurers have securitized excess risks from low frequency, high impact events such as hurricanes and earthquakes, by selling bonds to investors that can be traded on securities markets.[21] A typical cat bond yields considerably more than alternative investments in good years, but the investor stands to lose interest payments and sometimes principal if insurance losses exceed a specified amount. Cat bonds essentially follow the path already developed for packaging mortgage loans, auto payments and credit card debts into tradable financial instruments. Although their income streams are less predictable than are those for conventional securities, they can be attractive to investors as a distinct asset class for portfolio diversification. Cat bonds represent a growing part of the reinsurance market, but they have not yet been used to reinsure cyber policies. And absent traditional reinsurance or issuance of cat bonds, underwriters will continue to limit their commitments to cover IT security risks.[22]

Policy Exclusions

Like other property/casualty policies, those covering breaches of IT security typically exclude claims resulting from acts of war, riot, civil commotion and similar disasters known as *force majeure*. Yet these may be precisely the risks that businesses fear most and want to insure against. Moreover, unlike the case with most other property losses, it may be difficult to distinguish coordinated information attacks by terrorists or state-supported agents, which might be excluded under *force majeure*, from fortuitous events that would be covered. Such unresolved questions inject additional uncertainty into coverage of IT security risks that vex insurance underwriters and reinsurers, as well as prospective clients.

No Strong Collaborative Processes or Institutions for Information Sharing

One approach to increasing the base of experience regarding IT security risks would be for insurers and other knowledgeable stakeholders to share more data about breach of security incidents, claims and losses. There is relatively little sharing of such information today within the insurance industry, primarily for competitive reasons (IT security consultants, too, consider their databases to be highly proprietary and are reluctant to share them). Insurers also express concerns about possible antitrust violations if they exchange information with competitors.

In terms of collaborative institutions, no ISAC has been established solely for the insurance industry, although the financial services ISAC includes AIG, Chubb and other large financial firms that have insurance subsidiaries. The Financial Services Roundtable, a consortium whose members represent large, integrated US financial services companies, recently established a Working Group on 'Insurance in E-Commerce Risk Management' as part of its BITS Technology Group,[23] but what recommendations this Working Group may make about ongoing collaborative activities remain to be seen.

In 1999, The Financial Services Roundtable launched the BITS Financial Services Security Lab to test and certify hardware and software for online banking and related financial services.[24] This consortium-run Lab is modelled on the highly successful Underwriters Laboratories, Inc., which tests and certifies electric and electronic equipment for fire protection and related safety features, but it faces an uphill struggle to stay abreast of IT technology.[25] So far, the BITS Security Lab has certified only one product, a secure web transaction server (called the 'Virtualvault') produced by Hewlett Packard.[26] ICSA Labs, a division of TrueSecure Corporation (publisher of *Information Security Magazine*), certifies firewalls and other Internet security products and is trying to position itself as an industry-wide leader in developing IT security standards. However, ICSA Labs appears to function today more as a commercial consultant than as an independent standards organization. Finally, Congress recently appropriated $3 million to establish an Institute for Information Infrastructure Protection ('I3P') at Dartmouth University, whose mission is to develop an R&D agenda for IT security, support security product and service evaluations, facilitate public/private information sharing, and expand the education and training of IT security experts.[27] While not yet operational or focused specifically on insurance-related issues, a successful I3P could help support collaborative efforts by insurers in all the above areas.

Possible Moral Hazards

Insurance has always had to deal with cases of fraud, as well as problems that, once insured, policyholders may be less careful than they would be otherwise. For example, IT insurance covering extortion might encourage an employer to pay off a fired information systems employee who threatened to corrupt the firm's databases. As a second example, an insured might claim large damages from database corruption resulting from an unknown hacker's breach of IT security. The insurer might then respond that the covered loss is much less, since the insured should have had backup records the hacker could not reach. The insurer's argument would be that the hacking event was fortuitous but the resulting data corruption was non-fortuitous, requiring the insured to take active protective measures.[28]

Insurers have dealt successfully with moral hazards in other areas through mandating protective measures and procedures designed to reduce losses. Mandating that covered structures pass local fire codes is an obvious example. As another illustration, 'special crime' policies covering kidnapping and ransom demands may require the insured to report an event immediately and use designated crisis management specialists. Again because of rapid technology changes, however, such standard codes and practices are much more difficult to develop and implement for IT security.

Inadequate Accountability for IT Security Flaws and Vulnerabilities

A growing number of experts believe that uncertain liability and inadequate accountability for security flaws exacerbate network externalities and thus represent core obstacles to improving IT security.[29] US case law has not yet clarified who bears responsibility for losses when a breach of IT network security occurs upstream from the damaged party; e.g., when a hacker exploits a security weakness at site A to launch an attack over backbone network B through Internet service provider C which results in damages to company D's information stored on a server maintained by company E. To what extent are A, B, C or E liable for D's damages? If no such liability exists, then the parties will not invest in IT security beyond their own direct needs nor purchase third-party insurance with attendant incentives to improve security. This is the basic externality issue which leads to a familiar 'tragedy of the commons' result.

Perhaps even more important, software suppliers are generally not subject to product liability laws and regulations, unlike the situation for other manufacturers. This is because software suppliers sell licences to use their products rather than ownership of them. Opening a shrink-wrapped package or clicking on a website's 'I accept' button exempts the software vendor from liability if hackers subsequently exploit the program's flaws or vulnerabilities to cause damage. The lack of product liability for software providers is not an insurance problem *per se*; but it exacerbates the negative externalities associated with IT security and makes it more difficult to use insurance to address these externalities.

POTENTIAL GOVERNMENT ROLES TO STRENGTHEN CYBER INSURANCE MARKETS

Given the obstacles described above, are there constructive ways for government to help spur or strengthen private markets for cyber insurance to encourage greater private investment in IT security? Although government intervention inevitably affects market dynamics and results in costs as well as benefits, potential government roles in cyber insurance could include:

- Setting IT security standards;
- Mandating incident reporting or other information sharing;
- Mandating cyber insurance or financial responsibility;
- Facilitating reinsurance by limiting and/or indemnifying catastrophic losses;
- Providing insurance directly;
- Legislating liability.

These are discussed briefly in turn.

Setting IT Security Standards

Returning to the fire insurance analogy, local governments routinely pass ordinances detailing fire codes that then generally serve as minimum standards for insurance underwriting. Could similar government-set minimum standards for IT security facilitate underwriting of cyber insurance? One federal precedent would be 'airworthiness certification' of aircraft and other aviation equipment by the Federal Aviation Administration (FAA). Insurance companies require such certification before planes can be insured.

Although minimum IT security standards could aid in insurance underwriting, government-mandated standards seem difficult to achieve and likely to be counterproductive. Government-directed standards processes tend to be slow and process driven, and consequently poorly matched to the frenzied pace of information technology. Government support for non-government standards, analogous to supporting the development of Internet technical standards through the Internet Engineering Task Force (IETF), would seem a better approach. However, the federal government may be able to play useful roles in standards development through such actions as:

- Serving as a neutral forum to bring stakeholders together;
- Requiring security testing and certification, developed in cooperation with industry, for government procurement of IT equipment, systems and services;
- Providing some financial support, perhaps through institutions such as the newly formed Institute for Information Infrastructure Protection.

Mandating Incident Reporting or other Information Sharing

Although the financial services ISAC includes some insurers, it has not focused on or encouraged information sharing for insurance underwriting purposes. A separate ISAC for the insurance industry seems unlikely to broaden the underwriting experience base substantially unless reporting of threats, incidents and losses were made mandatory rather than voluntary.

Civil aviation offers such a model: the FAA requires air carriers and airports to report aviation accidents and serious incidents, as specified in FAA and National Transportation Safety Board (NTSB) regulations. For example, hard landings that result in 'substantial damage' must be reported to the FAA and NTSB;[30] records of other hard landings need not be reported but are used by the air carriers themselves for maintenance, pilot training and general quality assurance. In addition, a separate, voluntary call-in system (funded by NASA, not the FAA) encourages anonymous reporting of aviation problems and incidents.

Financial service firms and other businesses would strenuously oppose mandatory reporting of IT incidents. Consequently, mandatory reporting seems a political non-starter, unless Congress passes legislation giving the federal government prime responsibility for IT security, as it has done for aviation safety. As a more modest step, since insurance industry representatives often cite antitrust concerns as a barrier to information sharing, Congress could consider exempting sharing of IT security information from antitrust enforcement, similar to is proposed by the *Critical Information Infrastructure Security Act of 2001*.

Mandating Insurance or Financial Responsibility

Government insurance mandates are quite common. Governments at all levels demand that contractors carry specified liability coverage as a condition for receiving contract awards. Many states now require vehicle owners to document insurance coverage or equivalent proof of financial responsibility before their vehicles can be licensed. State regulated banks must carry 'bankers bonds' covering losses from fraud and embezzlement. And, as discussed further below, Congress has legislated that private owners of nuclear power plants and space launch operations carry primary liability insurance up to a specified limit.

Extending liability insurance mandates to cover breaches of IT security would seem most readily justified for firms doing business with government. Implementing such mandates, however, would require clarification of, and agreement on, the difficult issues surrounding who bears liability for security breaches on parts of the IT network not under the contractor's direct control.

Facilitating Reinsurance by Limiting and/or Indemnifying Catastrophic Losses

For nuclear power plants and space launches, the federal government has intervened to cap private liabilities and mandate financial responsibility up to that stipulated limit. The Price Anderson Act of 1957 limits the liability of nuclear power plant owners to $560 million for any single event. The Act (as amended) requires each nuclear plant to carry $200 million of primary insurance; secondary coverage for liabilities between $200 and $560 million comes from premiums assessed retroactively and shared by all US nuclear power plant owners. If damages exceed $560 million, Congress must determine whether and how compensation will be paid. The Commercial Space Launch Act of 1984, as amended, mandates that commercial operators must obtain $500 million of primary liability insurance before receiving a license to launch a space vehicle. The Act also provides that Congress may appropriate up to $1.5 billion to cover additional liabilities from the launch. Although the federal government essentially serves as the insurer of last resort, it has never been called on to cover excess liabilities for either nuclear power plants or space launches.

When IRA terrorist attacks in the early 1990s on commercial buildings in London threatened to make property insurance unavailable to building owners, the UK government worked with British insurers to maintain property damage and business interruption insurance coverage. Pool Re was established by Parliament in 1993 as a mutual reinsurance company owned by the insurers and backed by the UK Treasury as reinsurer of last resort.[31] Pool Re has succeeded in stabilizing UK property insurance markets over nearly ten years without requiring further government assistance.

Pool Re also served to inform discussion in the US about how to maintain property and casualty insurance protection against terrorism risks after the attacks of 11 September 2001, which prompted many insurance carriers to exclude or severely restrict coverage for acts of terrorism. The result is the Terrorism Risk Insurance Act of 2002, signed into law by President Bush on 26 November 2002. This new law requires property and casualty insurers to provide coverage of losses due to acts of terrorism, while providing a three-year government reinsurance backstop for such claims. After the industry has paid out $10 billion in the first year (increasing to $12.5 billion the second year and $15 billion the third year), the federal government will pay 90 per cent of remaining claims up to a ceiling of $100 billion. The three-year limit is intended to 'allow for a transitional period for the private markets to stabilize, resume pricing of such insurance, and build capacity to absorb any future losses'.[32] While the Terrorism Risk Insurance Act will apply principally to workers' compensation and property insurance claims, it should also be examined as a model for coverage of IT security risks, since the lack of adequate reinsurance appears a major obstacle to cyber insurance expansion.

Providing Insurance Directly

In a few cases where losses have become too great for private insurers and reinsurers to handle – notably floods and earthquakes – government has stepped in directly to provide property damage insurance.[33] Since 1968, the National Flood Insurance Program[34] has offered insurance for homes and commercial buildings in flood-prone areas, where coverage would otherwise be unavailable. Administered by the Federal Emergency Management Agency, federal flood insurance is mandatory in flood hazard areas for recipients of government-guaranteed mortgages or other construction assistance, and is linked to floodplain management measures.

Similarly, the California State Legislature established the California Earthquake Authority[35] in 1996 to write homeowners' policies when private insurers began pulling out of the state market after suffering heavy losses in the 1994 Northridge earthquake. Insurance companies have not as yet incurred large losses from IT breach of security claims, however, and there seems little interest in or incentive for federal or state governments to provide cyber insurance at this time.

Legislating Liability

Given the diffuse and limited accountability for IT security vulnerabilities, as well as the uncertainties surrounding existing case law on liability, Congress or state legislatures could clarify who bears what responsibility for losses due to security breaches. The most recent National Research Council report on cyber security recommends that:

Policy makers should ...[c]onsider legislative responses to the failure of existing incentives to cause the market to respond adequately to the security challenge. Possible options include steps that would increase the exposure of software and system vendors and system operators to liability for system breaches and mandated reporting of security breaches that could threaten critical societal functions.[36]

However, legislation introduced at the state level would move in the opposite direction by guaranteeing software vendors greater immunity from liability for product defects. This Uniform Computer Information Transaction Act (UCITA) was enacted in Maryland and Virginia in 2001 and remains under consideration in several other states.

REWARDING IT SECURITY IN THE MARKETPLACE

Since 11 September US industry and government have taken some steps to increase commitments to and improve incentives for investing in IT security. The most notable industry development was Bill Gates' internal memo to employees in January 2002 stating that Microsoft will emphasize security over functionality in its software.[37] Although many have expressed scepticism over the depth of Microsoft's commitment, the company has moved quickly to focus on security and train its developers in 'secure coding practices' as part of its new Trustworthy Computing initiative.[38]

Well-publicized vulnerabilities, customer complaints and threatened litigation no doubt have influenced Microsoft's change in policy. Going further, a Fortune 50 company has recently adding language to a contract with a large software firm making the vendor responsible for security breaches connected with its software, according to trade reports.[39] And Wurzler Underwriting Managers has reportedly 'tacked a 5 to 15 percent surcharge on cyberinsurance premiums for users of Windows NT on IIS servers, citing their poor security track record'.[40]

On the government side, the President's Critical Infrastructure Protection Board, chaired by Richard Clarke, developed and released for comment in September 2002 a draft of 'The National Strategy to Secure Cyberspace', with a recommendation that:

Corporations should consider active involvement in industrywide programs to (a) develop IT security best practices and procurement standards for like companies; (b) share information on IT security through an appropriate information sharing and analysis center (ISAC); (c) raise cybersecurity awareness and public policy issues; and, (d) work with the insurance industry to expand the availability and utilization of insurance for managing cyber risk.[41]

However, the draft National Strategy contains no recommendations for government actions to mandate such industry initiatives or otherwise address the market failures surrounding IT security. Supporting R&D and standards development, removing disincentives for industry information sharing, mandating cyber liability insurance or similar financial responsibility for government contractors, and facilitating cyber reinsurance markets are some of the government actions that seem worth consideration today.[42]

In the end, rewarding IT security in the marketplace will probably require legislative changes to define liabilities more clearly and relate them to risk management principles and practices. Responsibility for IT security should reside primarily with those stakeholders who can best take preventive and protective measures. This means making software manufacturers liable for product flaws and vulnerabilities, while making network and system operators and users liable for fixing vulnerabilities that they discover or that are known to exist. Cyber insurance can then provide the means to transfer liabilities among stakeholders in an economically efficient manner. Placing liabilities with the parties best able to manage the risks associated with them creates the appropriate societal incentives for private decisions about investment in IT security, or insurance against security failures.

NOTES

1. Computer Science and Telecommunications Board, *Cybersecurity Today and Tomorrow* (Washington D.C.: National Research Council, 2002), p.7.
2. L. Jean Camp and Catherine Wolfram, 'Pricing Security', *Proceedings of the CERT Information Survivability Workshop* (Boston, MA: 24–26 Oct. 2000), pp.31–9.
3. President Clinton established the CAIO and the NIPC in response to the Report of the President's Commission on Critical Infrastructure Protection (PCCIP), *Critical Foundations* (Washington D.C., 1997).
4. World Wide ISAC Frequently Asked Questions, <http://www.wwisac.com/faq.cfm>. Other ISACs support specific industry sectors such as financial services <http://www.fsisac.com, telecommunications>, <http://www.ncs.gov/ncc>, information technology <https://www.it-isac.org>, electric power <http://www.esisac.com/>, surface transportation>; <http://www. aar.org>, oil and gas <http://www.aar.org/Newsroom/ISAC.asp>, chemicals, <http://

chemicalisac.chemtrec.com>, food <http://www.fmi.org/isac>, and water supply <http://www.waterisac.org>.

5. <http://searchsecurity.techtarget.com/sDefinition/0,,sid14_gci519405,00.html>.

6. S. 1456, the 'Critical Information Infrastructure Security Act of 2001', would limit the Freedom of Information Act and the antitrust laws as applied to security information. Introduced in Congress after the terrorist attacks of 11 September 2001, the bill has received support from the Information Technology Industry Council, The Financial Services Roundtable and other IT stakeholders. See Ben Polen, 'Tech Groups Pledge to Share Info', *Wired News*, 19 Oct. 2001.

7. Bruce Schneier, 'The Insurance Takeover', *Information Security* (Feb. 2001), <http://www.infosecuritymag.com/articles/february01/columns_sos.shtml>.

8 Daniel E. Geer, 'Risk Management is Where the Money Is', Paper presented to the Digital Commerce Society of Boston, Nov. 1998, available at <http://catless.ncl.ac.uk/Risks/20.06.html>.

9. See, for example, Computer Science and Telecommunications Board, *Trust in Cyberspace*, (Washington D.C.: National Research Council 1999).

10. See James R. Garven, 'Risk Management and Insurance', lecture notes and transparencies, University of Texas at Austin, 1995.

11. Schneier, 'The Insurance Takeover'.

12. Chana R. Schoenberger, 'Payout', *Forbes* (24 Dec. 2001).

13. *American Guarantee & Liability Insurance Co. v. Ingram Micro, Inc.*, 2000 US Dist. LEXIS 7209 (DC Ariz. 18 April 2000).

14. Ibid.

15. Alex Salkever, 'Who Pays When a Business Is Hacked?' *Business Week*, 23 May 2000; Adam H. Fleischer, 'What's Wrong with Ingram Micro', *PLUS Journal*, Feb. 2001.

16. Some of the IT security consultants who perform audits and risk assessments for insurance underwriting include Counterpane Internet Security, Unisys, Global Integrity (now part of Predictive Systems), IBM Global IT Security Services and Information Risk Group (a Pinkerton unit).

17. Robert Bryce, 'Insurers Offer Incentives to Buy Hacker Insurance', *Interactive Week* (5 March 2001).

18. Risk and Insurance Management Society, '2001 RIMS Benchmark Study', quoted at <http://www.iii.org/media/lateststud/>. See also Lynna Goch, 'Study: E-Risk Coverage Stagnates', *Property/Casualty BestWeek* (7 Aug. 2000), p.12.

19. Dimitry Elias Leger, 'Why Internet Insurance Isn't the Best Policy', *Fortune* (10 July 2000).

20. Colleen Brush, '2002 Industry Trends: Cyberinsurance', *Information Security Magazine* (Nov. 2001), <http://www.infosecuritymag.com/articles/november01/industry_cyberinsurance.shtml>.

21. See, for example, Joe Niedzielski, 'Catastrophe-Bond Market Appears Poised for Growth', *The Wall Street Journal*, 12 June 2000; Hal R. Varian, 'The Case for Catastrophe Bonds', *The New York Times*, 25 Oct. 2001.

22. Insurance covering communications satellites faced similar obstacles when commercial space launches began in the 1970s. See Frank Seitzen, jr., 'Space Launch Indemnification Renewal Critical to Industry', *Space Policy Digest* (May 1999), <http://www.spacepolicy.org/page_fs0599.html>.

23. <http://www.bitsinfo.org/orginsurance.html>.

24. <http://www.bitsinfo.org/fslab.html>.

25. Scott Berinato, 'A UL-Type Seal for Security? Don't Bet on It', *eWeek*, 15 Oct. 2000. Bruce Schneier, CTO of Counterpane Internet Security, is quoted in this article as downplaying the prospects for a UL-type organization for IT security: 'The sheer complexity and cost …[suggests] you could never get ahead of the problem'.

26. <http://www.bitsinfo.org/sltestedmark.html>.

27. David R. Graham *et al.*, *A National R&D Institute for Information Infrastructure Protection (I3P)* (Alexandria, VA: Institute for defense Analysis, IDA Paper P-3511, April 2000). The I3P concept initially was proposed by the President's Council of Advisors on Science and Technology in December 1998, in response to the 1997 Report of the President's Commission

on Critical Infrastructure Protection.

28. Nicolas Pasciullo, personal communication, 2001.

29. For example, see Computer Science and Telecommunications Board, *Cybersecurity Today and Tomorrow*, p.14; Hal R. Varian, 'Managing Online Security Risks', *The New York Times*, 1 June 2000; 'A Lemon Law for Software?' *The Economist Technology Quarterly*, 16 March 2002, p.3; Ira Sanger and Jay Greene, 'The Best Way to Make Software Secure: Liability', Business Week, 18 March 2002, p.61; Bruce Schneier, 'Liability and Security', Crypto-Gram newsletter, 15 April 2002, <http:www.counterpane.com>.

30. Notification and Reporting of Aircraft Accidents or Incidents', National Transportation Safety Board Regulations, 49 CFR830.

31. Association of British Insurers, 'ABI Opens Discussions with Government on Terrorism Insurance for Commercial Property', 21 Dec. 2001.

32. *H.R. 3210, Terrorism Risk Insurance Act of 2002*, 'Congressional Findings and Purpose', Title I, Sec. 101.

33. For an excellent treatment of government as the insurer of last resort, see David A. Moss, *When All Else Fails: Government as the Ultimate risk Manager* (Cambridge, MA: Harvard University Press, 2002). Flood and other disaster insurance are discussed in Chapter 9, 'Security for All', pp.253–91.

34. <http://www.fema.gov/nfip>.

35. <http://www.earthquakeauthority.com>.

36. Computer Science and Telecommunications Board, *Cybersecurity Today and Tomorrow*, p.14.

37. The Gates memo stated: 'when we face a choice between adding features and resolving security issues, we need to choose security'. Dennis Fisher, 'Gates: Security Over Features', *eWeek*, 21 Jan. 2002.

38. Craig Mundie *et al.*, 'Trustworthy Computing White Paper', Microsoft Corporation, 31 January 2002, <http://www.microsoft.com/presspass/exec/craig/01-31trustworthywp.asp>; Paul Boutin, 'Anti-Trustworthy Computing', *Salon*, 9 April 2002.

39. 'Dennis Fisher, 'Contracts Getting Tough on Security', *eWeek*, 15 April 2002.

40. Brush, '2002 Industry Trends: Cyberinsurance'.

41. President's Critical Infrastructure Protection Board, 'The National Strategy to Secure Cyberspace', Draft for Comment, September 2002, Recommendation R2-5, p.22.

42. However, additional government intervention in cyber insurance, or government regulation of private investments in IT security more generally, must contend with well-known political–economic problems of regulatory dynamics. These include slow regulatory decision-making processes that conflict with fast-moving IT developments, regulatory processes and procedures that generally favour incumbents over new entrants, rules that protect certain groups such as households and rural areas, and outcomes that favour political effectiveness over economic efficiency. Government initiatives in IT security inevitably will tend to be slow, incremental and designed in ways that skew markets in order to protect regional and other important political constituencies. Peter Cowhey, University of California – San Diego, private communication, 2002.

Thinking About New Security Paradigms

JOHN ARQUILLA

Exactly 50 years ago, the newly installed Eisenhower administration began a systematic process of rethinking national security strategy. To be sure, the Truman Doctrine of containment of Soviet aggression continued to be relevant. But Eisenhower and many of his advisors were convinced that the onset of the nuclear age implied profound changes for security affairs. Beginning with the secretive 'Project Solarium',[1] and continuing in more open and formal review processes, an attempt was made to imbue the containment process with new energy and muscle. Nuclear weapons were quickly seen as the catalysts for remarkable politico-military changes. For example, any communist aggression was to be opposed by 'massive retaliation', a threat to respond even to conventional attacks with nuclear weapons. The Army was to have a 'New Look'; i.e. it was to shed much of its traditional weaponry in favour of heavy reliance on nuclear arms. Both initiatives were in deep trouble from the very outset, but both took years to die before the inescapable truth of mutual assured destruction asserted itself.[2] It is something of a cautionary tale.

Today, we find ourselves in the early stages of an information age, in which computational power leaps beyond our wildest dreams routinely, and all-channel connectivity links the world economically, politically and socially. The focus this time is on the electron, not the atom. But unlike the preceding nuclear age, this is not a period of American control of the new technology, at least at the outset. Instead, advanced information systems have swiftly and widely diffused. And the technology itself, though inherently 'dual use', has none of the destructive potential of atomic weapons. Further, a nuclear shadow continues to darken the new era – particularly the resurgent threat of nuclear terrorism,[3] which has apparently played a large role in encouraging the Bush administration to articulate an essentially preventive new national security strategy.[4]

Despite this persistence of weapons of mass destruction – and here we must not forget the atomic bomb's weaker chemical and biological cousins – there is much value in thinking through the military and security implications of information technologies, as they carry the potential to forge intricate new weapons of 'mass disruption'. If they do not threaten Armageddon, they can nevertheless still take advanced societies and their economies on a costly sojourn to one of the rings of hell.[5] And the dependency of modern militaries on strong, secure information systems and flows suggests that the information revolution may have more impact on armed forces, ultimately, than nuclear weapons ever have.

With this in mind, we can see that the preceding articles have come to grips with some of the most salient issues that bear upon future security concepts. Our well-established notion of deterrence has grown frayed when confronted with non-state actors; and crisis management seems unimproved by advances in connectivity. For the military services, the organizational implications of the rise of new information systems have barely begun to be considered, while debates about the strategic utility of the cyberspace-based aspects of 'information warfare' seem eerily similar to the early musings of strategic bombing enthusiasts in the 1920s and 1930s.[6]

At the level of governance, the key issues have to do, it seems, with three fundamental questions: What should be done to ensure democratic accountability in overseeing (mostly covert and often deceptive) actions taken in the name of the 'war on terror?' What is the potential role of the private sector in providing for US national security? and How can the need for security be balanced against the desire to protect civil liberties? There are articles devoted to each of these questions, and all three are rich with insight.

In what follows I make a few more detailed comments about each of the articles in this issue of *Contemporary Security Policy*, dividing the discussion into three sections covering, respectively: deterrence and crisis management; military strategy and organization; and finally democratic oversight and public–private cooperation. Taken together, these articles provide the first real glimpse, in my view, of how the information revolution should alter our views of national security strategy.

DETERRENCE AND CRISIS MANAGEMENT

Deterrence is dying, apparently because of the rise of non-state actors – particularly networked ones – who wield increasing power, of both the destructive and disruptive variety. Simply put, this is the outgrowth of a century-long trend toward the empowerment of small groups that began with dynamite and has culminated in the hydra-headed threats posed by destructive nuclear, chemical and biological weapons, and disruptive cyberattack capabilities. In the case of computer worms, logic bombs and viruses, this new power is even vested in the hands of individuals. Developing a capability for mass destruction remains a somewhat difficult goal for a small group to achieve, but mass disruption is readily available – at the click of a mouse.

The threat of swift, sure retaliation helped deterrence to work for half a century during the Cold War, because identifiable nation-states provided ready targets for punitive action. Not so with small groups or individuals, who may be working on their own. Richard Harknett notes in his article that it may also logically be the case that what he calls 'the few' could be working for a state, or in loose alliance with one – but we may have little way of knowing. To this I would add the complication that 'the few' may actively deceive us about who their masters – if they have any – really are, posing the possibility that retaliatory actions might be misdirected.

How are we to deter those who hide behind a veil of anonymity? Or who are willing 'cut-outs' for others? For Harknett, the solution is to 'integrate' national security strategy with elements that go beyond deterrence, to pre-emption, prevention and, if all else fails, consequence management. While each of these concepts was fielded during the Cold War, the first two were very narrowly construed in military terms, while the third was never considered seriously – at least not by the United States. The idea of pre-emption came to be associated with a military strike launched when one expected an imminent attack. In the nuclear realm, this led to notions of 'launch on warning' – which conjured up all sorts of nightmares, from being caught unawares by a 'bolt from the blue' to striking based on mistaken warning.[7]

The idea of preventive war – i.e. attacking before an enemy becomes too threatening – long predates the current Bush Doctrine. Indeed, Thucydides' classic formulation that the Peloponnesian War broke out because of 'the rising power of Athens and the fear this inspired in Sparta' is essentially a preventive rationale. At the outset of the nuclear age, the United States viewed, in turn, the 'growing power' of the Soviet Union and of communist China – and thought seriously about striking preventively against each. In both cases, planning for preventive war went on for years, and was only rejected at the highest levels after much deliberation.[8] More recently, during the administration of Bush *père*, a 'defense planning guidance' was written that called explicitly for preventing the rise of any challenge to American supremacy. This document was swiftly discredited, though its words and intent have reappeared in the current Bush administration's National Security Strategy.[9] Even the Clinton administration had its share of preventive thoughts, as it struggled to deal with the potential threat of a nuclear North Korea – a crisis barely averted in 1994 by the now-defunct Carter Accords.[10]

Consequence management, what Harknett calls recovery and what was known during the Cold War as civil defense, was given short shrift when the fundamental threat was of nuclear holocaust. Civil defense came to be represented by black-and-gold signs on public buildings and stale crackers in tin containers secreted away below ground. Everyone knew that there was no hope of recovery from a war in which hundreds or thousands of nuclear warheads had been set off. But today the threat of all-out nuclear war has abated, being replaced by the possibility of terrorist attacks with biological and chemical devices, or possibly one or a few nuclear weapons.

Against this threat, it seems that an emphasis on consequence management – not just 'recovery', but rapid response as well – might sharply reduce the amount of damage done. Today, much attention is being given to this matter, with a 'shadow government' having been formed to limit disruption caused by terrorist attack. But far more can be done to pull together a 'rapid response network' of public, private, federal and local organizations. At this writing (fall 2002), it appears that high hopes are being placed on the creation of another cabinet-level department – but this may prove to be just another balky hierarchy, ill-suited to the nimble networking that will be required to stage effective 'response and recovery' to attack.[11]

Beyond the new problems that have arisen for deterrence, Damon Coletta has advanced the argument that the information revolution has done little and is unlikely ever to do much for crisis management. His analysis suggests that it is all too easy to think that advanced communications technologies will enhance decision making in a crisis. Instead, he affirms the value of counsel given by trusted advisors who have seen the crisis for themselves in the field. This is a powerful observation, suggesting that, in diplomacy, the new technologies may have far less impact on outcomes than they do in battle. I would also add that technology has sometimes been manipulated in crisis, Bismarck's subtle manipulation of the Ems Telegram, to foment war with France, being the prime example.

Nonetheless, there may still be a way to think about using advanced systems during a crisis to prevent escalation – if we look beyond a strictly statist perspective. The various new media that have come into being over the past decade, largely Web- and Net-based, can be characterized as many-to-many in their architecture. That is, they allow anybody interested in a particular issue area to become involved, at very low personal transaction cost. This new technological capability to mobilize mass publics has often been harnessed by NGOs, which have proliferated right along with the new media. The result has been that, in some crises, civil society actors have played crucial roles in tamping down violence – on both sides of a dispute. The archetypal case of this sort of civil society intervention occurred during the Zapatista uprising in Mexico, which began in 1994. NGOs are acknowledged to have constrained the Mexican army from violently repressing the EZLN.[12] Here, then, may be a way in which the new technology might spark a true revolution in diplomatic affairs.

To be sure, the rising power of civil society actors will be seen as threatening to states' autonomy of action, in general – and to the United States in particular. Indeed, the abortive 'Office of Strategic Influence' and its successor, the 'Office of Global Communications', are both tacit recognition by the United States that the 'battle of the story' is growing as important as the battlefield itself. Beyond the possible constraints that civil society actors might impose upon states, NGOs and their minions should also be seen as effective early warning systems, and might work very effectively *with* states in heading off incipient genocides and other types of crises endemic to failed and failing states. The point is that non-state actors may constrain states, sometimes, but may also catalyse them to take emergency action as well. Would that this had happened in Rwanda in time to spark an intervention heading off the mass slaughter there in 1994.

MILITARY STRATEGY AND ORGANIZATION

Thirty years ago, Russell Weigley argued that the American way of war has always tended to emphasize 'annihilation'.[13] Given that the United

States came into existence right along with the industrial revolution, it seems unsurprising that we have tended to think about conflict in terms of producing and placing as much mass as possible on the battlefield, then destroying our enemies with it. In part, the reliance on mass was an artefact of the inherent inaccuracy of our weapons systems (e.g., the perceived need for carpet bombing grew from the large circular error probable of the basic gravity bomb). Today, though, weapons consist not only of mass and energy, but also of information. In fact it is possible to see, as Colin McInnes has noted, that the rise of advanced guidance systems means that 'accuracy is no longer a function of range'.[14] It might also be hypothesized that the more information content the weapon has, the less mass it needs. In the case of cyber weapons (logic bombs, viruses, worms, etc.), we have systems that are almost all information and no mass.

This is where information warfare (IW) enters, at least the technical variant that Matt Bishop and Emily Goldman have so masterfully summarized. For it seems that, whether the target is a field army's or a fleet's critical information systems, or those that support civil infrastructure, there is a new class of virtual weaponry that can cause much disruption. In the field, this may mean making enemy forces easier targets for other weapons. In the hinterland, it likely means imposing large economic costs on an adversary society. Either way, we are looking at an important new manifestation of war that can only be ignored at our increasing peril.

It is fascinating to observe how closely the debates about the uses of IW today parallel the discussions about the future of air power in the 1920s and 1930s. Back then, most theorists supported the idea that the primary use for air forces would be to bypass field forces in favour of striking directly – and decisively – at homelands.[15] This is true of IW discussions today as well, with most focusing on what James Adams calls the 'strategic attack paradigm'.[16] Only the Germans fully appreciated the tactical and operational uses of air power at the time.[17] No military today, in my view, has properly appreciated the battlefield implications of IW – yet it is likely to cast a shadow on twenty-first century conflict approaching in size the one cast by ground attack aircraft on twentieth century battlefields. The irony, of course, is that strategic bombing has seldom worked – if ever.[18] The major policy implication for us, then, ought to be to stop fixating on strategic IW and start concentrating on how to use IW in battle.

Another reason to tamp down our ardour for the IW strategic attack paradigm is the observation by Bishop and Goldman that the advanced state most technically adept at IW is also likely to be the one most vulnerable to strategic-level disruption of its information systems. This paradox is further complicated by the rise of non-state cyberwarriors (Harknett's 'few' – perhaps more aptly described as the 'small and the many'), who probably cannot be deterred, and who can easily mount and remount costly attacks on infrastructure. Bishop and Goldman correctly observe that these non-state actors will have less capability, relative to states – but this will still leave them with substantial disruptive power, in absolute terms. A truly frightening prospect.

Encompassing IW, and extending widely beyond it, is the other domain of information-age conflict: information operations (IO). Balky Pentagon definitions aside, the most important aspect of IO is what John Diebold identified, back in the 1980s, as 'information management'.[19] Chris Demchak has focused on this issue in her call for creation of a military information 'Atrium' – a place both virtual and physical where raw data can be structured into knowledge that is needed to support military operations. The Atrium is a place of all-channel connectivity where new insights can be generated and then passed on to task and expeditionary forces immediately. If the US military, or any other, is ever to transform itself into the kind of organization implied by the information revolution, then it is just this sort of vision of institutional redesign that will enable change.

Sadly, the principal focus of leading militaries remains on the technologies themselves,[20] as Demchak notes, leading, among other things, to a disturbing tendency to try to overcentralize command and control of field forces. This leaves militaries open to a variety of serious problems, especially 'clogged circuits' from having just too much information to process. Just as great a problem is having a central command meddling in tactical decision making – a problem that bedevilled American operations in the first weeks of the campaign in Afghanistan, and which has surfaced again during the current counter-guerrilla endgame. Only in the middle phase – when special operations forces were given very free reign to connect with attack aircraft overhead and even with unmanned aerial vehicle data feeds – did we see a useful model of what I like to call 'command and decontrol'. The lesson of those brief, bright weeks is being unlearned rapidly.

Beyond the organizational conservatism that acts as a 'cosmological constant' in security affairs, why is it so hard to transform a military?

Demchak trenchantly notes that part of the problem is that global politics has changed as rapidly as weapons systems. Militaries are not yet habituated to thinking in terms of dealing with newly empowered non-state actors (like Al Qaeda), which will likely prove nearly impossible to destroy – but which may be disrupted. Thus, the focus remains on nations, not networks. Given that armed services' institutional interests lie in maintaining or growing their budgets – which are overwhelmingly tied to costly, industrial-age systems designed for fighting advanced militaries of nation-states – the prognosis for transformational change remains poor. The best we can hope to see is incremental advances toward a capability for waging what Demchak calls 'wars of disruption'.

DEMOCRATIC OVERSIGHT AND PUBLIC–PRIVATE COOPERATION

The most vexing questions about information-age security policy arise from IW's fundamentally covert, non-lethal nature. How does the constitutional separation of powers affect such a form of war? Can the public be informed adequately of its onset and progress on those occasions when conflicts are waged entirely in the information domain? These issues pose serious dilemmas for democracies, and Miroslav Nincic has analysed them with dispassionate clarity. He finds that IW, in both its technical, cyberspace-based form, and in its 'soft' perception management guise poses stiff challenges to democratic governance.

The IW of computer viruses, worms and distributed denial-of-service attacks against adversary societies and their infrastructures may be war, but of a form that can be waged both covertly and non-lethally. In effect, it may prove an attractive nuisance for senior political and military leaders, simply because of its apparent ease of use. Nincic finds the right analogy here – to the use of covert operations – and quite sensibly suggests that oversight of IW might follow similar lines.[21]

Beyond this, I would simply add the practical constraint that I have observed over the past decade – there is real concern among American policymakers about 'going first' with this form of war. After all, the United States is replete with inviting targets for hostile cyber-warriors; and any signal that this form of warfare was casually acceptable to us might unleash a greater storm upon ourselves. We simply don't know whether strategic IW will have real coercive power, or if it will have more effect when inflicted on others than it will have when we are attacked.

For the present, practical concerns of this sort have acted as a real constraint.[22] But this state of affairs can hardly be the solution over the longer term, suggesting the need to explore Nincic's recommendations for more formal oversight.

The softer dimension of IW, that which aims at shaping beliefs and behaviours, is more concerned with message than medium. This is the realm of 'perception management', and American strategists have approached it much in the fashion of political campaigners, i.e., emphasizing 'spin control'. Hence the rise of the ill-fated Office of Strategic Influence (OSI) – which during its brief life was commanded by an Air Force colonel whose formal training was in astrophysics. Nincic is concerned about the potential for abuse of this aspect of IW, either inadvertent or intentional. For example, deceptive influence techniques employed against an adversary's mass public, when disseminated in an open way (e.g., by radio, television, or Internet), would also act upon the American mass public, misleading them or shaping their views by improper means.

Once again, though, practical constraints have emerged to mitigate this problem. When it was openly reported that the OSI would occasionally engage in disinformation, the public storm of protest quickly led to the Office's closure. Defense Secretary Rumsfeld himself got into trouble for quoting Churchill's Second World War-era comment that 'sometimes the truth must have a bodyguard of lies'. In short, there is little tolerance for official lies, so strategies that aim at influencing perceptions of adversaries, or international mass publics, should focus instead on disseminating information about our core values and beliefs. Indeed, this is the stated mission of the Office of Global Communications that has risen, phoenix-like, from the ashes of the OSI. If this new office stays on the right path, then perhaps we'll stand a chance of actually persuading much of the world – including the large Muslim portion – that the terror war is *not* a 'clash of civilizations'. Rather, it is a fight to build a global civil society based on individual freedom and security for all.

Nincic's concern about guarding against official truth-twisting has a corollary in Patrick Morgan's systematic investigation of the issue of 'who watches the watchers'. Morgan notes that technical advances in surveillance systems, coupled with the sense of total vulnerability that has come with the terror war, have combined to create permissive conditions for abuse. Specifically, he is worried that the pursuit of security will sacrifice some portion of our liberty. Indeed, this seems to be one of the most important tensions of the information age. While the possible outcome is hardly likely to be Orwellian, the dystopian future envisioned by William Gibson in his *Idoru*, where data can be easily mined about all the details of every individual, seems more and more plausible.[23]

There appear to be three strategies for dealing constructively with this security–liberty tension. First, as Morgan notes, there must be improved oversight of all surveillance activities. Given the sorry abuses of the Cold War era, and the perverted use of intelligence and legal agencies' capabilities for domestic political ends by Nixon, the willingness and ability to exert appropriate control over the watchers should be good. Morgan is less hopeful about a second solution, that individual access to strong (i.e., virtually unbreakable) encryption will diffuse widely – due to complex implementation, high cost and official resistance. His concern on this point is reasonable, as US policymakers have long resisted the spread of encryption to the people. But this battle is being won right now by private sector actors who are making strong codes available to the mass public, at modest cost.

This private-sector outflanking of the opponents of encryption is an example of Morgan's third strategy for mitigating the risks of over-intrusion upon civil liberties. In Morgan's view, there will be a market-based solution featuring private companies developing new technologies aimed at ensuring individual privacy. Of course, it is possible that terrorists and criminals will eventually get their hands on these products as well. Indeed, they already employ very strong encryption routinely, which has sparked a reaction from both law enforcement and intelligence – both of whom are developing ever stronger, 'clandestine technical collection' tools (i.e., those that are web- and net-based), like 'Magic Lantern'. The real point here may be that, in the action–reaction process surrounding new security technologies and the countermeasures against them, the private sector is doing most (in the range of 90 per cent-plus) of the research and development. We have come quite far from the Cold War, during which the ratio was exactly the reverse.

It is this fundamental shift toward private-sector solutions to security problems on which Walter Baer focuses. In particular, he considers primarily market-based solutions to the threats posed by costly, disruptive attacks – especially cyberspace-based ones, which will undoubtedly grow in frequency and severity in the future. To the extent to which Baer sees a role for government, he argues that it lies in elaborating good standards and encouraging safe practices, much as the Occupational Safety and Health Administration (OSHA) is intended to.

Baer examines in detail the many types of insurance coverage that might indemnify against losses due to cyberterrorism. To this I would only add that insurers are already grappling with coverage questions about terrorist attacks in general. Baer's conception of healthy public–private cooperation may thus prove invaluable to thinking through the general problem of insuring against the perils posed by terrorism, in addition to its prime focus on cyberspace-based attacks. Indeed, his ideas seem so sensible that it seems at first quite puzzling that insurance companies have not already leapt at the chance to provide an actuarial solution to this problem set.

The stumbling block is yet another security-related 'tension'. Where Nincic has concerns about the trade-off between the need for security and maintaining good governance, and Morgan is focused on security and individual liberty, Baer confronts an apparent zero-sum situation between security and 'efficiency'. Basically, the problem is that good security practices impose financial and operational costs on both corporations and individuals. In highly competitive market sectors, or in tough economic times, there is little inducement to shell out precious funds to cope with a problem that just hasn't proven itself to be a potent threat.

This is the area that security analysts must turn to now. Why haven't the costs of hacking, cracking and cyberterror been higher? To be sure, there are many instances of attacks that have cost single companies dearly (i.e., in the tens of millions of dollars) – but these are few and far between. Yet, if one looks just a bit deeper, it is apparent that both the number and severity of incidents has been increasing – and there is growing evidence that those with advanced hacking skills are no longer just skylarking. There are an increasing number of terrorist groups that are investing in cyberspace-based capabilities,[24] and an increasing number of hackers who appear to be in the process of 'radicalizing' to the point of being willing to do more damage than ever before. The storms will come, so now is the time to think through how to insure against the damage they will likely inflict.

THINKING ABOUT NEXT STEPS

As Lenin once famously asked, 'What is to be done?' Based on the range of concepts developed in the preceding articles, there are several interesting implications for security strategy that may help outline effective policies and doctrines to replace the ever-less-relevant Cold War constructs that still guide us to such a substantial degree. One of the most trenchant insights has to do with Richard Harknett's notion of the rise of 'the few'. Small, interconnected groups are becoming increasingly empowered – for good or ill – and it behooves national security policy makers to begin thinking as much about nimble new networks as about old-style nations. This means recognizing that punitive deterrence rooted in retaliatory threats may well be in tatters, and suggests instead a shift in emphasis to deterrence based on an ability to demonstrate to the attacker that his aims can be effectively defended against.[25]

Thinking more about terrorist, ethnonationalist and other dark sorts of networks of 'the few' should not prevent us from thinking about the explosive growth of civil society networks which may have a profound potential to do good things – particularly in facilitating crisis resolution. Damon Coletta has cogently argued the case against being over-optimistic about the potential of advanced communications technology as a crisis management tool. Yet it is this same technology that allows individuals, non-governmental organizations and other affinity groups to weigh in powerfully. This potential is worth cultivating, and should form part of any overall shift toward thinking about the implications of non-state networks.[26]

Insofar as notions of networking speak to the importance of thinking about organizational redesign, Chris Demchak's 'Atrium' concept should be seen as vastly increasing the military's ability to generate knowledge and distribute it broadly and swiftly. Where the German General Staff may have been the apotheosis of industrial-age military administration,[27] the Atrium – or something very much like it – seems destined to guide and govern the intellectual life of the armed services in the information age. Given that conflict itself is morphing into something hardly recognizable by Cold War norms, the need to engage in thoughtful institutional redesign is becoming quite pressing.

As to the emerging 'logic' of information warfare, as Matt Bishop and Emily Goldman put it, there seem to be two particularly salient policy issues in play. First, there is the need to decide on which form of IW we shall emphasize – we cannot do both at once, and should probably not even try. One form of IW is akin to earlier notions of 'strategic bombardment', the other is more related to the 'close air support' of military formations that are engaging some adversary in battle. In my view, dreams of using IW to bring a society to its knees are even further from realization than the continuing hopes of air power theorists that we may yet witness a demonstrably decisive bombing campaign. Instead, an emphasis on the integration of IW into battles and campaigns is likely to generate real dividends, as modern armed forces simply cannot fight – even terror networks can't – without secure, available connectivity.

The second policy that should grow out of our burgeoning IW skills affects intelligence. Today, we rely heavily on satellite-based information gathering systems, and far, far less on human spies. Against terrorists and other irregulars (i.e., 'the few'), assets in orbit don't help much, as they are best used for counting tanks, planes and ships. And spies are very hard to infiltrate into terror networks. This is why we must begin to grow a new kind of intelligence that is Web- and Net-based. It holds out the promise of detecting, tracking and countering global terror networks with information that can be described as being a kind of 'virtual human intelligence'. Today, intelligence organizations call this 'clandestine technical collection'. It enjoys only a small slice of the intelligence budget, and wields an even smaller amount of organizational influence. But if we are to prevail in the terror war, and in other conflicts to come, this must change.

Of course, the rise of IW, particularly with its potential for intelligence gathering, implies a whole new set of thorny social, economic and political problems that three contributors to this issue have engaged directly. Miroslav Nincic has thoughtfully exposited the tension between national security and government oversight, while Patrick Morgan has extended the argument to security-based threats to civil liberties. Finally, Walter Baer has identified just how the pursuit of security might be driven, and sustained, by market forces and mechanisms. Policies that can master each of these seemingly intractable problems will require something beyond the usual 'balancing act' that is called for by policy analyses. Instead, it may be that the answer is to eliminate the apparent 'tension' between security and oversight, liberty and efficiency by decisively ruling in favour of individual rights and public welfare at every turn. In doing so, we may even find ourselves more secure.

Throughout the Cold War, it was commonly accepted that our government sometimes had to act in the greatest secrecy in order to protect us; and that the quest for security sometimes led to the trampling of privacy rights and other aspects of individual freedom. In retrospect, though, it seems clear that covert actions, as often as not, have proved inimical to our interests – the Bay of Pigs being perhaps the stand-out example of such folly.[28] And the willingness to tolerate undue and unregulated intrusiveness has often bred abuses, as the subversion of the FBI and CIA during Watergate demonstrated. Perhaps now is the time to recognize that a well-informed public is the basis for sound security strategy, and that the protection of the individual's rights is a reasonable approach to mitigating external threats.

Can this really be the case? I think so. In an era in which civil society actors around the world are exercising their increasing power, why shouldn't the citizens of great nations exert the same kind of influence on high-level policy? Particularly as it pertains to their security. Seen in this light, the tension between security and oversight is illusory. As Nincic has noted, this view goes back at least to the nineteenth century ideas of Condorcet, who took the position that 'obstacles to the direct expression of popular will should be removed wherever possible in the interests of the international order'.[29]

As to privacy rights, the case for favouring the individual is even stronger here. Simply put, the best protection of these rights lies in the broad dissemination of very strong encryption, which will secure individuals against undue intrusion. It will also vastly improve information security against cyberterror, providing a basis for Walter Baer's market-based notions of an insurance solution to the disruptive new threats coming our way. Sadly, the United States government followed an obstructive policy for years. First, it tried to outlaw strong encryption. Inevitably, this failed, but government still tried to ignore the fact that unbreakable encryption could be made available to a broad public – because this might curtail the ability of law enforcement and intelligence agencies to monitor communications. Today, we must realize that terrorists and trans-national criminals have access to the most secure information systems, and that to deny such security to our own people is a grave public disservice.

These policy implications – from empowering public oversight to enabling private security – will, I hope, come to form part of a 'new normal' in the years ahead. When I was a schoolboy, I ducked and covered, because I was told that this was how to survive a nuclear attack. And for nearly 50 years, whole generations have grown up who have had to live with the possibility of being just 30 minutes away from nuclear holocaust at any given time – with little more than 'duck and cover' notions to keep them safe. Indeed we now know that, over 40 years ago, the Cuban Missile Crisis came very close to ending in nuclear war. Nevertheless, we learned to compartmentalize our concerns and to live on a daily basis with the threat of Armageddon. For we lived in a Cold War world, replete with implacable, but identifiable, foes held in check by rock-solid deterrence. Now we must learn to live in a new 'cool war' world, where the threats are less cataclysmic, but impossible to deter and very hard to prevent. Yet, for all its uncertainties, I'll take this cool war world over the Cold War one. And I hold out the hope that the adoption of creative new security constructs and paradigms will help us to prevail in this conflict as well.

NOTES

1. An extensive discussion of Solarium can be found in Robert R. Bowie and Richard H. Immerman, *Waging Peace: How Eisenhower Shaped an Enduring Cold War Strategy* (New York: Oxford University Press, 2000).
2. Thomas Schelling, *Arms and Influence* (New Haven: Yale University Press, 1966) puts it very succinctly: 'As a doctrine, "massive retaliation" (or the threat of it) was in decline almost from its enunciation in 1954' (p.190). For a critique of the short-lived 'New Look', see John Lewis Gaddis, *Strategies of Containment: A Critical Appraisal of Postwar American National Security Policy* (London: Oxford University Press, 1982), especially pp.161–3.
3. Early on, nuclear weapons were seen as means disproportionate to terrorist aims. In Brian Jenkins' oft-cited view, 'terrorists want a lot of people watching, not a lot of people dead'. See his *The Potential for Nurclear Terrorism* (Santa Monica: RAND, 1977). Thomas Schelling, 'Thinking about Nuclear Terrorism', *International Security*, Vol. 6, No. 4 (Spring 1982), pp.61–77, however was already worried, noting that he found it 'hard to think of any use [of nuclear weapons] that would *not* be terrorist' (p.66) emphasis added.
4. See 'The National Security Strategy of the United States' (Washington: Government Printing Office, Sep. 2002).
5. Although just how costly cyberattacks might be is a subject of debate. Winn Schwartau, *Information Warfare: Chaos on the Information Superhighway* (New York: Thunder's Mouth Press, 1994) takes the gravest view of the threat. Gregory Rattray, *Strategic Warfare in Cyberspace* (Cambridge: MIT Press, 2001), pp.490–2, surveys recent cyberattacks and finds the damage done to be modest at best.
6. Rattray, *Strategic Warfare in Cyberspace*, devotes a long chapter to drawing out the intellectual links between the rise of air power and the emergence of strategic information warfare. Compare his description of the current wave of thinking about cyberwarfare to such air power classics as Giulio Douhet, *The Command of the Air* (New York: McCann, 1942) (trans. Dino Ferrari); and Alexander de Seversky, *Victory Through Air Power* (New York: Simon and Schuster, 1942).
7. On some of the near disasters of this period, see Scott D. Sagan, *The Limits of Safety* (Princeton: Princeton University Press, 1993).
8. For a thorough analysis of the heated debates about taking preventive action during the early

Cold War period – and the primacy of ethical considerations in setting policy – see David Alan Rosenberg, 'Nuclear War Planning', in Michael Howard, Geo. Andreopoulos and Mark R. Shulman (eds), *The Laws of War: Constraints on Warfare in the Western World* (New Haven: Yale University Press, 1994), pp.160–90.

9. The attempt to formulate a preventive strategy by the first Bush administration foundered in the wake of its being publicly reported. The first article about it was Patrick E. Tyler, 'Pentagon Imagines New Enemies To Fight in Post-Cold-War Era', *The New York Times*, 17 Jan. 1992, pp.A1,5. As Tyler put it, 'the documents call for a strategy to deter the re-emergence later in this decade of a global "adversarial rival".' The current Bush administration builds directly on this predecessor in its national security strategy, noting ominously that, 'in an age where the enemies of civilization openly and actively seek the world's most destructive technologies, the United States cannot remain idle while dangers gather' (p.15).

10. Leon Sigal, *Disarming Strangers: Nuclear Diplomacy with North Korea* (Princeton: Princeton University Press, 1998), describes the 1994 crisis as one that came very close to seeing the United States launch a preventive war against the regime of Kim Il Sung. In Oct. 2002, North Korea formally abrogated the Carter Accords, but also expressed its openness to a new round of negotiations about the curtailment of its nuclear program.

11. For more on this, see John Arquilla, 'It Takes a Network', *Los Angeles Times*, 25 Aug. 2002.

12. See David Ronfeldt, John Arquilla and Graham and Melissa Fuller, *The Zapatista Social Netwar in Mexico* (Santa Monica: RAND, 1998). Also examining this case, and going beyond it, is Alison Brysk, >*From Tribal Village to Global Village: International Relations and Indian Rights in Latin America* (Stanford: Stanford University Press, 1998).

13. See Russell Weigley, *The American Way of War* (New York: Macmillan, 1973).

14. Colin McInnes, 'Technology and Modern Weapons', in John Baylis and N.J. Rengger (eds), *Dilemmas of World Politics* (Oxford: Oxford University Press, 1992), p.148.

15. A comprehensive survey of the air power debates in Britain and America during this period can be found in Tami Davis Biddle, *Rhetoric and Reality in Air Warfare* (Princeton: Princeton University Press, 2002).

16. James Adams, *The Next World War* (New York: Simon and Schuster, 1998), p.97.

17. On this point, see Richard R. Muller, 'Close Air Support: The German, British, and American Experiences, 1918–1941', in Williamson Murray and Allan R. Millett, eds), *Military Innovation in the Interwar Period* (Cambridge: Cambridge University Press, 1996), pp.144–90.

18. See Robert Pape, *Bombing to Win* (Ithaca: Cornell University Press, 1995) for the full, sorry listing of failed bombardment campaigns.

19. John Diebold, *Managing Information* (New York: American Management Association, 1985).

20. This tendency itself may grow from widespread ignorance about the early definitions of 'military revolutions' advanced by historians, who have always looked beyond the technology to issues of strategy, doctrine and organization. See especially Michael Roberts' Oxford lecture, given almost half a century ago, in which he contends that all these elements must be present for there to be revolutionary change. The example of revolutionary change he used was of the rise of mass volley fire in the seventeenth century Swedish army, his original concept can be found in Michael Roberts, *Essays in Swedish History* (London: Weidenfeld and Nicolson, 1967).

21. On the history of US covert operations since George Washington, and their oversight – with which there have been problems – see Stephen Knott, *Secret and Sanctioned: Covert Operations and the American Presidency* (London: Oxford University Press, 1996). See also Gregory Treverton, *Covert Action: The Limits of Intervention in the Postwar World* (New York: Basic Books, 1987).

22. Anecdotally, I was present at and involved in high-level Pentagon discussions of this very point early on during the Kosovo War. The discussions resulted in a decision to act with great circumspection about the use of IW against the Serbian people – and their individual leaders.

23. See William Gibson, *Idoru* (New York: G.P. Putnam's Sons, 1996). Falling between Orwell and Gibson is David Brin's more hopeful vision of the use of advanced technology for protective monitoring (e.g., to reduce crime in public places). See Brin, *The Transparent Society: Will Technology Force Us to Choose Between Privacy and Freedom?* (Reading, MA: Addison-Wesley, 1998).

24. See *Cyberterror: Prospects and Implications* (Monterey: Center on Terrorism and Irregular Warfare, 1999).

25. On the fundamental distinction between punitive- and denial-based deterrence, see Patrick Morgan, *Deterrence: A Conceptual Analysis* (Beverly Hills, CA: Sage Publications, 1973), and John J. Mearsheimer, *Conventional Deterrence* (Ithaca: Cornell University Press, 1983).

26. Important recent studies of the empowerment of 'the few' include Manuel Castells, *The Information Age: Economy, Society, and Culture*, Vol. II, *The Power of Identity* (Malden, MA: Blackwell Publishers, 1997), and Howard Rheingold, *Smart Mobs: The Next Social Revolution* (New York: Perseus Publishing, 2002). An interesting analysis of non-state actors trying to stop nineteenth-century imperialist depredations can be found in Adam Hochschild, *King Leopold's Ghost: A Story of Greed, Terror, and Heroism in Colonial Africa* (Boston: Houghton Mifflin, 1998).

27. See Walter Goerlitz, *History of the German General Staff* (New York: Praeger, 1953), and Trevor N. Dupuy, *A Genius for War: The German Army and General Staff, 1807–1943* (Englewood Cliffs, NJ: Prentice-Hall, 1977).

28. On the general tendency of covert action to fail – particularly its military and para-military variants – see Lucien S. Vandenbroucke, *Perilous Options* (New York: Oxford University Press, 1993). See also Treverton, *Covert Action*.

29. Miroslav Nincic, *Democracy and Foreign Policy: The Fallacy of Political Realism* (New York: Columbia University Press, 1992), p.10.

Abstracts

Integrated Security: A Strategic Response to Anonymity and the Problem of the Few *by Richard J. Harknett*

Historical trends involving technological development have led to an emerging strategic environment that undercuts the viability of traditional models of security – defense and deterrence. The potential for small numbers of people to inflict great damage and disruption is a dimension of conflict that must be considered alongside (and which interacts with) state and state proxy dimensions of conflict. A condition of multidimensional conflict requires a multi-approach response. The notion is offered of Integrated Security in which success lies in the interconnectedness between a continuum of security approaches: preventive offense, preemption, defense, deterrence, and recovery. The strategic goal of Integrated Security is to move conflict away from network and proxy dimensions, since the state dimension of conflict is easier to manage.

Revolution's End: Information Technology and Crisis Management *by Damon Coletta*

Despite the general enthusiasm for applying information technology to military affairs, insufficient work has been done on the question of how new systems will facilitate the management of international crises. Crises often set the initial conditions under which military competition must take place. The prevailing wisdom treats them as a less intense form of military conflict, so the same gains that revolutionary technologies have achieved in combat should obtain during crises. However, crisis management has its own dynamics apart from war-fighting. Wars are fought to eliminate competition, while crisis managers seek to induce cooperation – producing a favorable agreement while avoiding war. Crises call upon leaders' political intuition, their personal style of information processing, and their capacity to respond after surprises in different measures than combat does. A historical comparison of US crisis management during the Berlin crises – 1948–1962 and the crises in the former Yugoslavia – 1992–1999 shows that information age capabilities for the collection, analysis, and distribution of information neither reduced the difficulty nor lowered the intensity of crisis dilemmas for decision-makers.

Wars of Disruption: International Competition and Information Technology-Driven Military Organizations *by Chris C. Demchak*

The US military's vigorous development of force multiplying information technologies during the late Cold War period set the stage for the emergence of a new form of warfare, one seen as legitimate even though it lacks the formal declaration of war – 'wars of disruption'. 'Wars of disruption' are not inevitably lethal. Over the 1990s, however, military leaders channeled a traditional emphasis on lethality into many novel operations. New technologies were justified by the proposition that ultimately their test of effectiveness was their contribution to rapid, accurate applications of lethal force. This predilection was unfortunate since today's environment is filled with state and non-state actors whose mix of incentives to act may not be as sensitive to the application of lethal force as they might to a policy response mix of other levers. This piece discusses the evolution and the underlying focus on lethality that was used expediently by military leaders for budgetary purposes but came to dominate the modernization vision. This essay proposes a theory for assessing when actors have sufficient incentive to disrupt the status quo and when major power policies should employ a war of disruption against the recalcitrant actor, and with what degree of lethality.

The Strategy and Tactics of Information Warfare *by Matt Bishop and Emily O. Goldman*

What makes warfare in the information age a departure from the past is that information *as* warfare has become as important as information *in* warfare. Information is no longer just a means to boost the effectiveness of lethal technologies, but opens up the possibility of non-lethal attacks that can incapacitate, defeat, deter or coerce an adversary. The information age has also expanded the domains of IW – on the battlefield, in the marketplace, and against the infrastructure of modern society – and its purveyors –individuals and private groups in addition to national militaries. Yet despite these differences, the logic of warfare remains the same – sequencing and coordinating attacks to achieve lower order technical or 'cyber' goals, which are part of a broader campaign to achieve higher order political, material and/or symbolic goals. Moreover, despite the leveling affect of information technology, states and state-sponsored groups will retain certain advantages in waging information warfare because a capacity for sustained attack still requires a level of organization, intelligence about the target, and sustainability not likely to be possessed by the lone individual.

Information Warfare and Democratic Accountability *by Miroslav Nincic*

This essay explores how the expansion of information technology may affect two defining features of democracy: how power and accountability are structured at the apex of the political system, and how government and governed interact. *Offensive* information warfare may carry consequences for democracy at two levels. First, by rendering ambiguous the very definition of warfare, it makes it harder to ensure democratic controls over its conduct. Second, tools of offensive information warfare may seek to influence an adversary's will and capacity to fight through 'perception management'. As this often means manipulating the adversary's perceptions with a view to distorting his view of reality, it may convey the distortions to a domestic audience, undermining the public's ability to form an autonomous judgment of government actions and to hold it accountable for these actions. *Defensive* information warfare poses a different threat, that of civil liberties. Government's efforts to ferret out threats to critical information infrastructures may involve a level of monitoring and surveillance that threatens Fourth Amendment protections and other norms limiting governmental intrusiveness into the lives of its citizens. The broad concerns crystallize into the following three problems: (1) the implications of information warfare for decisions to initiate war, (2) its potential to distort judgments that are at the roots of public control of its leaders, and (3) the possibility that the requisites of defensive information warfare may lead to excessive government intrusiveness into the lives of its citizens.

Information Warfare and Domestic Threats to America Security
by Pat Morgan

Much concern has been expressed about disturbing domestic developments associated with the "War on Terrorism" that represent some erosion of American values - the general theme being that if the terrorists lead us to abandon or compromise some of our fundamental freedoms then they have won. However, there is an older theme in American political history that has been neglected: a national preoccupation with foreign affairs leads to bearing heavy burdens in national security and expands the power and capabilities of the state at the expense of the citizens. National security concerns tend, over time, to enlarge the threat to America from their own state and various elements in their society. This emerges more sharply when the nation is at war because then domestic support for government intrusions into or impositions on the lives of the citizens grow markedly, as do impositions by certain private entities. This trend seems inherent in many of the capabilities that are being developed to maintain US dominance in information warfare and expand the "Revolution in Military Affairs" of which it is a part. To identify what we may be up against and better understand the possible responses to it, this paper examines past instances of developments of this sort.

Rewarding IT Security in the Marketplace *by Walter Baer*

Improving information technology security demands greater efforts from both the public and private sectors, as well as better coordination and cooperation between them. US initiatives include creating a series of industry-specific Information Sharing and Analysis Centers to encourage government/industry collaboration on information security. Private sector firms also need stronger incentives to invest adequately in IT security. Moving from trust management to risk management, with widely available and well-functioning markets for insurance covering IT security risks, could go a long way toward strengthening such incentives.

Although the insurance industry has developed new forms of cyber insurance, coverage is limited, and few businesses now purchase these policies. Problems include lack of underwriting standards, little experience on which to base premiums, numerous exclusions and limits on liability, and an underdeveloped reinsurance market. Possible ways for government to spur insurance market expansion are explored, such as participating in standards development, mandating cyber insurance, facilitating reinsurance, or indemnifying catastrophic losses. In the end, rewarding IT security in the marketplace will likely require legislative changes to define liabilities more clearly and relate them to risk management principles and practices.

Notes on Contributors

John Arquilla is Associate Professor of Defense Analysis at the Naval Postgraduate School and, most recently, co-author of *Networks and Netwars: The Future of Terror, Crime, and Militancy.*

Dr Walter S. Baer is Senior Policy Analyst at RAND and Professor of Policy Analysis at the RAND Graduate School in Santa Monica, California. His research focuses on public/private sector collaboration and market-based approaches to information security and related policy issues.

Matt Bishop is an Associate Professor in the Department of Computer Science at the University of California, Davis. His research areas include vulnerabilities analysis and formal modeling of systems and software.

Damon Coletta is Assistant Professor of Political Science at the United States Air Force Academy near Colorado Springs, CO.

Chris C. Demchak teaches 'Governance and Security' and 'MIS for Poets' at the University of Arizona. She holds a UC Berkeley PhD and masters degrees in energy engineering and economic development. A US Army Reserve officer, she has published a book and several articles on comparative military transformations, complex systems, and knowledge management.

Emily O. Goldman is Associate Professor of Political Science at the University of California, Davis and Director of the UC Davis Washington Center. Her research focuses on the diffusion of military technology and ideas, the social and cultural foundations of military transformation, and strategic planning under uncertainty.

Richard J. Harknett is Associate Professor of Political Science at the University of Cincinnati and holds a professorial lectureship at the Diplomatic Academy, Vienna, Austria.

Pat Morgan is Professor of Political Science and Thomas and Elizabeth Tierney Chair in Peace and Conflict Studies at the University of California, Irvine. His book, *Deterrence Now*, was published by Cambridge University Press in May 2003.

Miroslav Nincic is Professor of Political Science at the University of California, Davis. His most recent book (co-authored with Joseph Lepgold) is *Beyond the Ivory Tower: International Relations Theory and the Issue of Policy Relevance* (Columbia University Press, 2002).

Index

and the expansion of state power, 163, 164,
  168
historical rates, fn 11
Wars of German Unification, 113
Washington, D.C., 65
Weapons of mass destruction (WMD), 29, 36,
  41
Weber, Max, 23, 24, 44
Wenk, Edward, 159
West Berlin, 64, 67
West Germany, 49

Western European Union, 71
White House, 178
Wilkenfeld, Jonathan, 51, 52
Wiretapping, 170–73 passim, 183
  Federal Wiretap Act of 1968, 170
  Trap and trace capabilities, 172
Woodward, John D., Jr., 188n
Worst case analysis, 163, 184

Yugoslavia 49–54 passim, 59, 68–9, 72

Other Titles in the Series

Why Wars Widen

A Theory of Predation and Balancing

Stacy Bergstrom Haldi, US Navy War College

The fear that a conflict will spread is often used as a justification for
'peacekeeping' operations. But why and under what conditions is war
likely to widen? When are concerns warranted and justified?

Why Wars Widen: A Theory of Predation and Balancing offers a
theoretical explanation for war widening based on the decisiveness of
warfare in a given era. It argues that conflicts are most likely to spread
when the effects of warfare are limited, as states seek limited gains with
a low cost. In an era where warfare is decisive, in other words, an era
of total war, wars are less likely to widen. Great powers will only enter
such a conflict to redress the balance of power.

The explanation of war widening is developed through four historical
cases: The Seven Years' War, the French Revolution/Napoleonic Wars,
the Crimean War and the First World War.

224 pages 2003
07146 5307 1 cloth

FRANK CASS PUBLISHERS
Crown House, 47 Chase Side, Southgate, London N14 5BP
Tel: +44 (0)20 8920 2100 Fax: +44 (0)20 8447 8548 E-mail: info@frankcass.com
NORTH AMERICA
920 NE 58th Avenue Suite 300, Portland, OR 97213-3786 USA
Tel: 800 944 6190 Fax: 503 280 8832 E-mail: cass@isbs.com
Website: www.frankcass.com

Terrorism and Grand Strategy

Paul B Rich, University of Cambridge and
Thomas R Mockaitis, De Paul University, Chicago (Eds)

This collection of essays examines the strategic dimensions of contemporary terrorist threats. It evaluates the changing nature of modern terrorism in the light of the events of September 11 2001. The collection argues that terrorism now promises to enter the terrain of global 'grand strategy'.

160 pages 2003
0 7146 5313 6 cloth
0 7146 8268 3 paper

FRANK CASS PUBLISHERS
Crown House, 47 Chase Side, Southgate, London N14 5BP
Tel: +44 (0)20 8920 2100 Fax: +44 (0)20 8447 8548 E-mail: info@frankcass.com
NORTH AMERICA
920 NE 58th Avenue Suite 300, Portland, OR 97213-3786 USA
Tel: 800 944 6190 Fax: 503 280 8832 E-mail: cass@isbs.com
Website: www.frankcass.com

Deterrence in the 21st Century

Max G Manwaring, US Army War College, Carlisle, PA (Ed)

Part One re-examines the broad concept of deterrence as it applies to the 'Russian Bear, Asian Dragons, and 1000 Snakes' and argues the need for a new and broader deterrence policy and strategy that can and will respond to the diverse threats looming on the none-too-distant horizon.

Part Two analyses a series of troubling issues – from 'Some Possible Surprises in Our Nuclear Future', to 'Deterrence and Conventional Military Forces', to questions of terrorism and information warfare – that make the case for change.

Finally, Part Three provides some strategic-level ideas regarding possible new deterrence policy and strategy.

160 pages 2001
0 7146 5133 8 cloth
0 7146 8160 1 paper

FRANK CASS PUBLISHERS
Crown House, 47 Chase Side, Southgate, London N14 5BP
Tel: +44 (0)20 8920 2100 Fax: +44 (0)20 8447 8548 E-mail: info@frankcass.com
NORTH AMERICA
920 NE 58th Avenue Suite 300, Portland, OR 97213-3786 USA
Tel: 800 944 6190 Fax: 503 280 8832 E-mail: cass@isbs.com
Website: www.frankcass.com

Asymmetries of Conflict
War Without Death

John Leech

Foreword by **Lord Judd**

> *'It is an arresting view of potential trends in modern warfare and deserves a wide audience. John Leech is keenly aware of how much we need to rethink.'*
>
> **Lord Owen**

Territorial defence – including protection from terrorism – must remain paramount. Yet most of today's challenges come from those unwilling to adjust to a global society. Even though small groups of men have access to huge destructive forces if they couple small material resources to their ferocious ingenuity, future threats to security are likely to concern not our immediate safety but the proper management of the world in which we have an interest. For that we need soft power, but always with a hard edge. Warfare must remain the last resort.

Europe and the USA represent a powerful combination of diplomacy and might, but they still have to fully comprehend their differing roles within a common defence. The NATO alliance should agree on a sensible re-balancing of functions, acknowledging the global investment each is already making in their common security.

Decisions about defence and security are becoming increasingly open to public influence. This book aims to give both the voter and the decision-maker a new vision of how to manage crises and avert hostilities through non-traditional means.

220 pages 2002
0 7146 5298 9 cloth
0 7146 8260 8 paper

FRANK CASS PUBLISHERS
Crown House, 47 Chase Side, Southgate, London N14 5BP
Tel: +44 (0)20 8920 2100 Fax: +44 (0)20 8447 8548 E-mail: info@frankcass.com
NORTH AMERICA
920 NE 58th Avenue Suite 300, Portland, OR 97213-3786 USA
Tel: 800 944 6190 Fax: 503 280 8832 E-mail: cass@isbs.com
Website: www.frankcass.com